KENTUCKY Keepsakes

Compiled, Annotated and Illustrated

by

ELIZABETH ROSS

McClanahan
Publishing House

ISBN 0-913383-38-4
Library of Congress 95-80007

Cover design and book layout by James Asher Graphics.
Line drawings by Elizabeth Ross
Back cover photograph by Nancy Lee Ross
Editor: Gloria Stewart

Manufactured in the United States of America.

All book order correspondence should be addressed to:

McClanahan Publishing House, Inc.
P. O. Box 100
Kuttawa, KY 42055
(502) 388-9388
1-800-544-6959

KENTUCKY
Keepsakes

Dedication

I wish to dedicate this collection of recipes and drawings to my late mother, Florence Hamilton Ross, who was a fine cook and hostess. It was at her table that I acquired my appreciation of fine Southern cooking. Also, I want to acknowledge all the good friends and family members who have contributed to my dining pleasure.

Introduction

Many of the origins of the recipes presented here are lost in the mists of culinary history. The majority have come down to us through local traditions and will be familiar to most Kentuckians. I wanted to record these regional foods for those who wish to carry on their own traditions so they will not be forgotten in our present day fast food culture. I have tried and tested many, and combined others with good results. The following recipes were collected over a period of about 30 years. The reason for including several versions of some of them is that it is interesting to note the variety of ingredients and techniques and it is worth noting where and who should be credited for presenting them. Read through them and pick or combine the ones that appeal to you. I sincerely hope that you enjoy my effort to record and preserve the historic recipes that make up Kentucky's traditional food heritage.

Foreword

Elizabeth Ross, in this closely packed book of long loved Kentucky recipes, has done what many intend to do with cherished family recipes, but never do it. Moreover, in this book she has done it for the whole of Kentucky.

Nor does she stop with one version of a recipe. Over 30 years of collecting she has accumulated versions of each dish—so similar, yet with subtle variations that make each special to someone. Have you ever made a chess pie—or a corn pudding—or a mint julep—for a native Kentuckian, who approached it with delighted anticipation, only, at first taste, to lamely say, "This is nice—but—it's not quite the way I remember it?"

Surely, in this ample collection the most determined searcher will find one that, to her or him, is the REAL THING. No matter how eager you may be to get your mixing tools into these recipes, please take a 30-minute segment of uncluttered time to leisurely read the section about Kentucky cuisine. If you're a stranger to this area, it will be a revelation. If you're a native it will revive cherished memories of dishes now forgotten in today's fast-food-on-the-run culture.

In case you haven't time to count these blessings, how about 48 cornbreads (including 11 hushpuppies)? Or 22 beaten biscuits? Or 13 grits dishes? Or 13 Kentucky Hot Brown Sandwiches; 21 guides for cooking country ham; 8 chess pies; Old-Fashioned Stack Cake; Blackberry Jam Cakes; Kentucky Bourbon Pecan Cake? Among the 9 versions of Mint Juleps, surely you'll find comfort if your horse limps in last in the Kentucky Derby.

If your favorite long-lost Kentucky dish isn't here, it's not because Elizabeth Ross hasn't tried. She has solved my future gift problems—shower, birthday and Christmas. For this and a wealth of revived memories, I thank her ... Kentucky will surely thank her.

Fern Storer
Retired Food Editor of *The Cincinnati Post*
Author of *Recipes Remembered*

Kentucky Cuisine

HISTORY

The Indians, Scotch, Irish, and English gave Kentucky its traditional food heritage. Later, other people of different ethnic backgrounds, Blacks, Germans, Dutch and French added their foodways traditions. Early Kentuckians learned from the Native Americans what food was edible and how to procure, prepare and preserve it. The Indians, a hunting and gathering society, had domesticated corn, pumpkins, squash, beans and various herbs. The early settlers used these foods and learned methods of preserving and preparing them.[1]

From the first settlements, Kentucky country was designed to be pastoral and agrarian. The family farm has been the backbone of Kentucky, having its roots in the Jeffersonian agrarian ideal, envisioned as a landscape of small family-oriented farms in clusters forming small communities. The German-American families who settled along the Ohio River tended small farms as had their ancestors and these intensive-style truck farms produced a variety of vegetables and fruits. The eastern mountains also produced small farms, but because of the terrain, subsistence farming was the rule for most mountain families. The rolling pastures of the Bluegrass area attracted the aristocratic second and third sons of Virginia plantations - men who had no prospect of inheriting family lands. They established their own plantations in central Kentucky. The early pioneer farmer, however, typically owned from 50 to 200 acres of land within the small agrarian communities.[2]

The land law of 1776 provided "that no family shall be entitled to the allowance granted to settlers..., unless they have made a crop of corn in that country, or resided there at least one year since the time of their settlement." Because it was easy to grow, very edible and easily transportable as whiskey, corn became the new country's staple crop and has been the mother crop from 1775 to the present.[3]

The most important technique of food preservation the pioneers learned from the Indians was how to dry corn and it was milled, roasted, boiled and baked. It was served as hominy, mush and grits. It could be dried, parched and pickled and could be utilized in breads, porridges, cakes and of course, whiskey. The prevalent form of corn was as cornmeal. An old Kentucky adage is that "The less you have to eat, the more you know about cooking," and cornmeal stretched the skills of the pioneer cook. Cornmeal mixed with water made ash cake, cornpone, mush, griddle cakes, cornbread or Johnnycake (a colloquialism for journey cake which traveled well).[4] Kentucky farmers also grew wheat, rye and oats and Kentucky streams were once lined with creekside gristmills.[5] These mills for grinding corn also processed wheat into flour which was used for gravies, biscuits, pie crusts, yeast breads and cakes. Since early cooks did not have proper ovens they assembled stack cakes with thin layers and filled with jam or stewed dried fruits.[6]

Nearly every party of settlers entering Kentucky brought with them cattle, hogs and sheep. Of all the farm animals, none was more self-sufficient than the hog. It thrived in the wilderness and supplied the settlers with lard and pork. Cured pork, especially country hams, became a commercial staple from 1789 on.[7]

In addition to using pork for hams, sausage, salt-pork and rendered lard, hocks and fat bacon were used to flavor wild greens and some home-grown vegetables. Along with pork, domestic cattle and poultry enriched the diet with butter, eggs and a wider variety of meats. By the nineteenth century, cultivated vegetables in Kentucky included tomatoes, green beans, carrots, cabbage, pumpkins, potatoes, turnips, peas and cucumbers. Fruits available were apples, cherries, peaches, plums and strawberries.[8]

The broad plains of central Kentucky, with an amenable climate and good rainfall, made an excellent environment for growing a bountiful variety of foods. It was, according to the pioneers, "a land flowing with milk and honey."[9]

The butter, home-butchered meats, deviled eggs, pastries and vegetables cooked according to traditional recipes are still much in evidence at family reunions, community picnics, gospel singings and dinners-on-the-grounds observed by many rural Kentucky church groups.[10] With a more sophisticated society Kentucky foodways changed, but many pioneer foods still hold a special place in the hearts of Kentuckians. For example, if you are looking for genuine country ham, barbecue, roasting ears of corn, cornbread and, of course, bourbon whiskey, the best place to find them is in Kentucky.[11]

TRADITIONAL HOSPITALITY

Kentucky hospitality has always been a major positive characteristic of the region. It is almost a sacred custom. Fond memories of home, family and guests in Kentucky have been captured in both verse and song. Even the ladies of the Methodist Church in Maysville, Kentucky, proclaimed in their 1884 cookbook, "Bad dinners go hand in hand with total depravity, while a well-fed man is already half-saved."[12] Salvation or satisfaction? Entertaining in the home is a strong tradition and a Kentucky host will tell you to "make yourself at home" all the while presenting the best of his or her kitchen. On the first Saturday of every May, Derby Day will exemplify the best of Kentucky hospitality. The "greatest two minutes in sports" starts with the Governor's Breakfast on the capitol grounds at Frankfort. For other Kentuckians, elaborate Derby brunches or television "watch-parties," complete with mint juleps, are a part of the weekend celebration. The hospitality of the "Happy Hunting Ground" is a strong and continuing tradition.

THE OLD INNS

Amazingly, some of Kentucky's early inns are still in business. Doe Run Inn, 1792, at Brandenburg serves meals in a rustic setting; Duncan Tavern, 1788, at Paris is now an historical library, museum and the Kentucky DAR headquarters; Old Stone Inn, 1791, once a stagecoach inn at Simpsonville, serves regional foods and is known for its corn fritters; and the Old Talbott Tavern, 1779, at Bardstown is still serving excellent meals. More recently, Beaumont Inn, 1917, at Harrodsburg is famous for it's "yellow-legged" fried chicken, country ham and corn pudding; Boone Tavern, 1909, operated by Berea College is famous for its spoonbread and Jefferson Davis pie; The Georgian Room of Science Hill Inn, Shelbyville, is known for its hot browns, hot-water cornbread and lemon chess pie; and the Trustee's Office Inn at Shakertown at Pleasant Hill serves Shaker-inspired and regional foods - try the Shaker lemon pie for a delicious taste experience. [13]

FAMOUS KENTUCKY COOKS AND WRITERS

Among Kentucky's early restaurants one of the most famous was Miss Jennie Benedict's in Louisville. Miss Jennie began in 1893 catering school lunches and private parties. She went to the Boston School of Cooking and in 1900 opened her tearoom where she created Benedictine cheese, a sandwich spread of cucumbers and cream cheese. In 1911 she moved to larger quarters on Fourth Street and a trip to Louisville was considered incomplete without luncheon or dinner at Benedict's. In 1904 she published her *Blue Ribbon Cook Book*, which, unfortunately, is now out of print. [14]

A resident of Louisville, Mrs. Marion Flexner wrote six cookbooks. The fourth, *Out of Kentucky Kitchens*, is considered a classic. It was first published in 1949 and reprinted in 1989 by The University Press of Kentucky. It contains Southern recipes with anecdotal material about Kentucky's culinary history. [15] Her son, Dr. John Flexner, told me that she was working on a cookie cookbook at the time of her death.

"Cissy" Gregg was a native of Cynthiana and a University of Kentucky graduate in home economics and agriculture. In 1942 she became "home consultant" for the Louisville *Courier-Journal* and for 20 years cooks waited for her daily food columns. She was much in demand as a speaker and as a judge for food competitions. She wrote two cookbooks issued in paperback by the newspaper. These books are now out of print. [16] Fortunately, I was given permission by the newspaper to use them in compiling this cookbook.

A food critic, Duncan Hines, was born in Bowling Green. He and his wife, Florence, traveled widely in the United States and in 1935 mailed a Christmas list of "superior eating places" to their friends. The responses resulted in the 1936 publication of *Adventures in Good Eating*, a guide to recommended United States restaurants. A companion book, *Lodging for a Night*, was published in 1938. The sign "Recommended by Duncan Hines" became the seal of approval for travelers. [17]

Kentucky has contributed more than its share to the foodways of America in verse and other endeavors. Irvin S. Cobb, humorist and journalist, often wrote about food and drink, especially the mint julep; Thomas D. Clark, historian and writer; and cookbook writers, Emma Allen Hayes (one of America's first black cookbook authors, in 1912), Lillian Marshall and Camille Glenn have all celebrated the foods of the region. [18] One of the early books of food preparation was Lettice Bryan's *The Kentucky Housewife*, 1839, which was followed by Minerva Carr Fox's *The Blue Grass Cook Book* published in 1904.[19]

BOURBON

From the first Kentucky corn harvest in 1775, settlers from Virginia, Maryland and Pennsylvania began producing whiskey and the distilling of whiskey has become an important part of the state's economy. Corn, the staple crop for early Kentuckians, had little cash value until it was distilled into whiskey. It was a medium of exchange in a cash-starved economy...a pack horse could carry only 4 bushels of corn as grain but up to the equivalent of 24 bushels distilled into whiskey. Jacob Meyers and Jacob Froman from Lincoln County, Marshall Brashear of Jefferson County, Elijah Craig of Scott County or Jacob Spears of Bourbon County may have produced the first bourbon. There were a number of distillers in Bourbon County and that is generally believed to be where it got its name. Bourbon is produced from a fermented mash made of at least 51% corn and lesser amounts of wheat, rye and barley, yeast and distilled limestone water. It is distilled at no more than 160 proof and then aged in charred oak barrels which give the bourbon its reddish color and distinctive flavor. Bourbon has become the standard by which all other whiskeys are judged and Kentucky is now considered the bourbon capital of the world. On May 4, 1964 Congress recognized bourbon whiskey as a distinctly American product.[20]

THE MINT JULEP

The celebrated mint julep came from the Kentuckians' taste for distilled spirits. The average American consumed 2 1/2 gallons of spirits a year when Kentucky became a state in 1792. A "julap" taken before breakfast was deemed a healthful way to avoid fevers arising from night air and hot climates. The words julap or julep appears to have derived from the Persian word "gulab" and the Arabic "julab," both of which mean rosewater. Later it came to mean a nonalcoholic medicinal herb syrup. By the mid-eighteenth century in America it was a beverage made of spirits frequently containing mint.[21] One legend is that a nineteenth century Kentucky boatman on the Mississippi River went ashore in search of spring water to mix with his bourbon. On a whim, he is said to have added some mint growing by the spring.[22] Nineteenth century juleps frequently contained wine or brandy, however, impoverished postbellam Southerners turned to bourbon whiskey, which is still the ingredient of choice in Kentucky. It has remained much in favor with genteel Kentucky society and is a tradition associated primarily with the Kentucky Derby.[23]

Now, we must define the mechanics of making a mint julep, a subject more controversial than the curing and cooking of a country ham. Traditionally the whiskey used is, without fail, straight aged Kentucky bourbon. The chilled cup in which the mint julep is served is, also by tradition, made of sterling silver (originally coin silver), about 4" tall and 3" in diameter. A specially designed julep cup is presented to the Kentucky Derby winner each year.[24] In the absence of silver, a tall glass is acceptable. The water must be cold and, if possible, from a limestone spring. The sugar is either granulated or powdered, and the ice is usually crushed but may be shaved. Some prefer to sip the concoction through a straw while others drink straight from the cup, being careful to hold the cup only by the rim so as not to disturb the frost on the silver. Now, to the serious issue here, the handling of the mint. To crush or not to crush, to bruise instead of crushing, all subjects of controversy in many newspaper columns and a few books. The only consensus seems to be that the sprigs of mint must be only the freshest. How best to extract the flavor of the mint is the question. There are those who agree with the Southern judge of the late 1880s who said, "Like a woman's heart, mint gives its sweetest aroma when bruised." On the other hand, there are those who cite Francis Parkinson Keyes who said, "Never insult a decent woman, never bring a horse hot to the stable, and never crush the mint in a julep." [25] Perhaps we could follow the lyrical directions of Henry Clay whose recipe, found in an old diary, follows:

> "The mint leaves, fresh and tender, should be pressed against a coin-sil
> ver goblet with the back of a silver spoon. Only bruise the leaves gently
> and then remove them from the goblet. Half fill with cracked ice. Mellow
> bourbon, aged in oaken barrels, is poured from the jigger and allowed to
> slide slowly through the cracked ice. In another receptacle, granulated
> sugar is slowly mixed into chilled limestone water to make a silvery mix
> ture as smooth as some rare Egyptian oil, then poured on top of the ice.
> While beads of moisture gather on the burnished exterior of the silver
> goblet, garnish the brim of the goblet with choicest sprigs of mint." [26]

Obviously, the rite of making a julep is not to be taken lightly, although I would say that after sipping the first concoction, whatever technique used would seem of little import and all this would seem like a bunch of foolishness. At any rate and all differences aside, on the first Saturday in May, when they play *My Old Kentucky Home* at Churchill Downs, stand and raise a cup in honor of "The Run for the Roses."

COUNTRY HAM

Among the prime culinary experiences you have in Kentucky is enjoying how good cured ham can be along with baked beaten biscuits as they are supposed to taste. Kentucky country hams are recognized as one of the world's best preserved meats, equal to those of Smithfield, Virginia, the Ardennes, Parma and Krakow, Poland, and are proud bearers of a centuries-old tradition. The basic curing process originated in England, but over 200 years numerous variations have developed[27] and the secrets of raising hogs, butchering, trimming, smoking, aging and cooking have been passed down from generation to generation. These practitioners are proud to give real country ham the time, effort and knowledge it demands.[28]

Southern-style country ham makes an impressive main course for any occasion. There is something about the complex smoky flavor of a Kentucky country ham that cannot be found in any other. It is richer, more nut-like and delicate than those of other states. Country hams are produced with a dry cure of salt or a combination of salt, sugar and nitrates. When cured, the hams are aged, which reduces their moisture content by as much as 30 percent. Then they are usually smoked. The whole process is required by Federal law to be at least 70 days, although 1 to 1 1/2 years is probably best. The flavor of Kentucky hams depends in part on the clover or grain the hogs were fed. Aging and smoking with hickory adds to the flavor, saltiness, firm texture and the rich color of the meat. Most smokehouses offer both uncooked and fully cooked country hams. Cooking a country ham involves removing some of the salt acquired in curing and restoring some of the moisture lost through aging. Consequently the ham is usually boiled rather than baked. After boiling, it is sometimes baked briefly in order to set a glaze on the outside. A whole ham generally weighs between 13 and 18 pounds, although prize specimens often weigh from 18 to 25 pounds. Often, they are lightly coated with mold. This mold is a natural, desirable result of curing and aging. This is not harmful and can be scrubbed off before cooking. It will also develop white spots through it during aging. These won't hurt you either. The ham is now ready to be cooked and when done, ready to be served, sliced paper thin, on that most elegant Southern speciality, the beaten biscuit.

BEATEN BISCUITS

No special social occasion, such as a Derby party, a wedding reception, a holiday meal or tea would be complete and proper without beaten biscuits served with country ham. "Beaten biscuits are great to eat but hard to beat."[29] They are small and hard, the result of vigorous beating to get all the air out of the dough. This "beating" ranges from 200 to 500 strokes, or 30 to 45 minutes, to get the dough to a satiny, blistered stage. Traditionally, the dough was placed on a hard wooden surface such as a tree stump and beaten with the flat side of an ax, mallet, rolling pin or, depending on the endurance of the cook, the heel of the hand.[30]

Enterprising cooks (and it seems as many men as women enjoy building the culinary reputation by making them) developed the beaten biscuit machine. This contraption is a sort of Southern version of a hand-cranked Italian pasta machine. With this device the dough could be more easily turned, rolled and beaten. Most often, the beaten biscuit machine is a washing machine wringer mounted on a marble slab attached to the base of an old Singer treadle sewing machine. Some have an electric motor for the turning of the rollers.[31] Find one of these at a reasonable price and you have a jewel in the crown of Kentucky cooking.

There is a profitable cottage industry built around making these gems for those who prefer to husband their energy. Beaten biscuits are available at many supermarkets in central Kentucky.

BIBB LETTUCE

Kentucky Bibb lettuce is considered by gourmets to be the finest in the world and is the pride of a Kentuckian's garden. Originally called limestone lettuce, it has a lovely compact head with crisp deep green leaves of single serving size that cluster like loose rose petals. Its flavor is delicate and sweet[32] and although tender and easily bruised, it is resistant to plant lice.

Sometime after 1865 John B. Bibb, an amateur horticulturist, developed this lettuce in his garden in Frankfort. He did not market it and it might have been lost had he not given seeds to his friends and neighbors. It was then grown by regional farmers and after 1919 was widely marketed by the Grenewein Greenhouse in Louisville.[33] It is the lettuce most often used for wilted lettuce salad, a Kentucky favorite.

HOT BROWN

Of special note is the Brown Hotel at Louisville. Opened in 1923, it shortly thereafter introduced the "Hot Brown." (The word sandwich is not used.) Created by chef Fred K. Schmidt, the original hot brown consisted of sliced roast turkey, open-faced on white toast, topped with Mornay sauce and sprinkled with Parmesan cheese. It was then broiled and garnished with crossed strips of cooked bacon and pimiento. An immediate success, it is consumed all over the country and has been imitated by home cooks and professional chefs with different degrees of success. Acceptable substitutions include cheddar and even American cheese in the sauce and an additional garnish of tomatoes. After closing in 1971, the Brown Hotel reopened in 1985 and the hot brown is again being served in its place of origin.[34] It is as satisfying as it is rich.

BARBECUE

The word comes from barbacoa, the term conquistadors used to define the wood frame on which the Carib Indians roasted meat over open fires. Barbecue today means meat, fowl or fish roasted over coals from nut-bearing trees, most likely hickory. The seasonings, bastings and sauces and the social event that occurs while the food is roasting are also called barbecue. In Kentucky, pork and beef are the most popular meats with the exception of the western part of the state where the number of sheep farms make mutton the favorite choice. Burgoo or Brunswick stew is often served with barbecue. The cooking and tradition of barbecue came to Kentucky with the early Virginia settlers and during the nineteenth century they became a major social event at religious, fraternal, charitable and political gatherings. In the twentieth century, restaurants became popular and barbecue appeared on menus. One of Kentucky's first commercial barbecue stands was opened in 1890 in Owensboro by Henry Green; and today, Owensboro is home to the pit-barbecue of the Moonlite Inn. The annual International Barbecue Festival has been held in Owensboro since 1980.[35]

BURGOO

Bean soups were eagerly borrowed from the Indians by the Scots, English and Black Kentuckians. The Indians most certainly made soups with a wide variety of wild meats cooked with herbs and vegetables, but so did the pioneers.[36] The word "burgoo" possibly comes from burghul, now bulgar, a term for a Turkish wheat pilaf. Burgoo as the name of a Kentucky stew came from Gus Jaubert, a member of John Hunt Morgan's cavalry, who used it to describe field rations he served and later for political gatherings. James T. Looney, a Lexington grocer known as "The Burgoo King," carried on the tradition with a recipe for 1,200 gallons of burgoo: Lean meat (not game), fat hens, potatoes, onions, tomatoes, tomato puree, carrots and corn, seasoned with red pepper, salt and his secret sauce.[37]

FANCY FARM PICNIC

Thousands have been fed on occasions such as the Annual Fancy Farm Picnic, an annual community and political event held in Graves County. The picnic has been held since 1880. Gradually it has become an important speech-making opportunity for Kentucky state politicians who make a special effort to be at this heavily publicized event. Since 1956, the picnic has been held on the first Saturday in August. The consumption of 15,000 pounds of mutton, pork and chicken at the 1982 Fancy Farm Picnic earned recognition in the 1985 Guinness Book of World Records. [38]

CABBAGE PATCH SETTLEMENT

Of special note is the Cabbage Patch Settlement founded in 1910 by Louise Marshall in a truck-farming area of Louisville known as the Cabbage Patch. Established to alleviate urban poverty, the Settlement house offers a total social service program in the Old Louisville area. Alice Hegan Rice, a board member, used the setting for one of her most popular novels, *Mrs. Wiggs of the Cabbage Patch*. Their cookbook, *Cabbage Patch Famous*

Kentucky Recipes is still in print and is very popular in Kentucky kitchens. [39]

SWEETS

Some of the edible wild plants growing in Kentucky are as tasty as some cultivated plants. These are blueberries, papaws, persimmons, black walnuts, certain hickories and pecans. But, the tastiest are blackberries - one of Kentucky's most common shrubs.[40] They mature in July and there is nothing better than biscuits served with homemade jam of Kentucky-grown blackberries. The Blackberry Festival at Carlisle has been held on the first weekend of July since 1948. Blackberry jam, jelly, pie, cobbler, cake and even ice cream is sold.[41] Black cake, found in many family cookbooks, is a molasses and spice cake made with the addition of fruit and nuts, and of course, bourbon. Spice cake is also the basis for the old favorite, Kentucky blackberry jam cake. Fried apple pies are another long-time Kentucky favorite, as is chess pie. The authors of *Virginia Cookery Past* and Present say that chess pie may have been the result of a careless cook who left out the cheese and misspelled the name.[42] Not a bad mistake, considering its popularity. Perhaps, some other cook said it was "jess" pie.

BOURBON BALLS

Kentucky Colonel is not only an honorary title bestowed on citizens of note; it is also the name of Kentucky's most famous candy, the bourbon ball. It is made with a fondant center generously laced with bourbon, encased in pecan halves and dipped in thin, dark chocolate. The candy was developed by the late Mrs. Ruth Booe of Frankfort, co-owner of Rebecca-Ruth Candy, Inc. The idea of making candy with bourbon was the result of a chance remark during Frankfort's sesquicentennial celebration in 1936. A friend commented that the two best tastes in the world were a sip of bourbon and Mrs. Booe's mint candy. She worked on the formula for two years and perfected the secret process for blending bourbon and candy.[43] This confection makes an elegant, delicious gift from the Bluegrass state.

Two other confections are worth noting here. In the 1870's Helen Mojeska performed at the Macauley Theater at Louisville. Busatti's Confectionery created a marshmallow-caramel candy in honor of the actress and called it a Mojeska, now known as Modjeska.[44] At Lancaster, "Mom" Blakeman had a family-style restaurant on the town square. A great cook, she also made Cream Pull Candy and sold it throughout central Kentucky. It is still sold by a younger woman who continued making it after Mrs. Blakeman's death. It is an incredible "melt-in-your-mouth" tasting experience.

In the spirit of this collection of recipes I want to start with the following song - a favorite of my grandfather when he wanted to entertain my sister and me before Sunday supper.

OLD DAN TUCKER

I come to town the other night
I heard the noise and saw the fight;
The watchman was a-running round,
Crying "Old Dan Tucker's come to town."

Get out of the way for Old Dan Tucker,
He's too late to get his supper.
Supper's over and the dishes washed
Nothing left but a piece of squash!

Old Dan Tucker was a funny old man,
He ate his dinner in an old tin pan;
The pan had a hole and the dinner ran through.
And what was old man Tucker going to do?

Old Dan Tucker was a fine old man,
He washed his face in the frying pan,
He combed his hair with a wagon wheel,
And died with a toothache in his heel.

Old Dan Tucker came to town
Riding a billy goat, leading a hound.
Hound gave a yelp, goat gave a jump.
Landed Dan Tucker a-straddle of a stump!

Old Dan Tucker's still in town
Swinging the ladies round and round.
One to the east and one to the west
And then to the one he loves the best!

Old Dan Tucker he got drunk,
He fell in the fire and kicked up a chunk;
A red hot coal popped in his shoe
And bless you, honey, how the ashes flew.

An now Old Dan Tucker is a gone sucker,
And never can he go home to supper;
Old Dan he has had his last ride,
And the banjo's buried by his side.[45]

[1]Reprinted from John Kleber, *The Kentucky Encyclopedia*, © 1992 by The University Press of Kentucky, by permission of the publishers, Marty Godbey and Jeanette S. Duke, p. 338-339.

[2]IBID., Bob Gates, p. 306-307

[3]IBID., Thomas D. Clark, p. 6-10.

[4]Reprinted from John Kleber, *The Kentucky Encyclopedia*, © 1992 by the University Press of Kentucky, by permission of the publishers, p. 388-389.

[5]IBID., p. 6-10.

[6]IBID., p. 338-339

[7]IBID., p. 6-10.

[8]IBID., p. 338-339.

[9]Dr. Jay A. Anderson, Professor of History, Utah State University, Logan, Utah (Professor in Folklore Program, Western Kentucky University, 1980-1985), permission granted by telephone interview, 2-4-95.

[10]Reprinted from John Kleber, *The Kentucky Encyclopedia*, © 1992 by The University Press of Kentucky, by permission of the publishers, Lynwood Montell, p. 336.

[11]"Roots of Southern Food" by John Egerton, *Southern Living* magazine, Feb., 1990, p. 56, by permission of the author.

[12]IBID., p. 55.

[13]Reprinted from John Kleber, *The Kentucky Encyclopedia*, © 1992 by The University Press of Kentucky, by permission of the publishers, p. 64, Clay Lancaster, 273-274; author's experience.

[14]Reprinted from John Kleber, *The Kentucky Encyclopedia*, ©1992 by The University Press of Kentucky, by permission of the publishers, p. 70.

[15]IBID., p. 326.

[16]Reprinted from John Kleber, *The Kentucky Encyclopedia*, © 1992 by The University Press of Kentucky, by permission of the publishers, p. 392.

[17]IBID., p. 433-434.

[18]"Roots of Southern Food" by John Egerton, *Southern Living* magazine, Feb., 1992, p. 57, by permission of the author.

[19]Reprinted from John Kleber, *The Kentucky Encyclopedia*, © 1992 by The University Press of Kentucky, by permission of the publishers, p. 338-339.

[20]Reprinted from John Kleber, *The Kentucky Encyclopedia*, © 1992 by The University Press of Kentucky, by permission of the publishers, Flaget M. Nally, p. 103; Thomas H. Syvertsen, p. 266.

[21]IBID., Marty Godbey, p. 641.

[22]Dr. Jay A. Anderson, Professor of History, Utah State University, Logan, Utah (Professor in Folklore Program, Western Kentucky University, 1980-1985), permission granted by telephone interview, 2-4-95.

[23]Reprinted from John Kleber, *The Kentucky Encyclopedia*, © 1992 by The University Press of Kentucky, by permission of the publishers, p. 641.

[24]*Kentucky Derby Museum Cookbook*, Kentucky Derby Corporation, P.O. Box 3513, Louisville, Kentucky, 40201, 1986, p. 47.

[25]"A Mint of Southern Tradition," reprinted by permission of *Southern Living* magazine, p. 20S, April, 1990.

[26]Reprinted by permission of Terry Green, Director, "Ashland," Henry Clay Estate, 120 Sycamore Road, Lexington, Kentucky, 40502.

[27]Dr. Jay A. Anderson, Professor of History, Utah State University, Logan, Utah, (Professor in Folklore Program, Western Kentucky University, 1980-1985), permission granted by telephone interview, 2-4-95.

[28]John Egerton, *Southern Living* magazine, p. 96, Jan. 1990, by permission of the author.

[29]"Beaten Biscuits with Lard and Laughter," *Back Home in Kentucky* magazine, Jan./Feb. 1989, p. 7, reprinted by permission of Sarah C. Willis.

[30]*Beat Dough Hard for Biscuits You Can't Beat*, by Cammie Vitale. Reprinted by permission of the author.

[31]Sarah C. Willis, p. 8.

[32]Dr. Jay A. Anderson, Professor of History, Utah State University, Logan, Utah (Professor in Folklore Program, Western Kentucky University, 1980-1985), permission granted by telephone interview, 2-4-95.

[33]Reprinted from John Kleber, *The Kentucky Encyclopedia*, © 1992 by The University Press of Kentucky, by permission of the publishers, Camille Glenn, John S. Goff, p. 75-76.

[34]IBID., Marty Godbey, p. 443.

[35]Reprinted from John Kleber, *The Kentucky Encyclopedia*, © 1992 by The University Press of Kentucky, by permission of the publishers, Janet Alm Anderson, John Egerton, p. 50.

[36]Dr. Jay A. Anderson, Professor of History, Utah State University, Logan, Utah (Professor in Folklore Program, Western Kentucky University, 1980-1985), permission granted by telephone interview, 2-4-95.

[37]Reprinted from John Kleber, *The Kentucky Encyclopedia*, © 1992 by The University Press of Kentucky, by permission of the publishers, Marty Godbey, p. 142-143.

[38]IBID., p. 308.

[39]Reprinted from John Kleber, *The Kentucky Encyclopedia*, © 1992 by The University Press of Kentucky, by permission of the publishers, Gail Henson, p. 149.

[40]IBID, Max E. Medley and John W. Thieret, p. 329.

[41]Ms. Pat Allison, Carlisle, Kentucky.

[42]Dr. Shirley Snarr, Professor of Nutrition, Eastern Kentucky University, Richmond, Kentucky, permission granted by telephone interview, 2-13-95.

[43]Rebecca-Ruth Candy Inc., P.O. Box 64, Frankfort, Kentucky, 40602-0064.

[44]*Kentucky Derby Museum Cookbook*, p. 244.

[45]An old minstrel song, words and music by Dan Emmitt, 1843 or by H. Russell, 1836.

Beverages

Spiced Cider

3/4 c. sugar	2 t. whole allspice
3/4 c. orange juice	2 t. whole cloves
1 gal. apple cider	2 sticks cinnamon

Completely dissolve the sugar and the orange juice in the cider before pouring it in an electric coffee maker. Put spices in the basket and perk. Serves 30.

Thelma's Treasurers, p. 104

Shaker Spiced Apple Cider

1 stick cinnamon	3 qts. cider
1 whole nutmeg	1 whole clove
1/2 c. sugar	

Place spices in a cheesecloth bag. Put cider, sugar and bag in pan and simmer for at least 3 min. Serve hot in warmed cups.

We Make You Kindly Welcome, p. 57

Kentucky Coffee

1 pt. bourbon	1 pt. coffee ice cream
1 pt. cold espresso or strong	freeze dried coffee crystals
regular coffee	

Combine all but crystals in blender or food processor. Garnish each cup with coffee crystals. Serves 6.

Best of the Best from Kentucky, Let Them Eat Ice Cream, p. 19

Eggnog Superb

12 egg yolks	1 qt. bottled-in-bond Kentucky
2 1/2 c. sugar	bourbon whiskey
1 qt. double cream	

Beat the egg yolks very, very lightly with the sugar - an electric mixer helps. They should be spongy and lemon-colored. Add whiskey very, very slowly, beat between each addition, about 1 to 2 T. at a time. Beat the cream stiff, but watch carefully that it does not get buttery. It is better on the runny than the too-thick side. Fold this cream into the batter mixture and pour into a crystal or silver bowl. This bowl should be placed in a larger one and chipped ice put around it to keep it thoroughly chilled. Grate nutmeg over the top or put a little over each serving. To make this eggnog go a little farther and be a little less rich, take the 12 egg whites you did not use, beat them to a stiff froth and fold into the mixed eggnog. Serves 20.

Out of Kentucky Kitchens, p. 38

Kentucky - Georgetown Eggnog

6 eggs, beaten separately	1 pt. whiskey
1 c. sugar, divided	1 qt. heavy whipping cream

Separate eggs and beat yolks until light. Add 2/3 c. of the sugar and beat and beat and beat. They should be thick and lemon-colored. When the egg yolks and part of the sugar have been the beating effort, turn your attention to the egg whites, which should be beaten until stiff but not dry with the remaining 1/3 c. of sugar. Then slowly pour the whiskey-sugar-egg-yolk mixture into the whites, folding it in gently. If you do this the eggnog mixture will not sepa-rate. Next, whip the cream and fold it into the eggnog mixture. Fold and fold and then let stand, folding again and again. Standing and gently moving the mixture helps to ripen it and that is important for a good eggnog. The other way we make eggnog combines the bourbon with 1/4 c. rum. Either way you make eggnog, it can or even should be made 2 or 3 days ahead of time, keeping it cool and stirring it occasionally.

Cissy Gregg's Cookbook, vol. 2, p. 14,
The Courier Journal & Louisville Times Co.,
reprinted with permission

Shaker Eggnog

6 T. sugar, divided   2 c. heavy cream
6 egg yolks   1 1/2 qt. milk
1/2 c. apple brandy or applejack   1/2 t. ground nutmeg
6 egg whites

Heat 4 T. of the sugar in a skillet until it is very warm, but has not browned nor melted. Gradually beat into the egg yolks until yolks are thick and lemon-colored. Beat in brandy. Beat egg whites until soft peaks are formed and gradually add the remaining 2 T. sugar, continuing to beat until stiff, moist peaks are formed when the beater is lifted. Pour the cream, then the milk into the beaten yolks gradually, folding gently as you pour. Pour into tall glasses and top with the beaten egg white meringue. Dust the top of each serving with nutmeg. Serves 6 to 8 tall glasses or 8 to 10 mugs.

The Shaker Cookbook, p. 143

Kentucky Mint Julep

simple syrup   crushed ice
mint leaves   100 proof Kentucky bourbon

To make simple syrup, mix 1 part boiling water to 2 parts sugar. Stir until dissolved. Place 3 to 4 mint leaves in julep glass. Add crushed ice. Press down with spoon to bruise leaves. Add 1 oz. bourbon and 1/2 oz. simple syrup. Stir well. Pack glass with crushed ice and fill with bourbon. Garnish with mint leaves. Traditionally, this is served in a frosted silver mint julep cup.

Best of the Best from Kentucky, To Market, To Market, p. 13, their p. 18

Kentucky Mint Julep

8 tender mint leaves   crushed ice
1/2 t. sugar   mint sprig sprinkled with
4 oz. bourbon   powdered sugar

In a 12 oz. glass, muddle mint leaves and sugar. Add 2 oz. of bourbon and 1/3 glass crushed ice. Stir. Add 2 more oz. bourbon and fill glass with crushed ice. Stir. Garnish with mint sprig.

The Crowning Recipes of Kentucky, p. 36

Kentucky Mint Julep

4 sprigs fresh mint   crushed ice
1 t. sugar   1 1/2 jiggers bourbon whiskey

Crush mint and sugar in a 12 oz. glass. Fill with crushed ice and add whiskey. Stir until glass frosts. Decorate with mint.

The Crowning Recipes of Kentucky, p. 36

Kentucky Mint Julep

1 t. sugar, or more to taste   2 oz. Kentucky bourbon whiskey
1 1/2 T. chopped mint leaves   1 sprig fresh mint
1 T. water   2 short straws
crushed ice to fill each cup

Place sugar and chopped mint in a small bowl and bruise the leaves with a wooden spoon until the mixture forms a paste. Add water and blend. Fill a julep cup half full of crushed ice. Add the mint syrup and the whiskey, add more crushed ice until the cup is full. Decorate with mint sprig and add straws. Put cup on tray and put in freezer to frost for about 1/2 hour. Serve at once. Serves 1.

A Taste from Back Home, p. 23

Churchill Downs Mint Julep

The julep you would be served at the Kentucky Derby.

1 to 2 oz. Kentucky bourbon whiskey	shaved or crushed ice to fill each cup
	1 small bunch fresh mint
1 T. chopped mint leaves	2 straws, cut short
1 T. water	1 t. sugar, or more to taste

Place sugar and chopped mint in a small crockery bowl. Bruise the leaves well with a muddler or the back of a wooden spoon until mixture forms a paste. Add water and continue stirring. There should be a thick green syrup by this time. Now you are ready for the whiskey. Fill a julep cup half full of crushed or shaved ice. Add the mint syrup and the whiskey. Fill the cup or glass with crushed ice. Slip the bunch of mint into the ice and beside it the straws. They should be no taller than the mint. Lift the cups onto a tray, being careful not to touch the sides with the fingers and put them into the icebox to frost. This will take from 1/2 to 1 hour. Serve at once. This is a potent drink and should be sipped slowly. Glass tumblers may be substituted for traditional silver julep cups but they will not frost. Serves 1.

Out of Kentucky Kitchens, p. 38

Burt Closson's Mint Julep

Mr. Closson of Closson's Interiors, Cincinnati, has a different technique for making mint juleps.

simple syrup*	1 qt. Old Rip Van Winkle bourbon
mint-flavored bourbon	fresh mint leaves, enough to stuff bottle

*Boil together equal amounts of sugar and water. Chill. Wash and dry mint leaves. Add to bourbon and let steep in the bottle for 3 days. Remove leaves and discard them. To serve fill julep glass with crushed ice. Pour 1 to 1 1/2 T. of simple syrup over ice. Fill glass with mint-flavored bourbon. Stir. Garnish with sprig of mint.

Kentucky Derby Museum Cookbook, p. 47

Irvin S. Cobb's Recipe For Mint Julep

"Take from the cold spring, some water, pure as the angels are; mix it with sugar until it seems like oil. Then take a glass and crush your mint in it with a spoon - crush it around the border of the glass and leave no place untouched. Then throw the mint away - it is a sacrifice. Fill with cracked ice the glass; pour in the quantity of bourbon you want. It trickles slowly through the ice. Let it have time to cool, then pour your sugared water over it. No spoon is needed, nor stirring allowed. Just let it stand a moment. Then around the brim place sprigs of mint, so that one who drinks may find taste and odor at one draught."

Historic Kentucky Recipes, p. 15

Pendennis Club Mint Julep

"A mint julep should be served in a 16 ounce metal cup. Dissolve 1 t. of granulated sugar in water - just enough to dissolve thoroughly. Add 2 or 3 tender sprigs of mint - not bruised. Fill cup with finely cracked ice. Add 2 jiggers of Old Forrester whiskey and stir gently. Refill with finely cracked ice and let stand to allow frosting. Place large bunch of mint, with cut to bleed slightly, on top of ice and force down firmly. Mint should be about 5 inches long. If straws are used, cut them so that the ends protrude just above the lip of the cup."

Provided with permission of the Pendennis Club, Louisville, Kentucky

Pendennis Old-Fashioned Cocktail

According to Irvin S. Cobb, the Old-Fashioned Cocktail originated at Kentucky's famous Pendennis Club.

"Using an old-fashioned glass, crush small lump of sugar in just enough water to dissolve thoroughly. Add 1 dash of Angostura and 2 dashes of Orange Bitters. Add large cube of ice and 1 jigger of whiskey. Twist and drop in lemon peel, and stir until mixed thoroughly. Remove ice and garnish with cherry." Serves 1.

Provided with permission of the Pendennis Club, Louisville, Kentucky

Pendennis Club Champagne Punch

juice of 1 doz. lemons
1 qt. carbonated water
powdered sugar to taste
2 c. strong tea, optional
1/2 pt. maraschino liqueur

1/2 pt. curacao
1 pt. brandy
2 qts. champagne
fruits for decorating

Mix lemon juice with carbonated water. Sweeten to taste with powdered sugar. The strong tea may be added if desired. Place a large block of ice in a punch bowl. Pour the mixture over it and add the maraschino liqueur, curacao, brandy and champagne. Mix well and decorate with fruits in season. Ladle into punch cups. Serves 35 to 40.

Out of Kentucky Kitchens, p. 37

Bourbon Slush

2 1/2 c. tea, 2 1/2 c. water
  and 2 small tea bags
12 oz. can frozen lemonade
1 6 oz. can frozen orange juice,
  thawed

2 c. Maker's Mark bourbon
1 c. sugar
6 c. water
thawed pineapple chunks,
  cherries or mint

Let tea cool. Then mix all together. Freeze in a plastic container. When ready to serve, scoop into a glass. Garnish with pineapple chunks or a cherry on a toothpick, or mint. Makes 3 qts.

The Kentucky Derby Museum Cookbook, p. 45

Minted Iced Tea, Old Kentucky Style

several sprigs of mint
6 T. lemon juice

6 c. hot tea
sugar to taste

Bruise the leaves of 4 to 5 sprigs of mint. Add lemon juice, the hot tea and sugar to taste. Let steep for about 1/2 hour then strain and chill it. Serve with crushed ice and sprigs of mint, also powdered sugar if you want it sweeter.

Cabbage Patch Famous Kentucky Recipes, p. 2

Fruit Juice Tea

1 tea bag
2 c. boiling water
1/3 c. sugar
1 T. honey
18 ice cubes

1 T. lemon juice
syrup from 1 20 oz. can pineapple,
   about 1/2 c.
1/2 c. orange juice, apple juice or
   apricot nectar
5 c. gingerale

Steep tea bag for 5 minutes. Stir in sugar and honey. Mix well. Add ice cubes, lemon juice, pineapple syrup and orange juice. Just before serving add gingerale.

Florence Ross, my Mother

Hot Spiced Tea

2 c. dry orange breakfast drink
1 c. sugar
1 1/4 c. dry lemonade mix

1/2 c. instant tea
1 t. cinnamon
1 t. ground cloves

Mix ingredients. Keep covered in a glass jar. Use 2 to 2 1/2 t. per cup of heated water.

Fountain Favorites, p. 93

Spiced Tea

14 cloves
14 whole allspice
1 stick cinnamon
2 qts. water

2 T. green tea
1 c. sugar
juice of 2 lemons
juice of 1 orange

Place the cloves, allspice and cinnamon in the water and bring to a boil. Pour hot water and spices over tea and let steep 7 minutes. Strain and pour over sugar and fruit juices.

Beaumont Inn Special Recipes, p. 139

Spiced Tea

16 whole allspice	3 tea bags
16 whole cloves	1 stick cinnamon
4 qts. boiling water	juice of 2 oranges
2 c. sugar	juice of 4 lemons

Put allspice and cloves in a cheesecloth bag. Place water, spice bag and sugar in a pan. Boil 10 minutes. Remove spice bag. Add tea bags and brew 3 to 5 minutes. Put in cinnamon stick while brewing. Remove tea bags and cinnamon stick. Add juices. Heat carefully before serving. Do not boil.

We Make You Kindly Welcome, p. 57

Kentucky Style Apple Toddy

6 apples	2 c. boiling water
1 c. sugar	sugar to taste
1 c. water	1 pt. bourbon whiskey
cinnamon, powdered	nutmeg, freshly grated

Pare and core the apples. Place them in a baking dish and pour over them a syrup made of sugar and water. Dust the apples with cinnamon and bake until done, about 1 hour. Baste frequently. Remove apples and juice from stove and mash in bottom of a silver or china punch bowl. Pour boiling water, sugar (to taste) and whiskey over apples. Grate nutmeg over this and ladle into cups.

Out of Kentucky Kitchens, p. 36

Kentucky Whiskey Toddy

1/2 t. sugar or 1 t. if you have a sweet tooth
1 T. tap water or more if you like a mild drink
a spilling jigger of bourbon whiskey, 2 to 2 1/2 T.

Mix sugar and water. Add the whiskey. Pour into an old-fashioned glass and fill with crushed ice, or add 2 ice cubes. Stir until chilled. Serve.

Out of Kentucky Kitchens, p. 41

Eggs, Cheese & Grits

Breakfast Souffle from Shakertown

1 1/2 lbs. pork sausage	1 t. salt
9 eggs, slightly beaten	3 slices bread, cut in 1/8" cubes
3 c. milk	1 1/2 c. cheddar cheese, grated
1 1/2 t. dry mustard	

Brown sausage and drain. Spread in a 9"x13"x2" greased pan. Mix all other ingredients and spread over sausage. Cover pan and refrigerate overnight. Bake uncovered at 350 degrees F. for 1 hour.

Food for My Household, Julia Ramey, p. 51

Egg Croquettes

7 to 8 eggs, hard-cooked	4 T. flour
1 small onion, or to taste	1/2 t. salt
4 to 5 sprigs parsley, chopped	1 c. milk
3 T. butter or margarine	

Peel eggs and put them through the meat grinder or chop very fine. If you use the meat grinder, run the onion and parsley through with the eggs. If you don't do this, chop the parsley fine and grate the onion. In a saucepan, melt the butter or margarine and blend in the flour and salt. Add milk gradually and cook, stirring until you have a smooth, thick cream sauce. If lumps form, beat sauce until they are gone. Add the ground egg, onion and parsley to the hot cream sauce. Let cool. Spread out in a pan and chill thoroughly in the refrigerator for several hours or overnight. Keep covered. When ready to cook, shape the mixture into croquettes. Place them on waxed paper. Dip them in beaten egg which has been diluted with 1 T. of cold water. Roll them in fine bread crumbs. These are soft, so work gently but quickly in coating them. Fry in deep fat until a good brown. Use a basket for best results and don't try to crowd them while they are browning or they may burst open. Serve at once with a sauce of your choice. Sauces come easy these days. The base can be a condensed cream soup; celery, asparagus, mushroom or one of the others, heated and thinned with milk or thin cream to sauce consistency. Makes 10.

Cissy Gregg's Cook Book, vol. 1, p. 14,
The Courier Journal & Louisville Times Co.,reprinted with permission

Deviled Eggs

6 eggs, hard-cooked
1/4 c. mayonnaise
salt and pepper to taste
1 t. prepared mustard

1 t. vinegar
1/4 c. sweet pickle relish, optional
curry powder, if desired
paprika

Hard cook eggs for 8 minutes turning often to center yolks. Chill and shell. Cut eggs in half, lengthwise. Remove yolks. Mash with a fork and moisten with mayonnaise. Season to taste with salt, pepper, mustard, vinegar and curry. If using the pickle relish omit the curry. Mix until light and fluffy. Pile lightly into egg white halves. Sprinkle with paprika. Makes 12 halves.

Elizabeth Ross

Goldenrod Eggs

6 eggs, hard-cooked
2 c. medium white sauce
6 slices toast

salt and white pepper
paprika

Chop egg whites. Combine with white sauce. Season to taste. Heat thoroughly. Pour over toast. Pile sieved egg yolks lightly over top. Sprinkle with paprika. Serves 6.

The Household Searchlight Recipe Book, p. 138

Pickled Eggs and Beets

40 oz. canned beets	3/4 c. vinegar
8 eggs, hard-cooked and shelled	1 1/2 T. salt
1 c. beet liquid	2 bay leaves
1 c. sugar	10 whole cloves

Combine all ingredients in a large jar with a tight fitting lid. Store in refrigerator.

Florence Ross, my Mother

Scrambled Eggs

6 eggs	2 T. butter
1/2 c. half & half or	salt and pepper to taste
1/2 c. cottage cheese	

Beat eggs and half & half together for 30 seconds. (This puts more air in the mixture and yields lighter and fluffier eggs.) Melt butter in a non-stick skillet until it begins to sizzle. Pour egg mixture into skillet. Lower heat and cook, scraping back and forth with a plastic spatula. Do not overcook. Eggs should be moist and fluffy. Season with salt and pepper and serve at once. Serves 3.

Elizabeth Ross

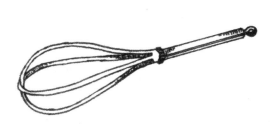

Beer Cheese

2 10 oz. sticks Cracker Barrel extra sharp cheddar cheese, grated	1/4 t. cayenne pepper
	1/4 t. Tabasco sauce
	1/8 t. salt
2 cloves garlic, minced	1 7 oz. bottle of stale beer, or less, to taste
1/2 medium onion, minced	

Combine all ingredients. Mix until thoroughly blended. The mixture will be soft but will harden in the refrigerator. It is better if made ahead of time. Cover and store in refrigerator. Serve with saltines, celery sticks and radish roses.

Cabbage Patch Famous Kentucky Recipes, p. 13

Beer Cheese

3/4 c. beer	2 T. butter
3/4 lb. sharp cheddar cheese	1/4 t. salt
1 1 1/3 oz. pkg. Roquefort cheese	1/4 t. hot pepper sauce or generous dash of cayenne pepper
1/2 small onion	1 t. Worcestershire sauce
2 cloves garlic	

Heat beer slowly in a small saucepan almost to boiling point. Cool to lukewarm. In the meantime, put cheddar and Roquefort cheese through food chopper along with onion and peeled garlic cloves. Grind all in large bowl of an electric mixer. Add butter to mixture and let stand at room temperature for 30 minutes to soften for easier blending. Add salt, pepper sauce and Worcestershire. Begin mixing at medium speed of electric mixer adding beer a little at a time. Beat at high speed as you add more and continue until mixture is smooth and fluffy. It should be quite smooth, but you may not need all of the beer. Put into jars. Cover tightly and store in refrigerator for flavors to blend. Flavor improves the longer mixture is refrigerated, however, plan to use within a couple of weeks or it will mold. Makes 1 3/4 c.

The Cincinnati Cookbook, Fern Storer, p. 290

Beer Cheese

1 lb. sharp cheese	1 t. dry mustard
1 lb. mild cheese	1/8 t. Tabasco
1 t. salt	2 cloves garlic, crushed
2 T. Worcestershire sauce	1 c. beer, or more

Grate or cut cheese into small cubes. Let stand until soft. Beat until smooth and add other ingredients except beer. Mix and add beer 3 T. at a time. Mix until fluffy. Refrigerate in covered container.

Civil Wah Cookbook from Boogar Hollow

Beer Cheese

1 lb. cheddar cheese, grated	1 T. dry mustard
1 lb. Swiss cheese, grated	2 t. Worcestershire sauce
1 clove garlic, crushed	1 c. beer

Combine all ingredients and mix well. Store in a covered jar in refrigerator. Serve with crackers. Makes 2 1/2 c.

The Crowning Recipes of Kentucky, p. 12

Beer Cheese

1 lb. sharp cheddar, finely ground	3 T. Worcestershire sauce
1 lb. mild cheddar, finely ground	4 to 5 drops hot pepper sauce or to taste
1 clove garlic, minced	1 t. dry mustard
1 t. salt	1 12 oz. can beer

Combine all ingredients, except beer, and beat with an electric mixer. Pour in beer slowly and beat until cheese is very smooth. Store in covered jar. Remove from refrigerator at least 30 minutes before serving. Beat once more. Serves 12 to 16.

The Kentucky Derby Museum Cookbook, p. 23

Beer Cheese

1 lb. aged sharp
  cheddar cheese
1 lb. American or "rat" cheese,
  bland
2 to 3 garlic pods, or to taste
3 T. Worcestershire sauce

1 t. salt or more to taste
1 t. powdered mustard
dash Tabasco sauce or
  cayenne pepper
3/4 of a 12 oz. can beer, 1 c.

Grind the cheese (do not use processed cheese) with the garlic pods. Mix with Worcestershire sauce, salt, mustard and Tabasco or cayenne. Put in a bowl in an electric mixer and slowly add enough beer to make a paste smooth enough to spread. Store in covered jars and keep in the icebox until needed.

Out of Kentucky Kitchens, p. 30

Beer Cheese

2 1/2 lbs. Ye Old Tavern cheese,
  ground
4 oz. stale beer

1 1/2 t. granulated garlic
1/2 t. cayenne

The cheese used is semi-soft. Commercial garlic and cayenne (which are extra strong) are used in this recipe. Mix all ingredients and refrigerate. It was the recipe used at Allman's Restaurant on the Kentucky River at Boonesboro.

Emily Utter

Colonel George M. Chinn's Beer Cheese

5 lbs. longhorn cheese
1/2 garlic (3 toes)
1 jar yellow peppers (sport)
2 bottles flat beer
  (pour beer into a receptacle
  and set a spell)

1/2 t. salt
1 oz. Frank's red hot sauce
  (2 if you're brave)

Put cheese through food grinder. Put garlic, peppers, beer, salt and Frank's sauce in blender; it will be a dark brown gloop. Blend the cheese and the liquid mixture together in an electric mixer, a little at a time. Horseradish, fresh ground only, can be added. Serve with crackers and a soothing, nonflammable drink.

Historic Kentucky Recipes, p. 17

Hot Beer Cheese

1 onion about the size of an egg
1 lb. Wisconsin sharp cheese
1 lb. cheddar cheese, not mild
2 bottles Michelob Classic
  dark beer, stale

1 t. garlic powder, to start
1 T. cayenne pepper, to start
7 to 8 shakes Tabasco
1 T. Worcestershire sauce

Chop onion very fine in food processor or blender. Cut cheese into small pieces and add to onion. Add some beer so machine will work smoothly. Add more cheese, more beer, garlic powder, cayenne, Tabasco and Worcestershire sauce. Process until the mixture is just right for a dip. You should have some beer left, but do not discard. Season to taste with a little salt and more hot pepper. After all is mixed and seasoned to taste, cover and refrigerate. After it has set overnight, it is usually too stiff to spread or dip so add remaining beer and more cayenne, if desired.

Cook's note: "My recipe is very much like everyone else's except I like the dark beer and Wisconsin sharp cheese and a good cheddar. Too much sharp cheese will make it bitter."

Katherine Giles, Versailles, Kentucky

Quantity Beer Cheese

6 cloves garlic, optional
2 T. garlic salt
1 T. red pepper
2 T. Accent salt,
  Lowery seasoned

1 small onion, chopped
1 bottle beer, stale
1 10 lb. carton Ye Ole Tavern
  cheddar cheese, softened

Mix first 6 ingredients together in blender. Add to softened cheese.

Faye Davis Maggard

Snappy Cheese (Beer)

1 large box Old English
  sharp cheese
1 can stale beer
2 to 3 cloves garlic, chopped

1 medium onion, chopped
1/3 bottle Tabasco sauce
paprika

Cut cheese into small pieces. Open can of beer and let sit for 24 hours. Mix cheese and beer in a large bowl. Beat until smooth. Add chopped garlic and onion and beat until smooth. Add Tabasco sauce. Add paprika for color.

Food for My Household, Joyce Turpin, p. 1

Snappy Cheese

1 10 oz. can beer	4 garlic buds or garlic powder
1 lb. rat cheese	2 t. red pepper
1 lb. sharp cheese	1/2 t. dehydrated horseradish or
2 medium to large onions	1 t. ordinary

Open beer the night before to become stale. Grate or grind the cheese and onions. Mix with other ingredients. Store in jars and refrigerate. This is the Jim Curry recipe from the Men's Bar, Lexington, Kentucky.

Florence Ross, my Mother

Snappy Cheese Spread

3 lbs. cheddar cheese	1 t. dry mustard
1 1/2 lbs. cream cheese	1 t. Worcestershire sauce
1/2 lb. butter	1 t. catsup
1/4 c. chicken broth	1/4 t. salt
1/4 c. paprika	1/4 t. pepper

Grind the first 3 ingredients then mix the remaining into broth and add to cheese mixture. Blend all together with an electric beater. Place in an earthenware jar and cover with waxed paper. This may be refrigerated for some time. Recipe may be cut in half.

Look No Further, p. 20

Benedictine

1 lb. cream cheese	1 t. white pepper
1 cucumber	1 T. dill weed
1 t. salt	green food coloring

Bring cream cheese to room temperature. Peel cucumber, slice in half lengthwise and seed. Shred the cucumber and squeeze dry. In a mixing bowl, beat the cream cheese until light and fluffy. Add the cucumber and seasonings and mix well. Add food coloring to give it a pale green color.

Donna Gill Recommends, p. 2

Benedictine

2 8 oz. pkgs. cream cheese,
  softened
1 large cucumber,
  peeled and minced

1 medium onion, minced
1 t. mayonnaise
1/4 t. salt
2 to 3 drops green food coloring

Beat the cheese in the mixer. Blend in the other ingredients well and chill.

Thelma's Treasures, p. 33

Benedictine Sandwich Spread

2 6 oz. pkgs. cream cheese
1 medium cucumber, grated
1 t. salt
1 small onion, grated

dash of Tabasco
mayonnaise, enough for spreading
2 to 3 drops green food coloring

Mash the cheese with a fork. Mix in other ingredients and enough mayonnaise to make a smooth filling. Add the green food coloring. Mix and spread on bread.

A Taste from Back Home, p. 62

Benedictine Cheese Spread

1 medium cucumber,
  peeled and seeded
1 8 oz. pkg. cream cheese,
  softened
1 small onion, finely ground

1/2 t. salt or to taste
dash of Tabasco sauce
mayonnaise
2 to 3 drops green food coloring

Grind cucumber pulp very fine. Put in a strainer or cheese cloth and press out juice until pulp is fairly dry. Mash cheese with a fork. Work pulp into cheese and add onion and seasonings. Add enough mayonnaise to make a smooth filling, easy to spread. Add food coloring; just enough to make the spread a pale green. Mix thoroughly. Use to make finger sandwiches or use as stuffing for celery.

Cabbage Patch Famous Kentucky Recipes, p. 14

Benedictine Sandwich Spread

2 large cucumbers	1/2 t. Worcestershire sauce
1 medium onion	salt and pepper to taste
1 8 oz. pkg. cream cheese	2 to 3 drops green food coloring

Peel the cucumbers, cut in half and remove all seeds. Peel the onion. Put the cucumber and onion through a food chopper. Squeeze out as much liquid as possible. Mix with the cream cheese, add Worcestershire and food coloring.

My Old Kentucky Homes Cookbook, p. 5

Benedictine Sandwich Spread

This spread was originated by Miss Jennie Benedict, a Louisville cateress of a generation ago. It is still a favorite at cocktail parties and weddings.

2 6 oz. pkgs. cream cheese	dash of Tabasco
1 medium cucumber,	1 saltspoon salt, or more to taste
pulp grated	mayonnaise
1 onion, grated	2 to 3 drops green food coloring

Mash the cheese with a fork. Work into them the grated pulp from a peeled, medium-sized cucumber, first extracting the juice by placing the pulp in a napkin and squeezing it fairly dry. Add the onion juice, more if a stronger onion flavor is desired, Tabasco, salt and enough mayonnaise to make a smooth filling, easily spread. (Miss Jennie used mayonnaise made of lemon juice, real olive oil and egg yolks.) Last of all, add the green food coloring; just enough to give a faint green tinge for too much will look unappetizing.

Out of Kentucky Kitchens, p. 30

Cucumber Sandwich Filling

green food coloring	1/2 medium onion,
1 8 oz. pkg. cream cheese	ground or grated
1 cucumber	salt to taste
	dash of red pepper

Combine desired amount of food coloring to cream cheese. Grind cucumber and squeeze in a cheesecloth to remove all juice. Add pulp and onion to colored cheese. Salt to taste and add a dash of red pepper.

Out of the Kitchen into the House, p. 2

Liptauer Cheese

5 3 oz. pkgs. cream cheese	2 t. paprika
3 T. capers	4 T. chives, chopped
2 T. onion, finely chopped	1 T. caraway seed
1 tube anchovy paste or to taste	beer
2 t. dry mustard	

Mix all together and soften with beer.

Kentucky Cooking New and Old, p. 2

Olive-Nut Cheese Spread

1/2 to 3/4 c. ripe or stuffed olives, chopped	1 8 oz. pkg. cream cheese, softened
1/2 to 3/4 c. pecans, chopped	mayonnaise

Mix together olives, nuts and cheese. Add enough mayonnaise to make a smooth spreading consistency. Salt and a small amount of prepared horseradish may be added to give it a more tangy taste. This spread may be made without the cheese to make a sandwich filling.

Lucille Vann, Elizabeth Ross

Pimiento Cheese

1 lb. sharp cheddar cheese, grated	1 2 oz. jar chopped pimientos
3/4 c. mayonnaise	1/2 t. salt
	1/2 t. Tabasco sauce

Grate cheese into mixing bowl. Add mayonnaise, pimientos with juice, salt and Tabasco sauce. Mix well. Use to stuff celery sticks or as a sandwich spread. Makes 2 2/3 c.

Fountain Favorites, p. 21

Pimiento Cheese

1 lb. extra sharp cheddar cheese
1 8 oz. pkg. processed cheese spread
1 4 oz. jar chopped pimientos

salt to taste
mayonnaise

Grate cheese into a mixing bowl. Add pimientos with juice and mix well. Add salt to taste and enough mayonnaise to make a smooth but chunky spread.

Florence Ross, my Mother; Elizabeth Ross

Pimiento Cheese Spread

2 lbs. sharp cheese
3 cloves garlic
1 7 oz. jar pimientos
1/2 bottle Durkees dressing
2 c. mayonnaise

2 T. lemon juice
1/2 t. Worcestershire sauce
1/2 t. cayenne
1 t. dry mustard

Cut cheese into 1 1/2" cubes and grate 1/3 at a time in food processor using metal blade. Remove each 1/3 of grated cheese before adding the next. To the last 1/3 of grated cheese, add the garlic cloves and pimientos, juice and all. When well mixed, add the Durkees, mayonnaise, lemon juice, Worcestershire sauce, cayenne and mustard. Add remaining grated cheese and mix well. Keeps in the refrigerator indefinitely. Makes 2 qts.

Cooking with Curtis Grace, p. 22

Pimiento Cheese Spread

1 lb. sharp cheddar or
longhorn cheese, finely grated
1 4 oz. jar chopped pimientos
with juice
1 t. sugar

1/8 t. salt
1/8 t. pepper
1/2 c. mayonnaise
1 T. vinegar

Put grated cheese into mixing bowl. Add remaining ingredients and mix thoroughly with a fork. If mixture is not spreading consistency, add a bit more mayonnaise. Don't use a food processor if you want it a bit chunky with pimiento bits through it. Makes 2 1/2 c.

Southern Style

Kentucky Cheese Fondue

4 t. margarine or butter	1/4 t. salt
4 pieces of bread	1/4 t. dry mustard
3 eggs	dash of cayenne pepper
2 c. milk	4 slices yellow cheese
2 t. Worcestershire sauce	(aged cheddar) cut 1/4" thick,
1/4 t. paprika	enough to cover 4 slices of bread

Soften margarine or butter and spread the pieces of bread on one side only. Beat the eggs with the milk, Worcestershire sauce, paprika, salt, dry mustard and dash of cayenne. Set aside. Grease a rectangular baking dish with butter or margarine. Pour 1/2 of the liquid mixture into this. Place 2 slices of bread, buttered side up, in this mixture in the baking dish. Completely cover the buttered slices of bread with sliced sharp cheese to a thickness of 1/4". Now put the other 2 slices of bread over the cheese, buttered side next to the cheese, making 2 sandwiches. Pour the rest of the liquid mixture over these top slices, then top each slice with another slab of cheese. Place the baking dish in a hot 400 degree F. oven and cook until the cheese melts and bubbles and all liquid has been absorbed. The bread will swell and puff and the cheese will give it a crunchy brown coating. It should be done in 35 to 40 minutes. Serve immediately. Serves 4.

Out of Kentucky Kitchens, p. 81

Cheese Straws

1/4 lb. butter	1 t. salt
1/2 lb. sharp cheddar cheese,	1/2 t. red pepper
grated	1 egg, beaten
1 1/2 c. all-purpose flour	pecans, optional

Let butter and cheese soften to room temperature. Mix well all ingredients except pecans and egg. Roll into 1 1/2" roll, about the size of a half-dollar. Refrigerate. Slice in 1/4" sections. Brush each slice with beaten egg and place pecan half on top. Bake at 350 degrees F. and serve warm. Makes 3 doz.

Best of the Best from Kentucky, Seasons of Thyme, Senator & Mrs. Wendell Ford, p. 21

Cheese Straws

2/3 c. butter
2 c. all-purpose flour
1 3/4 c. sharp cheese, grated

dash of red pepper
3 T. cold water

Cut butter into flour with pastry cutter. Stir in cheese and pepper. Sprinkle with water. Stir with fork and work into dough. Roll out on floured board. Cut in narrow strips with fluted pastry wheel, 3" long. Bake at 350 degrees F. for 10 minutes. These are extra good sprinkled with Parmesan cheese before baking. Makes 150.

Cabbage Patch Famous Kentucky Recipes, p. 8; *Welcome Back to Pleasant Hill*, p. 68

Cheese Straws

1/2 c. butter
1 c. New York cheese, grated
1 to 1 1/2 c. flour
dash of Tabasco

3 t. water
dash of salt
dash of cayenne pepper

Cream butter and cheese. Add flour and seasonings. Run through pastry tube. Bake at 300 degrees F. for 5 minutes and sprinkle with salt while hot. Make them into small cookies with a pecan on top.

Civil Wah Cookbook from Boogar Hollow

Cheese Straws

10 oz. Cracker Barrel
cheddar cheese
1 t. cayenne pepper

1 t. salt
1 stick butter
1 1/2 c. flour

Work all ingredients together by hand. Roll out like biscuit dough. Cut into strips with a pastry cutter or a knife. Cook on an ungreased cookie sheet for 8 to 10 minutes in a preheated 350 degree F. oven. Feel with your fingers; the sticks should be slightly hard. Don't get them brown. They will stay crisp in the refrigerator for a week. Makes 5 to 6 doz.

Thelma's Treasures, p. 27

Cheese Wafers

1 stick butter	1 t. salt
at room temperature	1 c. flour
1/2 lb. grated medium sharp	1/2 pkg. dried onion soup mix
cheese, room temperature	

Mix all ingredients together and make into a roll and wrap in foil. Freeze. Slice thin when ready to bake. Bake at 425 degrees F. for 10 to 15 minutes.

The Crowning Recipes of Kentucky, p. 16

Shakertown Cheese-Pecan Wafers

1 c. butter, softened	1 egg, beaten
2 c. flour	pecan halves
1/2 lb. sharp cheese, grated	salt

Mix butter, flour and cheese together with your hands. Roll out on floured board and cut with a very small biscuit cutter. Place on a cookie sheet and brush tops with beaten egg. Put pecan half on top of each wafer and bake at 350 degrees F. for 10 minutes. As soon as you take them out of the oven, sprinkle with salt and remove from cookie sheet. Makes 70.

Note: I have found that New York sharp cheddar tastes best.

We Make You Kindly Welcome, p. 59; *Weisenberger Cookbook II*, p. 161

Cheese Sauce

3 T. butter	1 c. milk
1/3 c. all-purpose flour	1 c. American cheese, grated

In a double boiler, melt butter and stir in flour. Add milk slowly, stirring constantly, until well blended. Add cheese and continue to stir and cook until sauce is thick and smooth. Serve over Brussels sprouts, green beans, cauliflower or any other vegetable or entree, as desired.

Beaumont Inn Special Recipes, p. 37

A Set of Grits (long way)

6 c. water	1/8 stick butter
1 t. salt	1/4 pt. cream
1 c. grits	

Pour water in top of double-boiler. Add salt. Bring to boiling and slowly add grits. Boil and stir until it begins to thicken so that the steam bubbles pop. Set this saucepan in the double-boiler. Let cook 15 minutes, then stir. Let cool 15 minutes. Put in butter and cover. Do not stir. Let set for 10 minutes and add cream. Stir vigorously. Let cook in double-boiler for 15 to 20 minutes. When ready to serve, beat in small pat of butter.

Source unknown

Grits

4 c. water	1 c. washed grits
1 t. salt	

Bring salted water to a boil. Add grits slowly so that boiling does not stop. Stir. Cover and let cook 40 minutes. Stir often. Serve hot with butter. Serves 4.

Fort Lauderdale Recipes, Recipe Selection Committee, p. 215

Grits Casserole

1 c. grits	2 eggs
4 c. boiling water	2/3 c. milk
1 t. salt	dash Tabasco
3/4 c. grated cheddar cheese	salt to taste
1 small roll garlic cheese	corn flakes, buttered and crushed
1/4 stick butter	paprika

Preheat oven to 350 degrees F. Cook grits in boiling salted water for 25 to 30 minutes. Add cheddar cheese, garlic cheese and butter. Stir until melted. Beat eggs with milk, add Tabasco and salt and mix together with grits mixture. Pour into well-greased 2 qt. casserole and sprinkle with buttered, crushed corn flakes and paprika. Bake for 45 minutes. Serves 6.

Kentucky Derby Museum Cookbook, p. 86

Cheese Grits

2 c. instant grits	1 6 oz. tube garlic cheese spread
3 c. boiling water	1 t. salt
1 stick butter	2 eggs, well beaten

Stir grits into boiling water. Remove from heat and add butter, cheese, salt and beaten eggs. Pour into well-greased casserole. Bake for 45 minutes at 350 degrees F. until set and light brown on top.

Cookbook of Treasures, Jane Cobb, p. 55

Cheese Grits

1 1/2 c. quick grits	1/2 lb. shredded sharp cheese
1 t. salt	3 eggs
1 1/2 sticks margarine	dash of Tabasco sauce
1 1/2 lbs. processed cheese loaf	1/2 t. paprika

Cook grits in boiling water with salt for 3 minutes until thick. Drop margarine, processed cheese and sharp cheese into hot grits and stir until melted. Add eggs, one at a time, mixing well after each egg. Add Tabasco and paprika. Pour into greased baking dish. Bake for 45 minutes at 400 degrees F.

Cookbook of Treasures, Marian Dykes, p. 55

Cheese Grits

4 c. boiling water	8 oz. mild cheddar cheese, grated
1 t. salt	1/2 t. garlic powder
1 c. instant grits	3 eggs
1 stick butter	3/4 c. cream

Bring salted water to a boil and slowly stir in grits. Cook for 3 minutes, stirring constantly. Remove from heat and stir in butter, cheese and garlic powder. Beat eggs and cream together and add to grits. Pour into a greased 2 qt. casserole and bake at 300 degrees F. for 1 hour.

Donna Gill Recommends, p. 26

Cheese Grits

1 c. quick cooking grits	1 lb. processed cheese loaf
3 c. boiling water	2 eggs
1 stick butter	sprinkle of garlic salt

Cook grits in boiling water. When thick, add butter and cheese. Stir until both are melted. Beat eggs lightly and stir into grits and add garlic salt. Pour into buttered oblong glass dish. Bake at 300 to 325 degrees F. for at least an hour. Put a container of water under baking dish in oven.

Speedwell Christian Church Cook Book, Louise Hensley, p. 24

Cheese-Garlic Grits

3 1/2 c. milk	1 t. salt
1 c. grits	2 eggs
1 stick margarine	1/2 c. milk
1 6 oz. roll garlic cheese	1/2 c. cheese, grated

Bring to boil milk and add grits. Cook over medium heat, stirring constantly, for 8 to 10 minutes. Add margarine, garlic cheese and salt. Stir until margarine and cheese are melted. Beat eggs and add milk. Add to grits mixture. Pour into a well-buttered 1 1/2 qt. casserole. Bake 30 minutes in a 350 degree F. oven. Remove from oven and sprinkle grated cheese on top. Return to oven and bake 15 minutes longer.

Cookbook of Treasures, Mary Keene, p. 54, 55

Garlic Cheese Grits

4 c. water	milk
1 t. salt	1 roll garlic cheese
1 c. grits (not quick-cook)	corn flakes
2 eggs	1 roll "nippy" cheese

Boil salted water and add grits. Cook, stirring constantly, until thick. Break the eggs into a cup measure and fill with milk. Add to cooked grits. Melt garlic cheese and add to grits. Mix thoroughly and pour into lightly-greased 1 1/2 qt. casserole. Cover with corn flakes. Cut "nippy" cheese into rounds and place on top of corn flakes. Bake at 350 degrees F. for 45 minutes or until top is brown.

Mrs. James C. Carr

Garlic Cheese Grits

4 1/2 c. water	1 1/2 rolls garlic cheese
1 c. quick grits	1 stick margarine
1 T. salt	4 eggs

Cook together water, grits and salt for 5 minutes. Add cheese, margarine and eggs. Bake at 350 degrees until set.

Speedwell Christian Church Cook Book, Mary L. Sewell, p. 24

Garlic Grits Souffle

2 c. grits	4 egg yolks, beaten
8 c. water	4 egg whites, beaten stiff
1/2 c. butter	bread crumbs
1 t. salt	1 c. sharp cheese, grated
1 tube garlic cheese	paprika

Cook grits in water with butter and salt until done. Add cheese and cook until cheese is melted. Add egg yolks and stir well. Fold in egg whites and pour into greased 3 qt. oven-proof casserole. Sprinkle crumbs, grated cheese and paprika on top. Bake at 350 degrees F. for 40 minutes. Serves 8.

The Crowning Recipes of Kentucky, p. 129

The Rat Takes the Cheese Grits

1 qt. milk	1 c. grits, uncooked
1/2 c. butter	3 squares Gruyere cheese
1/2 t. pepper	1/2 c. Parmesan cheese, grated

Bring milk to boil and add butter, pepper and grits, stirring until creamy. Remove from heat and add cheese. Beat with mixer until very creamy. Pour into greased casserole. Top with butter and Parmesan cheese. Bake at 400 degrees F. for 35 minutes.

Best of the Best from Kentucky, The Corn Island Cookbook, p. 91

Hominy Grits Casserole

1 c. hominy grits	1 t. salt
4 c. water, salted	2 eggs
1 c. sharp cheese, grated	1 1/2 c. milk, approx.
1/2 c. butter	corn flakes

Cook grits in boiling salted water until slightly thick. Add the cheese, butter and salt. Cool a little. Put eggs in measuring cup and add milk to make 1 1/2 c., then beat. Fold egg mixture into grits. Put in 325 degree F. oven for 15 minutes. Stir and sprinkle with corn flakes and cook until firm.

We Make You Kindly Welcome, p. 16

Buttered Hominy

canned hominy	salt and pepper
butter	

Simply empty the can of hominy into a strainer and run cold water through it to flush off the loose starch. Heat it with a bit of butter at a low temperature on conventional range, or in microwave on a low power setting, only long enough to heat through. High heat or over-cooking will shrivel and toughen it. Season with salt and pepper.

Recipes Remembered, p. 160

Soups
&
Sandwiches

Bean Soup

beans, brown or white	1 dried red pepper pod
salt to taste	country ham

Wash and pick through beans, discarding bad ones. Put beans in crock, cover with water and soak overnight. Drain, put in kettle and cover with clean water. Add salt and dried red pepper pod. Bring to a boil, then reduce heat and cook until done. After beans have cooked for an hour, add country ham for seasoning. Serve with fried cornbread.

Dining in Historic Kentucky, vol. 2, Our Best Restaurant, p. 111

Bean Soup

1 lb. dried Great Northern beans	1 t. salt
6 c. cold water	1/4 t. dry mustard
2 lbs. ham shank	1 clove garlic, minced
1/2 c. onion, chopped	6 peppercorns

In a large 5 qt. saucepan, combine beans with other ingredients in water. Simmer, covered, for 3 to 3 1/2 hours until beans are tender. Remove peppercorns and ham bone. Cut ham from bone and return to soup. A pinch of baking soda added to cooking soup is said to reduce the flatulence factor. Serve soup with hot-water cornbread.

Florence Ross, my Mother

Bean Soup

2 c. dried navy beans or	1 c. onion, chopped
other dried beans	4 ripe tomatoes, cut in quarters
1 ham bone,	1 c. potatoes, diced
not too well trimmed	salt and pepper to taste
3 qts. water	1 T. parsley, minced
2 c. celery, diced	

Place beans in cold water, cover and refrigerate overnight. Drain and add to ham bone and water and simmer slowly until beans are tender. Add vegetables and cook another 20 minutes. Remove bone and pass soup through a sieve or food mill. For variety in texture, do not puree soup, but leave beans whole. Season to taste and add minced parsley. Serves 6 to 8.

Note: If ham bone is unavailable, make a broth from 2 smoked ham hocks and 3 1/2 qts. water. Simmer 2 to 3 hours or pressure cook for 30 minutes.

The Shaker Cookbook, p. 31

Ham and Bean Soup

1 c. navy beans	1/2 c. onion, chopped
1 small meaty ham bone	3 1/2 c. canned tomatoes
1 1/2 qts. water	1 T. parsley, minced
1 c. celery, diced	salt and pepper

Soak beans overnight in cold water. Drain in morning. Cover beans and ham bone with water. Add remaining ingredients. Cover and simmer 4 to 5 hours. Season to taste with salt and pepper.

A Taste from Back Home, p. 55

Lake Cumberland Bean Soup

4 c. white navy beans, soaked overnight	1/4 c. chopped parsley or 1/2 c. dried parsley
ham bone with some meat on it	1 1/2 t. salt
4 medium onions, chopped fine	1 t. black pepper
6 stalks celery with tops, chopped fine	1 t. Accent or M.S.G.

Simmer the ham bone and soaked beans in 3 qts. of water for 2 hours. Add remaining ingredients and simmer 1 hour longer. Remove the ham bone. Chop pieces of meat and return to soup. Using a potato masher, mash enough beans to thicken soup.

Recipes from Kentucky State Resort Parks, p. 1

Soup Beans

1 lb. beans	1 T. salt
3 T. sugar	1 piece of pork meat,
	the size of your fingers

Wash and soak beans overnight. Use a large kettle so you can use as much water as possible without having it boil over while cooking. Add sugar, salt and meat. Stir often to prevent sticking. Add more water, if necessary, to have some juice in the beans. Test for taste; you may need more sugar or salt or both.

Ruth Ross Ballard

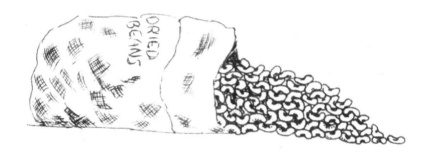

Beer Cheese Soup

2 cloves garlic, minced	1 can beer
2 T. butter	1 lb. sharp cheddar cheese, grated
4 c. rich chicken stock,	1 t. seasoned salt
fat removed	1/2 t. black pepper, freshly ground
1/2 c. flour	1/8 t. cayenne pepper

In heavy saucepan, saute garlic in butter. Over medium heat, add chicken stock and bring to a boil. Stir in flour that has been whisked in beer. Cook until slightly thickened, stirring constantly. Add grated cheese and seasonings. Stir constantly until cheese has melted. Serves 6.

Cooking with Curtis Grace, p. 37

Hearty Kentucky Beer Cheese Soup

4 slices bacon, diced
3/4 c. onion, chopped
1/2 c. celery stalks with tops,
  thinly sliced
1/2 c. carrots, grated

2 c. potatoes, grated
2 T. plain flour
1 t. salt
4 c. milk
8 oz. Kentucky beer cheese

In a large skillet or very heavy saucepan, cook bacon until crisp. Remove bacon and reserve 3 T. bacon drippings. To bacon drippings add vegetables and 2 T. water. Cook until vegetables are tender, stirring frequently. Sprinkle flour over vegetables and stir well. Remove from heat. Add salt and milk. Add bacon pieces and simmer over very low heat for 45 minutes. Remove from heat and stir in Kentucky beer cheese. Serve 6 to 8.

Castano Foods, Inc.

Old Kentucky Brunswick Stew

1 4 lb. young hen
1 veal shank
salt and pepper to taste
1 red pepper pod
2 large onions,
  peeled and chopped
1 lb. small lima beans

1 lb. fresh okra, sliced
1 doz. ears of white corn,
  kernels cut off cobs
1 t. sugar
1 dash seasonings
3 lbs. ripe tomatoes, peeled

Cook the hen and veal with salt, pepper and red pepper pod until meat falls off the bone. Cut meat into pleasant-sized pieces and return to pot in broth which has been strained. Add other ingredients and cook until the vegetables are soft, about 30 minutes. It is said that this recipe came through the Cumberland Gap with Virginians emigrating to Kentucky. Serves 10.

Recipes from Kentucky State Resort Parks, p. 16

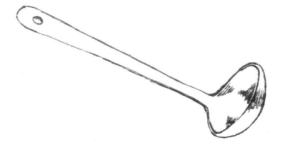

Kentucky Burgoo

1 4 to 5 lb. hen	1 T. Worcestershire sauce
1 lb. beef stew meat	1 1/2 t. black pepper
1 lb. veal stew meat	1/2 t. cayenne
2 lbs. knuckle bones	6 onions, finely chopped
1 stalk celery	8 tomatoes, peeled and chopped
1 carrot, peeled	1 turnip, peeled and chopped
1 onion, peeled	2 green peppers, chopped
6 sprigs parsley	2 c. butter beans, fresh
1 10 oz. can tomato puree	2 c. celery, sliced
4 qts. water	2 c. okra, sliced
1 red pepper pod	2 c. fresh corn
1/4 c. salt	1/2 unpeeled lemon, seeded
1 T. sugar	2 c. cabbage, chopped
1 T. lemon juice	

Combine first 17 ingredients in a large pot. Bring to a boil. Simmer for 4 hours; cool. Strain meat mixture, reserving meat and stock. Discard vegetables. Remove bone, skin and gristle from meat. Finely chop meat and return to stock. Refrigerate overnight. The next day remove layer of fat. Add remaining ingredients. Cover and simmer 1 hour. Uncover and simmer 2 hours, stirring frequently.

My Old Kentucky Homes Cookbook, p. 33

Kentucky Burgoo

2 lbs. pork shank	1 qt. tomato puree
2 lbs. veal shank	2 c. whole corn, fresh or canned
2 lbs. beef shank	2 red pepper pods
2 lbs. breast of lamb	2 c. okra, diced
1 4 lb. hen	2 c. lima beans
8 qts. water	1 c. celery, diced
1 1/2 lbs. Irish potatoes	salt and cayenne to taste
1 1/2 lbs. onions	Tabasco
1 bunch carrots	A-1 Sauce
2 green peppers	Worcestershire sauce to taste
2 c. cabbage, chopped	parsley, chopped

Put all the meat in the cold water and bring slowly to a boil. Simmer until it is tender enough to fall from the bones. Lift the meat out of the stock. Cool and chop up the meat, removing the bones. Pare potatoes, skin onion, and dice both. Return meat to stock and add potatoes, onions and all other vegetables. Allow to simmer until thick. Burgoo should be very thick, but still soup. Season along, but not too much until it is almost done. Add chopped parsley just before the stew is taken up. Stir frequently with a long-handled wooden paddle or spoon during the first part of the cooking and almost constantly after it gets thick. Cissy Gregg says "We made ours in a 4 gal. water bath kettle and all in all it cooked approx. 10 hours." Serves 25.

Cabbage Patch Famous Kentucky Recipes, p. 27; *Cissy Gregg's Cook Book*, vol. 1, p. 22, The Courier Journal & Louisville Times Co., reprinted with permission

Barren River's Famous Burgoo

This is the same as Cissy Gregg's recipe but in a much more manageable and a smaller amount.

1/2 lb. pork shank	1/4 c. celery, diced
1/2 lb. beef shank	1/2 c. whole corn, fresh or canned
1/2 lb. veal shank	1/2 c. cabbage, chopped
1/2 lb. lamb breast	1/2 c. okra, diced
1 lb. hen	1/2 c. lima beans
2 qts. water	salt to taste
3/4 lb. Irish potatoes	cayenne pepper to taste
3/4 lb. onions	Tabasco to taste
1/2 pt. tomato puree	A-1 sauce to taste
2 carrots	Worcestershire to taste
1/2 green pepper	parsley, chopped, to taste
1/2 red pepper pod	

Start cooking burgoo early in the day. Overall cooking time is approx. 10 hours. The time may be broken in half; cooking the meat the first day, then adding vegetables and continue cooking the next day. Put all meat into cold water and bring slowly to a boil. Simmer until it is tender enough to fall from the bones. Lift the meat out of the stock. Cool, chop up the meat, removing the bones. Dice potatoes and onions. Return meat to stock and add all vegetables, potatoes and onions. Simmer until thick. Burgoo should be very thick, but still soupy. Season along, but not too much, until it is almost done. As the burgoo simmers down, the seasoning will become more pronounced. Add chopped parsley just before the stew is taken up. Stir frequently with a long-handled spoon during the first part of the cooking and almost constantly after it gets thick. Serves 4 to 6.

Recipes from Kentucky State Resort Parks, p. 9

Cucumber Soup

1 medium cucumber,
  peeled and sliced thin
2 T. onion, chopped
1 T. butter
1 13 3/4 oz. can chicken broth
1/2 c. packed fresh parsley
  springs, coarsely cut

salt and pepper
1/2 c. half & half or
  whipping cream
2 to 3 fresh chives, finely snipped
fresh dill sprigs, finely snipped

Combine the cucumber, onion and butter in a 2 qt. glass bowl. Microwave on high, covered, for 5 minutes, stirring once. Add the broth and cook on high, covered, until vegetables are soft, stirring twice, for 12 minutes. Put the parsley in a blender container and add the hot soup. Blend on high speed then put through a medium-fine strainer or food mill. Taste and add salt and pepper as needed to season well; seasoning will be slightly diluted when half & half is stirred in. Partially cool, then refrigerate. When cold, stir in half & half or cream and refrigerate several hours or overnight. Thirty minutes before serving transfer soup to the freezer to chill until ice particles are forming around edges. Also chill punch cups. Serve lightly sprinkled with snipped chives and dill. It's best not to serve crackers with a chilled soup; they detract from the delicate flavor. Makes 5, 4 oz. punch cup servings.

My note: Add a drop or two of green food coloring to this soup to call it Benedictine soup.

Recipes Remembered, p. 43

Milk Toast (Graveyard Stew)

Prepare toast and butter. Cover with a generous amount of scalded milk which has been seasoned with salt and pepper. Serve at once. If desired, toast may be broken into a bowl of well-seasoned scalded milk. A good "stomach calmer."

The Household Searchlight Recipe Book, p. 45

Oyster Stew

1/2 pt. oysters	1/8 t. pepper
1/2 stick margarine or butter	butter or margarine
3/4 t. salt	1 qt. milk

Pick oysters for bits of shell. Place in colander and run cold water through oysters. Heat in skillet with salt, pepper and butter until edges of oysters curl. Pour into milk that has been heated, but not boiled. Simmer to near boiling point. Pour into soup bowls. More salt, pepper and butter may be added for individual taste.

Food for My Household, Mrs. Billy Cosby, p. 16

Mazzoni's Original Oyster Stew

2 to 3 T. butter	1 c. whole milk, room temperature
7 to 8 standard size oysters	salt and pepper to taste

Melt all but 1/2 T. of the butter. Place oysters in pan with butter. Saute briefly until oysters begin to lose some of their liquor. Add some of the remaining liquor from the package the oysters came in. When the edges of the oysters begin to wrinkle, add milk. Bring milk to foaming point. Move oysters from the pan to a bowl. Pour hot milk on top and add the reserved 1/2 T. butter. Salt and pepper to taste, taking care not to season too heavily. Serves 1.

Sharing Our Best, Christine Boone, p. 54

Pimiento Soup

(modified Boone Tavern recipe)

3 c. milk (may use skim milk)	8 or 9 level T. flour
4 c. chicken stock or broth	1/2 c. pimientos
1/2 T. onion, finely grated	pepper to taste
5 T. butter or margarine	

Mix milk, chicken stock or broth and onion and warm. If broth is unsalted, add 1 t. instant chicken bouillon. Mix butter and flour as for cream sauce. Increase heat and gradually add warm milk and chicken broth, stirring constantly until desired thickness. Add pimientos and pepper. Stir well. Allow to set for blending of flavors.

Cookbook of Treasures, Nancy Black, p. 26

Boone Tavern Pimiento Soup

2 T. butter
3 T. flour
1/2 t. salt
a few flecks of black pepper
3 c. milk

4 c. chicken stock
(fresh stock or stock made
by dissolving 5 bouillon cubes
in 4 c. boiling water)
1/2 t. onion, grated
1/2 c. pimientos

Melt butter, add flour and seasonings. Blend well. Add milk, meat stock, onion and pimientos that have been put through sieve. Cook 20 to 30 minutes, stirring constantly until mixture thickens. Serves 10.

Look No Further, p. 111

Cream of Pimiento Soup

1 c. potatoes, diced
1 c. boiling water
1 t. onion, minced
1/4 to 1/2 c. pimiento, minced

2 c. thin white sauce
salt and pepper
celery salt
paprika

Combine potatoes, water and onion and cook until tender. Rub through a sieve and add pimiento and white sauce. Season to taste with salt, pepper and celery salt. Heat to boiling. Garnish with paprika.

The Household Searchlight Recipe Book, p. 264; Elizabeth Ross

Cream of Tomato Soup

1 qt. canned tomatoes
1 onion, sliced, optional
3/4 t. soda
1 qt. milk

salt and pepper
4 T. butter
4 T. flour

Boil tomatoes in their own liquid for 15 to 20 minutes. Add onion and when it is done, remove from heat. Stir in soda. Scald milk and add salt, pepper, butter and flour. Add tomato mixture now and it won't curdle. Keep hot but do not allow it to boil. "Put the red in the white or you will be blue."

Florence Ross, my Mother

Herbed Tomato Soup

1/2 onion, finely chopped	1 T. parsley, chopped
oil for sauteing	1 T. basil leaves, chopped
4 c. tomato sauce	1 T. dried thyme, crushed
4 c. chicken stock	salt and pepper

In large saucepan, saute onion in oil until transparent. Add tomato sauce and stock and bring to a boil. Turn off heat and add herbs, salt and pepper. Serves 8.

Dining in Historic Kentucky, vol. 2; Courthouse Cafe, p. 14

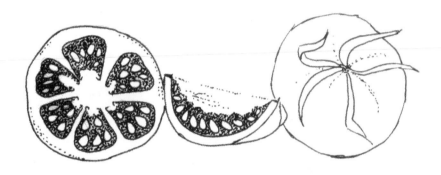

Tomato Celery Soup

1 sm. onion, chopped	1 t. sugar
1/2 c. celery, chopped	1/4 t. salt
2 T. butter	1/8 t. pepper
1 can condensed tomato soup	unsweetened whipped cream,
1 can water	for topping
1 T. lemon juice	1 t. parsley, minced, for topping

Saute onions and celery in butter until clear, but don't brown. Add remaining ingredients. Simmer for 5 minutes. Top with unsweetened whipped cream and parsley.

Cookbook of Treasures, Katherine Whitaker, p. 26

Vegetable Soup

2 1/2 lbs. short ribs
1 T. salt
1/8 t. thyme
6 peppercorns
1 bay leaf
2 allspice

2 beef bouillon cubes
6 c. hot water
1/2 c. onion, chopped
2 c. raw potatoes, cubed
1 1 lb. can tomatoes, undrained
1/2 large pkg. frozen mixed
    vegetables

In large 5 qt. saucepan, combine first 8 ingredients. Simmer, covered, for 3 hours or until meat is tender. Remove beef, peppercorns and bay leaf. Cut meat from bones into chunks and return to soup, adding remaining ingredients. Continue simmering, covered, for 30 minutes or until vegetables are tender. Serve with skillet cornbread.

Elizabeth Ross

The Real Hot Brown Sandwich

As served at the Brown Hotel in Louisville, according to Cissy Gregg, former food editor of the Louisville *Courier-Journal*.

There have been many spin-off versions of this recipe. A hot brown starts with a hen simmered in water with peppercorns, salt and a bay leaf. Cool in the broth and slice the meat thinly. Prepare a Mornay sauce (never cheddar) by starting with 2 c. of medium-thick white sauce. Saute some minced onion in the butter first, then stir in the flour, milk and seasonings (salt, pepper, flecks of parsley, dash of nutmeg). To turn into Mornay sauce, heat the white sauce and combine with 2 egg yolks, beaten to blend. (Stir a bit of the hot sauce into the yolks, then return all to saucepan.) Stir constantly and remove from heat as soon as it starts to boil. When hot and thick, add 1/2 c. grated Parmesan cheese and 1 T. butter. Do not let boil. Fold in 4 T. whipped cream (whipped topping, no way). To assemble sandwiches, fry as many strips of bacon as sandwiches as you are fixing. Saute a mushroom cap for each sandwich. Cut crusts from 2 slices of bread for each sandwich and toast. Put one slice of toast in an oven-proof shallow dish for each serving. Lay slices of chicken on top. Cover with a heaping portion of sauce. Place in very hot oven or beneath broiler until sauce gets a suntan. Cut the extra slice of toast diagonally and put the tips at each end. Top with bacon strips and the mushroom. A little more grated cheese mixed with bread crumbs can be sprinkled over the sauce.

(Note: Some prefer to use half chicken broth, half light cream for the white sauce and then you can skip the addition of whipped cream later. You may also use shredded Swiss cheese in the sauce and part Parmesan - egg yolks may be omitted.) And some would rather make "brown" sauce with a can of soup: In a saucepan, combine 1 can cream of chicken soup, 1/2 c. milk, 1/3 c. white wine, 1/2 c. shredded Swiss cheese, 2 T. Parmesan and 1 egg yolk. Cook, stirring until thickened. Serve over slices of chicken or turkey or asparagus.

The Louisville Courier-Journal & Times, Co.,
reprinted with permission, from the Food Section, many years ago

The "Original" Hot Brown Sandwich

4 oz. butter	salt and pepper
6 T. flour	12 slices toast
3 to 3 1/2 c. milk	roasted turkey breast, sliced
6 T. Parmesan cheese, grated	Parmesan cheese, grated
1 egg, beaten	12 strips bacon
1 oz. heavy cream, whipped	

Melt butter in skillet. Add flour and stir until absorbed. Stir in milk and cheese. Add egg. Do not allow to boil. Remove from heat and fold in cream with seasonings. For each hot brown, place 2 slices toast on oven-proof dish. Cover with sliced turkey and sauce. Sprinkle with additional cheese and broil until speckled brown and bubbling. Remove from broiler, cross 2 strips bacon on top and serve at once. Serves 6.

Dining in Historic Kentucky, vol. 2, The Brown Hotel, p. 134

Hot Brown

4 slices toast	Mornay sauce
4 slices cooked turkey breast	Parmesan cheese, grated
8 slices fried bacon	4 slices of tomatoes

In 4 individual gratin dishes, place a slice of toast and top with turkey and 2 bacon slices. Cover with Mornay sauce. Sprinkle with Parmesan cheese and top with sliced tomato. Place in 400 degree F. oven and bake 10 minutes or until brown and bubbly.

Mornay sauce: Melt 3 T. butter in a pan, remove from heat and stir in 3 T. flour. Pour in 2 c. milk and bring to a boil, stirring. Simmer 2 minutes, season and cool a little before beating in 1/4 c. grated Gruyere or cheddar cheese. Stir in 1/4 t. Dijon-style or prepared mustard and season to taste. Makes 2 c.

Donna Gill Recommends, p. 17

Hot Brown

8 large slices whole-grain toast	4 slices fresh tomato
10 oz. cooked turkey breast, sliced	8 strips bacon, cooked
4 oz. country ham, sliced	paprika
4 mushroom caps, carved and boiled 5 minutes	8 sprigs parsley

Sauce:

1/3 c. butter	1/8 t. nutmeg
2/3 c. onion, diced	1/2 c. sharp cheddar cheese, grated
1/3 c. flour	1/3 c. Parmesan cheese, grated
2 c. milk	2 egg yolks
1/4 t. white pepper	1/2 c. heavy cream

In a 3 qt. saucepan, melt the butter and add the onion. Saute until onion starts to brown. Add flour and mix thoroughly, bringing the mixture to a boil. Whisk in milk, pepper and nutmeg. Bring sauce to a boil for 1 minute. Remove sauce from heat and stir in the cheeses until melted. Add the egg yolks. Return to the heat and cook until the sauce reaches 176 degrees F. This will thicken the egg yolks. To loosen the sauce to the desired consistency, add up to 1/2 c. heavy cream.

To assemble sandwiches: Place baking rack on the top shelf of the oven. Preheat it to 350 degrees F. In 4 individual, oval-shaped, oven-proof dishes place 1 slice of toast on the bottom of each dish. Add the turkey and a T. of the sauce. Add the ham and divide the remaining sauce among the 4 sandwiches. Place a mushroom in the center of each and on each side place a tomato slice. Add strips of bacon and paprika. Bake on top shelf of the oven for 20 minutes and then broil until the cheese sauce starts to turn golden brown. Cut the remaining 4 slices of toast diagonally and place tips at each end of sandwiches. Garnish with parsley and serve. This traditional Kentucky sandwich is rarely served outside the state but is a popular dish with guests in town for the Derby. This recipe is an adaptation of the one by Cissy Gregg. Serves 4.

Mark Sohn, Pikeville, Kentucky

Hot Brown Sandwich

1 pat butter
1 c. cream sauce
1 egg yolk
Tabasco
1 T. cheese, grated

1 T. whipped cream, optional
1 piece toast
sliced chicken or turkey
2 slices bacon, cooked

Add butter to cream sauce and beat in the egg yolk. Add a dash of Tabasco sauce. Add cheese and whipped cream. Place toasted bread in individual baking dish. Cover with sliced white meat of chicken or turkey. Cover entirely with white sauce. Sprinkle more cheese over top. Place 2 strips of partially cooked bacon across and broil in oven until bubbly. Serves 1.

Cabbage Patch Cookbook, p. 63

Hot Brown Sandwich

One hen, cooked in water seasoned with peppercorns, salt and bay leaf and allowed to cool in broth. Slice thin, preferably the white meat.

Sauce One or Bechamel:

1/3 c. butter or margarine	1 t. salt
1/2 medium onion, minced	dash of red pepper
1/3 c. flour	parsley, optional
3 c. hot milk	dash of nutmeg

Melt butter in saucepan. Add onions and cook until light brown. Add flour and blend until a smooth paste. Add milk and other seasonings and cook 25 to 30 minutes, stirring constantly until sauce is thick and smooth and then occasionally. Strain.

Sauce Two or Mornay:

2 c. Sauce One	1 T. butter or margarine
2 egg yolks	1/4 c. whipped cream
1/2 c. Parmesan cheese, grated	

In the top of a double boiler, heat the Sauce One and combine with egg yolks. When hot and thick, add cheese and butter. Sauce must not boil or it will curdle. Fold in whipped cream.

Fry 1 strip of bacon for each sandwich and clean 1 mushroom cap for each sandwich, if desired. To assemble, cut crusts from 2 slices of bread. Toast the bread. Place 1 slice on oven-proof shallow dish and cover with chicken slices. Spoon sauce over and place in a very hot oven or under the broiler until sauce is a golden tan. Cut the second piece of toast diagonally and place at each end of the dish. Top the sandwich with bacon slice and mushroom and sprinkle with more grated cheese mixed with bread crumbs, if desired.

Cissy Gregg's Cook Book, vol. 1, p. 28,
The Courier Journal & Louisville Times Co., reprinted with permission

Hot Brown Sandwich

1/4 c. American cheese, grated	4 slices toast
1 c. cream sauce	8 strips bacon, fried crisp
4 slices baked chicken or turkey	4 T. Parmesan cheese, grated

Blend yellow cheese with cream sauce until cheese has melted. Place a piece of chicken on each piece of toast. Cover with 1/4 c. of sauce. Place 2 strips of crisp bacon on each sandwich and sprinkle with 1 T. of Parmesan cheese. Place in a pan under the flame until cheese melts and becomes a golden brown. Serve at once. Serves 4.

Note: If you have baking dishes, use them as this sandwich should be served in the dish in which it was browned.

Recipes from Kentucky State Resort Parks, p. 50

Hot Brown Sandwich

Sauce:

6 T. butter	1/2 c. Parmesan cheese
6 T. flour	2 egg yolks, whipped
3 c. milk	1/2 c. half & half
3/4 c. sharp cheddar cheese, grated	1/4 t. Worcestershire sauce

Melt butter in a saucepan. Add flour and stir well. Add milk, cheese, eggs, half & half and Worcestershire sauce. Cook, stirring constantly, until thick. Note: Make sure sauce is liquid enough so it won't dry out while baking.

Sandwich:

8 slices toast, trimmed	4 slices tomato
1 lb. cooked turkey or chicken breast meat, sliced thin	8 strips bacon, partially cooked
	4 oz. Parmesan cheese

Cut toast into triangles and place on a baking sheet or into individual baking dishes or ramekins, if you have them. Arrange turkey slices on the toast and cover with hot cheese sauce. Top with tomato slices and bacon strips. Sprinkle with Parmesan cheese. Bake at 425 degrees F. until bubbly. Serves 4.

Note: To freeze, omit tomatoes and wrap in foil. When ready to use, remove foil and bake at 375 degrees F. for 45 minutes.

Emily Utter

Hot Browns

2 T. butter	1/4 c. American cheese, grated
2 T. flour	4 slices chicken or turkey, 1/4" thick
1 c. milk	4 slices toast
1/4 t. salt	8 strips bacon, crisp
dash of white pepper	4 T. Parmesan cheese, grated

Melt butter, blend in flour, but do not brown. Add milk gradually, stirring until smooth. Add salt and pepper. Blend American cheese with cream sauce until cheese is melted. Place sliced chicken on toast, cover with 1/4 of the blended sauce. Place 2 strips of crisp drained bacon on each and sprinkle with Parmesan cheese. Place in a shallow baking pan under flame until cheese melts to golden brown. Serve at once in the dish in which it has been browned. Sliced tomato can be added for variation. Serves 4.

The Cincinnati Cookbook, Mrs. John Saindon, p. 40, 41

Hot Browns

2 slices toasted bread	1 can mushroom soup
cooked, sliced turkey or chicken	2 cans milk
1 T. flour, heaping	crisp bacon slices
1 c. cheese, grated	mushrooms, optional
1/2 stick butter	pimientos, optional

Arrange toast, cut diagonally, on plates. Place turkey or chicken on top of each piece of toast.

Sauce:
Stir flour, grated cheese and butter into mushroom soup. Add milk and cook until thickened. Pour sauce over open face sandwiches and garnish with crisp bacon slices. Add mushrooms and pimientos to the sauce, if desired.

Favorite Recipes, Mrs. Edgar Brandenburg, p. 28

Kentucky Hot Brown

2 T. butter	1/2 t. Worcestershire sauce
1/4 c. flour	1 lb. sliced turkey
2 c. milk	8 slices toast, trimmed
1/4 c. cheddar cheese, grated	4 slices tomato
1/4 c. Parmesan cheese	8 strips bacon, cooked
1/4 t. salt	4 oz. Parmesan cheese

Melt butter in saucepan. Add flour and stir well. Add milk, cheeses and seasonings. Cook, stirring constantly, until thick. Arrange turkey on toast and cover with cheese sauce. Top with tomato slices and bacon. Sprinkle with Parmesan cheese. Bake at 425 degrees F. until bubbly. Serves 4.

Cookbook of Treasures, Katherine Whitaker, p. 120

Kentucky Hot Brown

2 T. all-purpose flour	1/4 to 1/2 c. cheddar cheese, shredded
2 T. margarine, melted	chicken, sliced
1 c. milk	4 slices bread, toasted
1 t. salt	8 slices bacon, fried
1/8 t. white pepper	1/4 c. Parmesan cheese, grated

Combine flour, margarine, milk and seasonings. Cook over low heat, blending until thickened. Add cheddar and melt. Place chicken on toast and cover with sauce. Place 2 slices of bacon on each sandwich and sprinkle with Parmesan cheese. Bake at 400 degrees F. for 10 minutes, more if needed.

Speedwell Christian Church Cookbook, Brenda Bingham, p. 30

Louisville Hot Brown

This adaptation of Cissy Gregg's 2-sauce recipe is an old standard of unknown authorship.

1 small onion, chopped	1/4 c. Parmesan, grated
4 T. butter	8 slices toast, trimmed
3 T. flour	chicken or turkey breast,
2 c. milk	cooked and sliced
1/2 t. salt	bacon, fried crisp and crumbled
1/4 t. white pepper	mushroom slices, sauteed
1/4 c. cheddar, shredded	

Saute onion in butter until transparent. Add flour and combine. Add milk, salt and pepper and whisk until smooth. Cook on medium heat until sauce thickens, stirring occasionally. Add cheeses and continue heating until they blend. Remove from heat. Put 1 slice of toast in each of 4 oven-proof individual serving dishes. Top each piece of toast with slices of chicken or turkey. Cut remaining slices diagonally and place on sides of sandwiches. Ladle cheese sauce over sandwiches. Place sandwiches under broiler until sauce begins to bubble. Garnish with crumbled bacon and sauteed mushroom slices and serve immediately.

The Courier-Journal Kentucky Cookbook, p. 113

Cornbreads

Cornbread

"Perhaps no bread in the world is as good as Southern cornbread, and perhaps no bread in the world is as bad as the Northern imitation of it."

Mark Twain

Buttermilk Cornbread

2 c. cornmeal	1 c. buttermilk
1 c. flour	1 c. water
2 t. baking powder	1/2 t. soda

Combine all ingredients and pour into well-greased pan. Bake in hot oven until top is brown.

The Crowning Recipes of Kentucky, p. 55

Buttermilk Cornbread

2 c. white or yellow cornmeal	1/2 t. baking soda
1/2 c. flour	2 c. buttermilk
1/2 t. salt	2 eggs, well beaten
1 t. baking powder	4 T. shortening, melted

Sift cornmeal, flour, salt and baking powder together. Mix soda with buttermilk. Add to dry ingredients and beat well. Add eggs and beat. Add shortening and mix well. Pour into well-greased, smoking hot, large iron skillet. Place on lower shelf of oven at 450 to 500 degrees F. for 18 minutes. Move to upper shelf of oven and bake 5 to 10 minutes longer.

Recipes from the Miller's Wife

Claudia Sanders Cornbread

2 1/2 c. plain white cornmeal	1/4 c. baking powder
1/2 T. salt	1/2 c. sugar
6 eggs	1 c. shortening
2 c. flour	buttermilk to right consistency

Mix all ingredients together. Pour batter into hot, greased cornstick molds and bake at 450 degrees F. for 10 minutes or until golden brown. Makes 30, 1 1/2 oz. corn sticks.

Historic Kentucky Recipes, Claudia Sanders Dinner House, p. 96

Country Cornbread

1 c. self-rising flour	1 1/2 c. milk or buttermilk
1 c. self-rising cornmeal	1 egg, slightly beaten, optional
1/2 c. vegetable oil	

Mix together and pour into well-greased iron skillet. Bake at 400 degrees F. for 20 minutes.

Southeastern REMC Electric Consumer, April, 1989

Country Style Cornbread

2 c. self-rising cornmeal mix   1 1/4 c. milk
1/2 c. vegetable oil

Heat oven to 450 degrees F. Grease skillet, pan or molds and place in oven to heat. Measure meal into mixing bowl. Add oil and milk. Stir to blend thoroughly. Pour the batter into hot, greased pan. For muffins and sticks, fill pans approx. 2/3 full. Bake 15 to 20 minutes or until golden brown. Makes 1, 8" skillet; 1, 8" square pan; 12 muffins; or 16 corn sticks.

Martha White Cornmeal Mix package

Our Best Restaurant Egg Cornbread

2 c. self-rising cornmeal   2 c. cold milk
2 eggs   1/2 c. shortening, melted

Place cornmeal in bowl. Break eggs into cornmeal. Add milk and shortening and stir together. Fry in greased skillet or griddle. May also be baked in greased skillet in hot oven.

Dining in Historic Kentucky, vol. 2, Our Best Restaurant, Smithfield, Kentucky, p. 111

Lake Cumberland Spider Cornbread

1 c. white cornmeal   1 egg
1/3 c. flour   1 c. milk
1 T. sugar   1/2 c. rich milk
2 t. baking powder   1/4 c. water

Sift the dry ingredients together. Beat the egg and combine with 1 c. milk. Add to dry ingredients and mix well. Heat a lump of butter in an iron skillet and add batter. Over this pour the combined rich milk and water. Do not stir. Bake 30 minutes at 350 degrees F. Cut in pie-shaped wedges and serve piping hot.

Recipes from Kentucky State Resort Parks, p. 5

Sally Lunn Cornbread

1 c. unbleached flour
3 c. yellow cornmeal
1 T. sugar
1 t. salt

1 pkg. dry yeast
1 T. shortening
3 eggs, beaten
3 c. milk, lukewarm 110 degrees F.

In a large mixing bowl combine flour, cornmeal, sugar, salt and yeast. Cut the shortening into the dry ingredients with a pie dough blender. Blend in eggs and milk. Pour batter into greased 10" iron skillet and allow to rest 30 minutes before baking. Bake in preheated 350 degree F. oven for 30 to 40 minutes or until golden brown. Serve with honey and butter.

Old-Fashioned Bread Recipes, p. 21

Skillet Cornbread

3/4 c. cornmeal
1/2 c. flour
1 t. salt
1 t. baking powder

1/2 t. soda
1 c. buttermilk
2 T. vegetable oil or bacon drippings

Heat greased iron skillet. Combine all ingredients. Pour batter into heated skillet and bake at 400 degrees F. for 20 minutes.

The Crowning Recipes of Kentucky, p. 54

Skillet Cornbread

1 1/2 c. white cornmeal,
   preferably water-ground
3 T. all-purpose flour
1 1/2 t. baking powder

1 t. salt
2 T. butter or shortening, melted
1 1/2 c. milk
1 egg, beaten

Sift together cornmeal, flour, baking powder and salt into a bowl. For coarse texture, simply mix. Melt butter or shortening in a 10" iron skillet in a 450 degree F. preheated oven. Add milk and egg to dry ingredients, stirring to combine. Do not overbeat. Add melted butter from skillet to batter. Mix. Pour batter into very hot skillet. Bake at 450 degrees F. for 20 to 25 minutes. Makes 9 servings

Source unknown

Sour Cream Cornbread

1 c. self-rising cornmeal
2 eggs
1 8 1/4 oz. can cream-style
    corn, undrained

1/2 c. salad oil or bacon drippings
1/2 t. salt
1 c. sour cream

Combine and mix all the ingredients well. Pour into a greased 9" pan. Bake in a 400 degree F. oven for 20 to 30 minutes. Can be frozen after baking. Reheats well. Serves 4 to 6.

Best of the Best from Kentucky, Entertaining the Louisville Way, vol. II, p. 70

Southern Cornbread

1 1/2 c. cornmeal
3/4 t. baking soda
1 t. salt

1 1/3 c. buttermilk
2 eggs, separated
1/4 c. shortening, melted

Sift cornmeal, soda and salt together. Add buttermilk to well-beaten egg yolks and add cornmeal mixture. Beat well. Add hot melted shortening and beat well. Fold in stiffly beaten egg whites and pour into greased skillet. Bake at 450 degrees F. for 20 to 30 minutes.

Speedwell Christian Church Cookbook, Nell Pearson, p. 48

Yeast Cornbread (Cornmeal Sally Lunn)

1 c. flour
1 T. sugar
1 t. salt
3 c. cornmeal

1 T. lard or other shortening
3 eggs
3 c. milk
1 yeast cake

Sift together the flour, sugar, salt and cornmeal. Then put the siftings back in, you don't want to lose the coarseness of the water-ground cornmeal. Rub the cold lard into these dry ingredients. Beat in the well-beaten eggs. Scald the milk until it is lukewarm and crumble in the yeast. Stir until the yeast is dissolved. Beat the milk into the cornmeal mixture. This should make a moderately stiff batter. Pour batter into well-greased shallow baking pans, 8" square, or pie pans. Let stand in a warm kitchen until the batter begins to rise. Bake in a 375 degree oven for 30 to 40 minutes.

Cissy Gregg's Cook Book, vol. 1, p. 16,
The Courier Journal & Louisville Times Co., reprinted with permission

Cornbread or Cornsticks

1 c. cornmeal	1 c. buttermilk
1 t. salt	1 egg
1/2 t. soda	2 T. shortening
1 t. baking powder	

Sift dry ingredients together. Add buttermilk, well-beaten egg and shortening. Pour into well-greased frying pan or cornstick pan. Bake in hot oven at 350 degrees F. for 25 minutes or until brown. Can be made with sweet milk but omit soda.

Source unknown

Cornsticks

1/2 t. salt	1 egg
1/2 t. soda	1/2 c. flour
3 t. sugar, optional	1 c. buttermilk
1/2 t. baking powder	1 c. plus 2 T. cornmeal
2 T. oil	

Beat all ingredients together. Beat well. Heat greased irons until hot enough to sizzle. Fill irons to half full. Bake at 450 degrees F. in a preheated oven for 10 minutes or until golden. The secret of good cornbread is beating well and using hot irons.

We Make You Kindly Welcome, p. 45

Angel Cornsticks

3/4 c. cornmeal	3/4 t. baking powder
1/2 c. all-purpose flour	1/4 t. soda
1/2 pkg. dry yeast	1 egg, beaten
1/2 T. sugar	1 c. buttermilk
1/2 t. salt	1/4 c. vegetable oil

Combine first 7 ingredients in large bowl. Combine egg, buttermilk and oil. Add to dry ingredients, stirring until batter is smooth. Spoon the batter into well-greased cast iron corn-stick pans, filling half full. Bake at 450 degrees F. for 12 to 15 minutes. Makes 18.

Speedwell Christian Church Cookbook, Edna M. Hord, p. 51

Boone Tavern Cornsticks

1/2 c. flour	1/2 t. baking soda
2 c. white cornmeal	2 c. buttermilk
1/2 t. salt	2 eggs, well beaten
1 t. baking powder	4 T. lard, melted

Sift flour, cornmeal, salt and baking powder together. Mix soda with buttermilk. Add to dry ingredients. Beat well. Add eggs and beat. Add lard and mix well. Pour into well-greased, smoking hot cornstick pans on top of stove. Fill pans to level. Place on lower shelf of oven at 450 to 500 degrees F. for 8 minutes. Move to upper shelf and bake 5 to 10 minutes longer. It is important to heat well-greased cornstick pans to smoking hot on top of stove before pour-ing in your batter. Makes 1 doz.

Look No Further, p. 3

Hoe Cake Number One

2 c. water-ground white cornmeal	2 eggs, well beaten
1 t. salt	sweet milk, cold
boiling water	2 T. fat, melted

Combine cornmeal with the salt and mix well. Pour over it boiling water to make a thick paste and then cool slightly. Add the beaten eggs and enough cold milk to give a smooth pancake-consistency batter. Lastly, add the melted fat. Bake on a hot griddle in small batches. Bake on one side until bubbles form, then turn and bake on the other until brown. Serve hot with a generous supply of butter.

Cissy Gregg's Cook Book, vol. 1, p. 16,
The Courier Journal & Louisville Times Co., reprinted with permission

Hoe Cake Number Two

1 c. cornmeal	1/2 t. salt
1/4 c. flour,	2 eggs, well beaten
sifted before measuring	1/2 c. sweet milk
1 1/2 t. baking powder	4 T. butter or fat, melted

Mix dry ingredients together and combine the beaten eggs and milk. Stir until smooth. Last, add the melted fat. Bake as individual cakes on a hot, well-greased griddle on top of the stove, or in a skillet or heavy pan in a 400 degree F. oven, having the batter 3/4" thick.

Cissy Gregg's Cook Book, vol. 1, p. 16,
The Courier Journal & Louisville Times Co., reprinted with permission

Hoe Cake or Pone Bread

Mix 1 c. plain cornmeal with water to make a soupy mixture. Add 1 t. salt. Pour a thin layer onto a hot, well-greased frying pan. Allow to brown and turn once. Serve hot. If making pone bread, use less water and shape into pones. Cook in oven at 325 degrees F. until brown.

Source unknown

Hot-Water Cornbread

2 c. white cornmeal
1 t. salt
1 t. sugar

1 T. solid shortening
1/4 c. half & half cream
1 1/2 to 2 c. boiling water

Combine cornmeal, salt and sugar in bowl. Add shortening and cut into meal. Add cream and boiling water and stir to mix well. In a skillet melt shortening to a depth of 1/2". Heat to 325 degrees F. Using a large kitchen spoon scoop up a spoonful of the meal mixture and drop into the skillet. Fry, turning to brown on both sides, for 5 minutes. Serve warm with whipped butter.

Donna Gill Recommends, p. 39

Hot-Water Cornbread

2 c. white cornmeal
1 t. salt

boiling water,
    enough to make thick mush
solid shortening for frying

Mix cornmeal and salt. Add boiling water, stirring constantly until a thick mush forms. Add enough water so it can easily be spooned onto a hot griddle. Fry until golden. Turn and fry other side. Be sure one side is done before turning. Add extra shortening during frying if bread appears to be dry.

Food for My Household, Alene L. Tudor, p. 71

Hot-Water Cornbread

2 c. white cornmeal,
    preferably water-ground
1 t. salt
2 T. shortening or bacon grease

2 c. water
1/2 t. baking powder
2 T. milk, warmed

Combine cornmeal and salt in a bowl. Add shortening to water and bring to a rolling boil. Add to cornmeal mixture, stirring hard until mixture reaches consistency of a moist croquette. Let cool 20 minutes. Combine baking powder and milk and add to cornmeal mixture, stirring to combine. Shape dough into 1" balls. Press each ball between 2 fingers to make a

slight indentation on 2 sides. Heat an iron skillet containing 1/4" shortening until smoking.
Carefully slide shaped dough into hot (375 degree F.) shortening. Cook only a few at a time
until golden brown. Turn and cook on other side. Drain on paper towels and keep warm in
oven until all cakes are cooked. Serve hot with lots of butter. These are great with bean or
vegetable soup. Makes 2 1/2 doz.

Florence Ross, my Mother

Cornbread Pones

1 to 1 1/4 c. white cornmeal	2 1/2 t. shortening, melted
1/2 t. salt	1 c. buttermilk
1/4 t. baking soda	

Combine dry ingredients. Blend in shortening and milk. Shape into flat pones. Place in a
well-greased preheated skillet or baking sheet. Bake at 400 degrees F. for 15 to 20 minutes.
Makes 1 doz.

Recipes from the Miller's Wife

Cornmeal Batter Cakes

1 c. cornmeal ·	2 eggs, beaten
1/2 t. baking soda	1 1/4 c. buttermilk
1/2 t. salt	2 t. bacon drippings or shortening

Sift cornmeal, soda and salt together. Add beaten eggs, then buttermilk. Beat until smooth.
Dip a tablespoon of batter onto a greased hot griddle. Let brown on bottom then turn quickly and lightly brown on other side.

Beaumont Inn Cookbook Special Recipes, p. 89

"Batty Cakes" with Lacey Edges

1 c. white cornmeal,	1 egg
water-ground if possible	1 1/4 c. rich buttermilk
1/2 t. soda	from which no butter
1/2 t. salt	has been removed

Sift dry ingredients. Slowly add well-beaten egg mixed with milk, beating batter until very smooth. Drop by tablespoons on well-greased iron skillet allowing 1 t. lard, or substitute, for every 4 cakes. When brown on one side, turn with a pancake turner and brown on the other side. If batter gets too thick add a bit more milk a T. at a time. Serve with molasses or maple syrup. Serves 6.

Dixie Dishes, p. 23

Indian Griddle Cakes

1/2 t. salt	1 egg
1/2 t. soda	1/2 c. flour
3 t. sugar	1 c. buttermilk
1/2 t. baking powder	1 c. plus 2 T. cornmeal
2 T. oil	sweet milk

Mix, beating all ingredients except sweet milk. When the mixture is smooth, add enough sweet milk to make the consistency of the batter thin. Heat a griddle covered with melted shortening until very hot. Dip 1/4 c. batter to each cake. Fry until bubbly on the top and light brown on the bottom. Flip and cook until done.

We Make You Kindly Welcome, p. 4

Lonesome Pine Corncake

1/2 c. sifted flour	2 eggs, well beaten
2 c. white cornmeal	1/2 t. baking soda
3 t. baking powder	1 1/2 c. buttermilk
1/2 t. salt	5 T. lard, melted
1/2 c. milk	

Sift flour, cornmeal, baking powder and salt together. Add the milk to the beaten eggs. Add the egg mixture to the flour mixture and beat well. Mix the baking soda with the buttermilk. Add to the batter and mix well. Add the melted lard and beat together well. Heat a 9"x13" baking pan in a 475 degree F. oven until it is very hot. Grease the pan well with lard. Pour the batter into the pan and bake at 475 degrees F. for 30 minutes. The cornbread is also good to use in making dressing. Makes 12 to 18 squares.

More Hougen Favorites, p. 129

Lacey-Edged Cornmeal Cakes

2 eggs
2 c. milk
1 c. coarse water-ground
   white cornmeal

1 t. salt, scant
3 T. butter, melted

Beat eggs well. Add milk and beat again. Add cornmeal and salt. Add butter and stir batter. Spoon batter onto a well-greased hot griddle. Stir batter each time you do this and grease griddle between each batch. Turn cakes when broken bubbles appear on the surface and center seems dry. Turn only once.

The Cincinnati Cookbook, Mrs. T. Milburn Coutcher, p. 67

Spooncakes

1/2 c. white cornmeal
1/4 t. baking soda
1/2 t. baking powder
1/2 t. salt

1 c. buttermilk
1/4 c. water
4 eggs
4 T. butter, melted

Sift together dry ingredients. Add buttermilk and water and beat. Add beaten eggs and beat. Add melted butter last and beat all together. Drop by spoonfuls onto a hissing hot griddle which has been greased before cooking each cake. Use a large skillet if desired. Serve piping hot from the griddle.

These spooncakes are one of the favorite Boone Tavern hot breads. They are cut in half and eaten by buttering a bite and holding the cake in your fingers.

Look No Further, p. 15

Crackling Bread

1 1/2 c. white cornmeal
3 c. boiling water

1/4 t. salt
1 c. crushed cracklings

Cracklings are the crisp bits left after fat has been thoroughly rendered. Mix cornmeal, water and salt. Add cracklings. Form into cakes and fry in shallow fat until brown. Place in a hot oven for a few minutes to crisp.

Elizabeth Ross

Corn Dodgers

sour milk or buttermilk	1 t. salt
1 1/2 c. meal	1 egg
1 T. flour	1/2 t. soda

Add enough sour milk or buttermilk to next 4 ingredients to make a stiff batter and add soda to keep company with the sour milk. Mold into dodgers and cook in a greased pan in a 450 degree F. oven. Makes 8.

Cissy Gregg's Cook Book, vol. 1, p 25,
The Courier Journal & Louisville Times Co., reprinted with permission

Lacy Cornmeal Pancakes

1 c. cornmeal	1 egg, beaten
1/2 t. baking soda	1 to 1 1/4 c. buttermilk
1/2 t. salt	

Mix cornmeal, baking soda and salt together. Add the beaten egg and buttermilk, beating until smooth. The secret of having the cakes trimmed with lace is to get the batter thin enough. Sometimes, if the buttermilk is very thick, it is a good idea to thin it with sweet milk or water. Pour or dip a generous T. of batter onto a hot griddle. Bake until brown and turn only once. Also, don't stand by and "spank" the cakes after they have been turned, either. With these corn pancakes it is necessary to stir the batter each time before dipping or pouring.

Cissy Gregg's Cook Book, vol. 1, p. 16,
The Courier Journal & Louisville Times Co., reprinted with permission

Hushpuppies

1 1/2 c. plain white cornmeal
2 t. baking powder
1/2 t. salt
1 T. sugar
1 egg, beaten

1 onion, chopped
1/2 c. self-rising flour
3/4 c. sweet milk
oil, enough for deep frying

Mix together all ingredients except oil. Drop by spoonfuls into preheated oil. Cook until golden brown. Drain on paper towels.

Nancy Ballard McQuerry, Harrodsburg, Kentucky

Hushpuppies

1 c. cornmeal
1 c. all-purpose flour
2 t. baking powder
1 t. brown sugar

1/2 t. salt
1 egg, beaten
1/2 c. onion, chopped
milk

Combine cornmeal, flour, baking powder, sugar and salt. Beat in egg and onion. Add just enough milk to make batter stiff. Drop from a spoon into boiling fat and fry until golden brown.

Old-Fashioned Bread Recipes, p. 26

Hushpuppies

1/2 c. self-rising meal
1/2 c. self-rising flour
1 T. sugar
1/2 t. salt

1 large onion, chopped
1 egg
2/3 c. milk

Mix together all ingredients. Let stand for 30 minutes to 1 hour before frying. Drop by teaspoon into hot grease that has been used for frying fish.

Sharing Our Best, Agnes Humphrey, p. 82

Hushpuppies

2 c. cornmeal	onion, finely chopped
2 t. baking powder	2/3 c. milk
1 t. salt	1 egg

Mix cornmeal, baking powder and salt. Add onion to taste. Stir in milk and egg. Mold into balls about the size of a golf ball and fry in hot fish fat or hot oil.

We Make You Kindly Welcome, p. 65

Hushpuppies

2 c. cornmeal	1 egg
1 T. flour	3 T. onion, finely chopped
1/2 t. soda	1 c. buttermilk
1 t. salt	

Mix together dry ingredients. Add all other ingredients. Mix well. Drop by a teaspoon into hot deep fat. They will float when done. Makes 20.

Weisenberger Cookbook II, p. 153

Hushpuppies

2 c. cornmeal	1 t. sugar
1/4 c. flour	1/2 c. onion, chopped
1/2 t. soda	1 c. buttermilk (to use sweet milk,
1 t. baking powder	omit sugar)
1 t. salt	1 egg

Mix together dry ingredients. Add onion, then buttermilk. Add beaten egg. Drop into hot grease from spoon.

Note: This recipe was on the back of Weisenberger's cornmeal bags from the 1950's to 1979. They still get requests for it.

Weisenberger Cookbook II, p. 153

Kentucky Dam Village Hushpuppies

1 c. self-rising cornmeal	1/4 t. paprika
1/2 c. self-rising flour	2 t. dry chives, chopped
1 t. salt	1/4 c. onion, minced
1 t. garlic powder	3/4 c. buttermilk

Mix together all ingredients. Drop mixture into fryer, heated to 300 degrees F. using very small ice cream scoop or iced tea spoon. Cook for 5 minutes or until golden brown. Makes 12 to 16 hushpuppies.

Sample West Kentucky, p. 104

Tennessee Hushpuppies

2 c. cornmeal	1 T. baking powder
1 t. soda	6 T. onion, chopped
1 t. salt	2 c. buttermilk
2 T. flour	1 egg

Mix together dry ingredients. Add chopped onion, then milk and egg together. Drop by small spoonfuls into boiling hot fat. They will float when done. Drain on brown paper.

A Taste from Back Home, p. 41

Uncle Johnnie's Hushpuppies

1 c. plain cornmeal	1/2 t. pepper
2 T. onion, minced	1/2 t. baking soda
1/2 t. salt	1/4 c. buttermilk

Mix cornmeal, onion, salt and pepper. Dissolve soda in milk and add to meal mixture. Beat well and drop from spoon into hot fat and brown on both sides.

Source unknown

Hushpuppy Mix

1 c. self-rising corneal
1 c. self-rising flour
1/2 c. onion, chopped
2 1/2 t. sugar

1 1/2 t. salt
2 t. baking powder
2 eggs

Mix with buttermilk until the right consistency.

Recipes from Kentucky State Resort Parks, p. 5

Tavern Hushpuppy

1/2 t. salt
1/2 t. baking powder
1 c. white cornmeal
1/4 t. baking soda

1/2 c. buttermilk
1 egg
1/2 c. onion, grated

Sift salt, baking powder and cornmeal. Mix soda with buttermilk and add to cornmeal mixture. Mix well. Add beaten egg and mix well. Add grated onion. Shape into small balls and drop into deep fat. Fry until golden brown.

Look No Further, p. 162

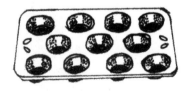

Johnnycake

Put 1 qt. cornmeal into a bowl. Add a heaping t. of salt. Stir in boiling water until it is all moistened. With your hands, mold it into cakes 1/2" thick. Bake cakes on a hot griddle rubbed with a bit of pork fat. Let them cook slowly. When one side is done turn the other. They may be baked in an oven for 20 minutes. Serve hot with plenty of butter. Sounds like another version of hot-water cornbread to me.

Prairie Recipes and Kitchen Antiques, p. 36

Elmwood Inn Corn Muffins

1 c. cornmeal	1/4 c. sugar, add more if you like
1 c. plain flour	1 stick butter, melted
4 t. baking powder	1 egg
1/2 t. salt	1 c. sweet milk

Sift together all dry ingredients including sugar. Pour melted butter on top. Mix egg and milk and pour on top of butter. Mix and bake in muffin tins at 425 degrees F. for 15 to 20 minutes. Makes 1 doz.

Recipes from the Miller's Wife

Indiana Corn Muffins

1 c. cornmeal	1 c. milk
1 c. all-purpose flour	2 eggs, beaten
1 t. salt	2 T. shortening, melted
2 1/2 t. baking powder	

Preheat oven to 400 degrees F. Sift dry ingredients into bowl. Combine milk with eggs and add to dry ingredients. Add shortening and stir until blended. Pour into 2" muffin tins and bake for 20 minutes. You can also use this recipe to make cornsticks.

Recipes from the Miller's Wife

Fried Cornmeal Mush

1/2 c. cornmeal   3/4 t. salt
2 3/4 c. boiling water

Sprinkle cornmeal into rapidly salted boiling water (using the top of a double boiler). Stir constantly. When thickened, cook over hot water at least 1 hour, stirring only occasionally. While hot, pour into a greased loaf pan. Smooth surface of mush. Chill overnight or until very firm. Cut into 3/4" slices and brown in hot fat on both sides. This is especially good with maple syrup.

The Household Searchlight Recipe Book, p. 111

Spoonbread

3 c. milk, scalded   2 T. butter flavor shortening
1 1/4 c. plain cornmeal   1 t. salt
3 eggs   1 3/4 t. baking powder

Boil milk to rolling. Add meal and beat well. Let cool. Add eggs, butter flavor shortening, salt and baking powder. Bake at 375 degrees F. for 30 minutes. Bake in a Pyrex dish that you can use to serve it in. Spoon out as you want.

Cookbook of Treasures, Jane Cobb, p. 71

Spoonbread

1 c. cornmeal   1 t. salt
3 c. milk   3 t. baking powder
3 eggs, beaten   2 T. butter or margarine

In saucepan, stir meal into 2 c. milk. Let come to a boil, making mush. Add rest of milk and well-beaten eggs. Stir in remaining ingredients. Bake at 350 degrees F. for 30 minutes.

Cookbook of Treasures, Katherine Powell, p. 71

Spoonbread

1 c. boiling water	1/2 t. salt
1/2 c. yellow cornmeal	1 egg, well beaten
2 T. butter	1/2 c. milk

Pour boiling water over cornmeal, stirring constantly. Add butter and salt. Cook briskly for 3 to 4 minutes. Remove from heat and add egg and milk. Beat with rotary beater to obtain smooth mixture. Pour into well-buttered shallow baking dish. Bake at 400 degrees F. for 20 to 25 minutes. Serves 6.

The Crowning Recipes of Kentucky, p. 69

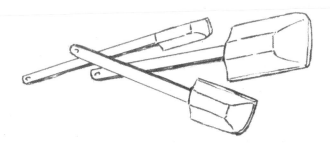

Spoonbread

2 c. milk	1 c. cold milk
1 c. white cornmeal	1 t. baking powder
1 T. brown sugar	3 eggs yolks, beaten
1 t. salt	3 egg whites, beaten stiff
3 T. butter	

Heat milk to the scalding point in a sauce pan. Gradually stir in the cornmeal, brown sugar, salt and butter. Remove pan from heat. Blend in the cold milk, then baking powder. Beat egg yolks in a separate bowl and stir a cup of the hot liquid into them. Stir yolk mixture into milk mixture. Beat egg whites to stiff-peak stage and fold into mixture. Pour into well-greased 2 qt. souffle dish or casserole. Bake in 325 degree F. oven for 50 minutes. Done when knife inserted in center comes out clean.

Old-Fashioned Muffins and Biscuits, p. 30

Spoonbread

1 qt. sweet milk	2 T. butter
1 c. cornmeal	1/2 t. baking powder
3 eggs, separated	1 3/4 t. salt

Scald milk and add meal gradually. Cook until thick. Pour small amount over beaten egg yolks, then add egg yolks to meal mixture. Return to heat and cook a few minutes longer. Add butter and fold in beaten egg whites, adding baking powder and salt. Pour into greased baking dish and cook at 325 degrees F. for 1 1/2 hours. Stir once after first 15 minutes of cooking.

We Make You Kindly Welcome, p. 65

Spoonbread

2 1/2 c. milk	1 1/2 T. butter, melted
1 c. cornmeal	4 egg yolks, beaten
1 t. salt	4 egg whites, beaten stiff
3 t. baking powder	

Combine milk, cornmeal, salt and baking powder. Cook until thick, stirring constantly. Add melted butter. Cool this cooked mixture for 10 minutes. Add the beaten egg yolks and mix well. Fold in egg whites. Pour into a 1 1/2 qt. casserole. Bake 1 hour at 325 degrees F.

Speedwell Christian Church Cookbook, Edna Hord, p. 45

Kentucky Spoonbread

1 stick margarine	1 8 oz. can whole kernel corn
2 eggs	1 8 oz. can creamed corn
1 8 oz. carton sour cream	1 8 oz. pkg. corn muffin mix

Melt margarine. Beat eggs slightly in separate bowl. Add eggs to margarine. Mix and add sour cream. Mix and add corn. Mix and add corn muffin mix. Mix and bake in a 1 1/2 qt. casserole at 350 degrees F. for 30 minutes.

Speedwell Christian Church Cookbook, Janie McGraw, p. 46

Plantation Spoonbread

4 T. flour	1 egg, beaten
1 T. sugar	1 c. milk
1 t. baking powder	2 T. butter
1 t. salt	1/2 c. milk
3/4 c. yellow cornmeal	

Sift the flour, sugar, baking powder and salt into a medium-sized mixing bowl. Stir in corn-meal. Blend in egg and milk. Melt butter in the bottom of an 8"x8" baking dish and pour batter into dish. Pour the 1/2 c. milk over batter. Bake in a preheated 375 degree F. oven for 45 to 50 minutes. Top will be golden and crusty. Serve hot.

Old-Fashioned Bread Recipes, p. 22

Southern Spoonbread

This is the spoonbread for which Boone Tavern is so famous. Be sure to use white cornmeal for the true Southern bread.

1 1/4 c. white cornmeal	1 t. salt
3 c. milk	1 3/4 t. baking powder
3 eggs	2 T. butter

Stir meal into rapidly boiling milk. Cook until very thick, stirring constantly to prevent scorching. Remove from fire and allow to cool. The mixture will be cold and very stiff. Add well-beaten eggs, salt, baking powder and melted butter. Beat with electric beater for 15 min-utes. If hand beating, break the hardened cooked meal into the beaten eggs in small amount until all is well mixed. Then beat for 10 minutes using a wooden spoon. Pour into a well-greased casserole. Bake for 30 minutes at 375 degrees F. Serve from casserole by spoonfuls.

Look No Further, p. 16

To make Self-rising Cornmeal

1 c. cornmeal   1/2 t. salt
1 1/2 t. baking powder

Mix together. You will have 1 c. self-rising cornmeal.

Weisenberger Cookbook II, p. 13

To Season Cast Iron Cookware

Heat cookware in the oven or on top of stove. Using a paper towel or cloth, wipe cookware with a light coat of unsalted cooking oil. Reheat in oven or on top of stove. Repeat 1 to 3 times for best results. Do not wash in soap and water when cleaning. Wipe with a light coat of cooking oil.

Source unknown

Breads

Beaten Biscuits

4 c. flour	1 t. baking powder
3 t. sugar	4 T. lard, level
1 t. salt	2/3 c. milk and water, half and half

Mix dry ingredients together. Add lard and rub well into dry ingredients. Add the liquid, which should make a stiff dough. Put through the kneader 75 times, or beat with a mallet until it blisters. Roll out 1/2" to 3/4" thick and cut into discs approx. 2" in diameter. Stick in the center with table fork 3/4 of the way through. Bake at 400 degrees F. approx. 20 minutes, or until they rise and appear very light brown. Makes 3 doz.

Beaumont Inn Special Recipes, p. 88

Beaten Biscuits

5 c. flour	1 c. lard
1/4 c. sugar	1/2 c. ice water
1 T. salt	1/2 c. milk
1/2 t. baking powder	

Mix all together. Knead and beat. If you don't have a kneader, beat and fold over. Continue this for a while, then roll out and cut out. Bake at 350 degrees F. for about 30 minutes, then cut oven down to 200 degrees F. for 10 minutes. Cut off oven and let stand in oven for 5 minutes.

A Cookbook of Treasures, Jane Cobb, p. 62

Beaten Biscuits

7 c. White Lily flour,	2 T. sugar
plain all-purpose, 1 3/4 lb.	1 c. solid shortening, frozen
1 t. salt1	1/3 c. cold milk, just before
1 t. baking powder	measuring dry ingredients
	measure milk and place in freezer

Sift the flour, salt, baking powder and sugar together 3 times. Cut shortening into dry ingredients until almost like meal. Slowly add cold milk, working it in with a fork until a ball is formed. Work with hands until it holds together solidly. Place dough in a plastic bag in the freezer for 1 hour or in the refrigerator 2 to 3 hours. Roll on biscuit kneader 150 passes or for 30 minutes. After the first 100 passes, about 20 minutes, turn oven to 375 degrees F. After 150 passes, roll dough to 3/8" thickness and cut out biscuits with a 2" or smaller cutter. Place on pan with low sides or cookie sheet and pierce all the way through 3 times with a fork. Place on second from bottom rack in preheated oven and immediately turn oven back to 350 degrees F. Bake 30 minutes. Turn off oven and leave biscuits in for 5 minutes. Remove from oven. After pan is cool, transfer biscuits to wire rack to finish cooling. When cool, store in airtight container or in a plastic bag in freezer.

Cookbook of Treasures, Connie Congleton, p. 62

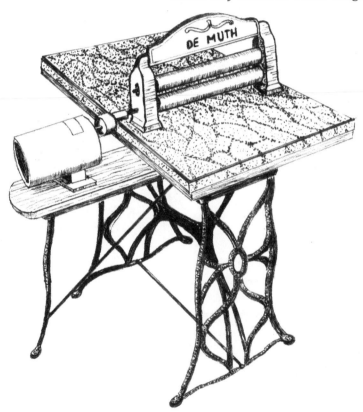

Using a Beaten Biscuit Machine

If using a beaten biscuit machine, fold the dough in half and feed, folded end last, through the rollers approx. 12 to 15 times. The dough is ready for cutting when the folded end emits a popping sound as it passes through the rollers.

Beat Dough Hard for Biscuits You Can't Beat, Cammie Vitale

Beaten Biscuits

7 c. flour	1 c. lard with 2 t. butter
1 t. baking powder	1 c. water
6 t. sugar	1/4 c. milk
2 t. salt	

Combine dry ingredients in a large bowl. Cut in lard with a pastry blender. Add water and milk and mix to make a very dry dough. Beat and fold dough for 30 to 40 minutes until it blisters and pops. Roll out dough to about 1/2" thickness. Cut out with a 1 1/2" biscuit cutter. Prick tops 3 times with a fork. Bake on a lightly greased cookie sheet in a preheated 350 degree F. oven for about 30 minutes or until done.

Mrs. Cecil (Louise) Dunn, Richmond, Kentucky

Beaten Biscuits

No leavening of any kind is used in these biscuits, which will keep perfectly fresh for almost a week. Preferably winter wheat should be used, although any kind will serve.

1/2 t. salt	1 T. leaf lard
2 c. sifted bread flour	ice water or chilled milk,
	as little as possible

Add salt to flour and rub in the lard with the hands. Add the iced liquid, (water or milk, or equal parts of each), to make a very stiff dough, kneading all the time. Wrap the stiff dough in a strong, clean, dry towel and beat hard with either a hatchet, a heavy stick or flat-iron for 25 to 35 minutes or more until you can hear the dough snap and crackle. Hard work, but it is what "makes" the biscuits. Cut dough into small biscuits and prick tops with the tines of a fork dipped in flour. Place on ungreased baking sheet and bake at 350 degrees F. for 35 to 40 minutes. Serve hot or cold, usually the latter. Makes 2 1/2 doz.

The Gold Cookbook, p. 1045

Beaten Biscuits

4 1/2 c. all-purpose plain four,	1/2 c. solid shortening, frozen
preferably White Lily	1/2 c. milk, placed in freezer just
1/2 t. salt	before measuring dry ingredients
1 1/2 t. baking powder	1/2 c. cold water
3 T. sugar	

Combine flour, salt, baking powder and sugar in a large mixing bowl. Cut in shortening with a pastry blender or 2 knives until mixture resembles coarse cornmeal. Add milk and water to flour mixture. Stir until blended. Dough will be very dry. Add 1 to 2 T. water, if needed, but no more. Knead the dough on a lightly floured surface for 5 minutes or until it is no longer sticky. Beat the dough with a rolling pin, folding it over often, for 20 to 30 minutes or until it is elastic or run it through the rollers of a pasta machine set at the widest setting for 20 minutes, at least 9 times, folding it constantly. Roll out the dough 1/4" thick on a lightly floured surface. Cut out rounds with a 1 1/2" cutter and place them on baking sheets. Prick 3 times with a 3-tined fork all the way through to baking sheet. Bake biscuits in batches in the middle of a preheated 350 degree F. oven for 1 hour or until they are pale golden. Makes 26, 1 1/2" biscuits.

Elizabeth Ross, thanks to many

Beaten Biscuits

2 c. flour	1/3 c. shortening
1 t. salt	milk

Sift flour with salt and cut in shortening thoroughly. Add enough milk to make a stiff dough. Work dough for 20 minutes on floured board by beating dough with mallet or rolling pin, folding it, then beating and folding again over and over until dough is blistered and pops. Roll out 1/3" thick and cut with 2" round cutter. Prick with fork 3 times. Bake on ungreased cookie sheet for about 15 minutes at 400 degrees F. Makes 2 doz.

Old Farmer's Almanac Colonial Cookbook, p. 13

Beaten Biscuits

4 to 5 c. flour	1/2 c. shortening, heaping
3 t. sugar	1/2 c. water
1 t. baking powder	1/2 c. milk
1 t. salt	

Combine ingredients and work on beaten biscuit kneader until dough is smooth and forms blisters, about 30 minutes. You can hear it pop. Cut out with small biscuit cutter and prick all the way through the biscuits 2 to 3 times with a fork. Bake at 300 degrees F. for about 30 minutes.

Out of the Kitchen into the House, p. 10

Beaten Biscuits

2 c. flour	1/4 c. lard or solid shortening
1 t. salt	1/4 c. ice cold milk
1 t. baking powder	1/4 c. ice cold water

Combine dry ingredients. Cut lard into mixture until it resembles cornmeal. Stir in milk and water to make a very stiff dough. Turn out on a lightly floured board and form into a ball. Beat with a rolling pin about 500 times, turning and beating for at least 1/2 hour. Roll out to 1/2" thickness and cut out with a 1 to 1 1/2" biscuit cutter. Prick each biscuit with a 3-tined fork 3 times. Bake in a preheated 350 degree F. oven for 20 to 25 minutes until biscuits are lightly browned. Makes 2 doz.

Source unknown

Beaten Biscuits

7 c. White Lily flour, if available	5 T. sugar
1 t. baking powder	1 c. lard
1 t. salt	1 1/3 c. cold milk

Sift flour, baking powder, salt and sugar 2 to 3 times. Cut in lard, using pastry blender, until well mixed to the consistency of biscuits. Add milk in 2 or 3 additions, working well after each addition. Put through kneader or break many times, doubling dough over each time. Do this 10 to 15 minutes or until dough is smooth white and begins to "pop." Roll dough 1/4" thick and cut. Various cutters make interesting biscuits. Bake in a 300 degree F. oven on the top shelf for 55 to 60 minutes until lightly browned on bottom. I like them white on top. Makes 5 doz.

H. Thomas Tudor, Tudor Hall, Richmond, Kentucky

Beaten Biscuits

6 c. bleached flour	1 c. pure lard
4 T. sugar	2/3 c. sweet milk
2 t. salt	1/3 c. water
1 t. baking powder	

Preheat oven to 350 degrees F. Mix dry ingredients in a bowl. Cut in lard with a fork or pastry blender until texture resembles cornmeal. Add water and milk. Knead until dough is stiff and elastic. Beat the dough 10 to 15 minutes with a heavy rolling pin or other instrument, or put it through a beaten biscuit machine until smooth. Roll dough to about 1/4" thick. Cut out with a 2" round biscuit cutter. Prick each biscuit twice with a fork. Place on an ungreased cookie sheet. Bake until slightly golden, approx. 30 minutes. Biscuits should be crisp throughout and the insides should not be the least bit soggy. Makes 5 doz.

Beat Dough Hard for Biscuits You Can't Beat, Cammie Vitale

Beaten Biscuits

2 c. bleached flour	1 t. baking powder
4 t. sugar	1/4 c. lard or vegetable shortening
3/4 t. salt	1/3 c. sweet milk or more as needed

With the steel blade in place, put flour, sugar, salt and baking powder in the bowl of a food processor. Turn the machine on and off 3 or 4 times to blend the dry ingredients. Add lard or vegetable shortening, processing until mixture resembles cornmeal. Add milk only to the point that a ball is formed. Continue to process the dough in the machine for 2 to 2 1/2 minutes. Remove dough from machine and form into a flattened ball. Dough will be very warm from the action of the processor. Wrap in waxed paper and place in refrigerator for 1 1/4 hours or until slightly chilled. Preheat oven to 350 degrees F. Unwrap dough and place on a flat surface. Roll out to 1/4" thickness with rolling pin. Cut into rounds with a 2" biscuit cutter. Prick each biscuit twice with the tines of a fork. Place on an ungreased cookie sheet and bake until done, approx. 30 minutes. Biscuits should be crisp and slightly golden-colored with no soggy centers. Cool and store in an airtight tin. Makes 1 1/2 doz.

Beat Dough Hard for Biscuits You Can't Beat, Cammie Vitale

Beaten Biscuits

6 c. plain flour	1 t. baking powder, heaping
1/4 c. sugar, plus a little more	1/2 c. lard
1 T. salt	1 1/2 c. cold water and milk, mixed

Combine flour, sugar, salt and baking powder in large mixing bowl. Add lard and mix well with fingers until it feels like coarse cornmeal. Add cold milk and water and work and knead with hands until a damp, elastic dough is formed. Divide in three parts. Chill slightly, then run through kneader until a smooth dough is formed. When close to finished, a bubble or blister will pop when going through. It takes approx. 30 minutes. Cut with small biscuit cutter and place on cookie sheet. Use fork to prick through biscuits a couple of times. Bake at 400 degrees F. for 15 minutes. Turn oven down to 300 degrees F. for about 10 minutes. Biscuits will be slightly brown on bottom. Makes 6 doz.

Weisenberger Cookbook II, p. 148

Beaten Biscuits

8 c. flour	2 t. salt
1 c. shortening, full	1 T. sugar
1 t. baking powder, heaping	milk and water

Combine dry ingredients. Add enough cold milk and water to make a stiff dough. Put 2 ice cubes in milk and water so it will be ice cold. Knead until dough is smooth. Cut with forked biscuit cutter or use regular biscuit cutter and puncture top crosswise with fork 3 times. Place on greased cookie sheet. Bake 10 minutes in 400 degree F. oven. Reduce heat to 350 degrees F. and bake until done. Pinch sides of biscuits. If soft, leave in oven a little longer. Makes 5 to 6 doz.

What's Cooking in Kentucky, Mrs. Fred Francis, p. 18

Daisy's Beaten Biscuits

1 t. salt	3 T. solid shortening, level
2 T. sugar	1 1/2 t. baking powder
1/2 c. sweet milk, little more	3 c. flour
or less as dough must be dry	

Mix salt and sugar with milk until dissolved. Mix shortening and baking powder with flour and add the milk mixture. Knead until dough blisters and is smooth, using old fashioned biscuit kneader. Bake at 300 degrees F. until light brown. Turn off oven and leave biscuits until dry.

Favorite Recipes, Mrs. R.H. Turley, p. 62

Food Processor Beaten Biscuits

2 c. unbleached all-purpose flour	1/2 c. butter, cut into pieces
1 t. salt	1/2 c. ice water

Preheat oven to 350 degrees F. Adjust oven rack to center position. With metal blade in place, add flour and salt to work bowl of food processor. Turn machine on and off twice to aerate mixture. Add butter and process until mixture is consistency of cornmeal. With the machine running, pour ice water through the feed tube in a steady stream. Process until mixture forms a ball, then process for an additional 2 minutes. Carefully remove dough from blade and work bowl. Roll dough out on a lightly floured surface to a rectangle 1/8" thick. Fold dough in half to form layers. Cut through both layers of dough with a 1 1/2" round cutter with a fluted edge. Place biscuits on ungreased cookie sheets and bake in preheated oven for 25 to 30 minutes or until golden brown. Remove from oven and split biscuits immediately. If centers are soft, return split biscuits to oven for an additional 3 to 4 minutes to assure a crisp base for spreads. Makes 36 biscuits, 72 split.

Note: To shape biscuit dough in a more traditional manner use either of the following methods:

1. Roll out dough on a floured surface to 1/4" thickness and cut out with a 1 1/2" round cutter. Place biscuits on an ungreased cookie sheet and prick them 2 to 3 times with the tines of a fork. Bake as directed in recipe, but do not split before serving.

2. Pinch off pieces of dough about the size of a large walnut. Shape into a ball by gently pulling top surface to underside. Or squeeze dough between thumb and forefinger of one hand while pushing up from bottom with index or middle finger of other hand. Tuck ends neatly under and place rounded side up on an ungreased cookie sheet. Flatten biscuits slightly with a rolling pin and prick tops 2 to 3 times with a fork. Bake as directed in recipe.

The Pleasures of Cooking, vol. 1, no. 12, Suzanne S. Jones, p. 38, 39

Frankfort Beaten Biscuits

6 c. flour, sifted	2 T. sugar
1 t. baking powder	1 c. lard, scant
1 t. salt	1 c. cream, iced

Measure dry ingredients and work lard in until entire mixture is mealy. If any large pieces of lard are left unmixed, the biscuits will have flakes in them. Work in the c. of iced cream to a stiff dough. Do not get too much liquid in mixture. Work in kneader until the dough pops and is soft and velvety, folding each time the dough is put through the kneader or bread break. The dough will work easier if left to "soak" after a few turns through the kneader. Cut out biscuits and prick with a fork being sure the fork goes clear through the biscuits. Bake in a 375 degree F. oven for 45 minutes or until done. If you don't have a bread break or kneader, use a heavy plate to do the thumping. Just remember to turn the dough over in envelope fashion each time you redo the beating. It has always been said that beaten biscuits should be beaten 30 minutes for home folks, 45 minutes to an hour for company. The reason for this isn't that you have a grudge against the dough but by the beating and folding over, air is incorporated which provides the texture.

Cissy Gregg's Cookbook, vol. 2, p. 10,
The Courier Journal & Louisville Times Co., reprinted with permission

Kentucky Beaten Biscuits

2 T. grainy hog lard, heaping	1 t. salt
3 c. all-purpose flour	1 T. sugar
1 t. baking powder	1/2 c. water and 1/2 c.
	milk, mixed with ice cubes

Work lard into dry ingredients until consistency of coarse cornmeal. Add liquid, very little at a time, until dough is very stiff. Add as little of the liquid as possible. The stiffer the dough, the better the biscuits. Run dough through biscuit roller until it is satiny smooth. Cut biscuits approx. 1/2" thick with pronged cutter or cut and prick with silver fork. Bake at 350 degrees F. for approx. 45 minutes or until a delicate brown. Makes 2 1/2 doz.

The Cabbage Patch Famous Kentucky Recipes, p. 106

North Middletown Beaten Biscuits

7 c. flour	2 to 4 T. sugar
1 t. baking powder	1 c. lard
1 t. salt	1 1/3 c. cold milk

Sift flour and measure. Then sift flour, baking powder, salt and sugar together 3 times. Cut in the lard, using the finger tips or 2 knives or a blender, until these ingredients are of a finer consistency than when mixed for ordinary biscuits but not quite as fine as for pastry. Add the cold milk to make a stiff dough. If using the bread break, a hand-turned machine, get the dough in a ball, flatten it out and start running it through the machine, which looks like a clothes wringer. Fold the dough over and run back between the rollers. Repeat this process until dough is slick, glossy and "talks back to you." The talking back comes from popping the blisters that the air forms in the dough. Roll 1/4" thick and cut with a biscuit cutter, 2" or less in size. If the dough is beaten by hand, use a flat iron or the edge of a heavy plate. Beat the dough out until it is approx. 1/4" thick. Fold and beat again. Repeat until dough is smooth, glossy and has blisters. Roll the dough out to the 1/4" thickness and cut as suggested. Do not add any more flour in either method. By hand it takes approx. 30 minutes to beat them, or use the "200 beats for home folks and 500 for company" rule. It takes approx. 15 minutes using a machine or 30 minutes at most. All beaten biscuits must have pricked tops. Some say the best style is 3 rows, some say 4. When using a fork, make sure the fork goes clear through the biscuit and hits the pan. Look at the bottom of a biscuit to make sure. The reason for this is that the dough has been made into thin layers with the rolling or beating and folding. In baking, the air between these layers will expand and the fork pricks aid in holding the biscuit layers together. Many good cooks say a good beaten biscuit should "yawn" during the baking but this appearance isn't too attractive. To bake, this recipe calls for a 350 degree F. temperature for 20 to 25 minutes but it may take a little longer, perhaps 30 minutes. Other recipes call for a 325 degree F. oven for a baking time of an hour. This recipe can be halved. Makes 6 1/2 doz.

Cissy Gregg's Cookbook, vol. 1, p. 24,
The Courier Journal & Louisville Times Co., reprinted with permission

Mrs. Rice's Beaten Biscuits

3 t. sugar, level	1 t. salt
1 1/4 c. water, more or	1 t. baking powder, rounded
less to make a very stiff dough	3/4 c. lard
7 c. flour, sifted	

A soft Kentucky flour is best for beaten biscuits. Allow flour to age for at least 3 months. Dissolve sugar in water. Sift dry ingredients. Work lard into dry ingredients by hand until thoroughly mixed. Add water and again mix well. Run dough through beaten biscuit kneader* until dough holds together. Put dough back in mixing bowl and cover with a damp cloth for approx. 30 minutes to season. Preheat oven to 400 degrees F. Run dough through kneader rollers until it is very smooth and shiny, approx. 100 times. Place dough on bread board and roll to desired thickness. Cut with beaten biscuit cutter, or use regular biscuit cutter and pierce tops of each biscuit 3 times with a fork. Place biscuits close together, but not touching, on ungreased 15 1/2"x15 1/2" flat pan. Biscuits bake better if many small holes are bored in the baking pan. Put pan on bottom shelf in oven for 10 to 15 minutes, then move to top shelf and cook for a total of 40 minutes. Biscuits should be rotated during baking time from sides of pan to center of pan to insure even baking and browning. To make biscuits less white, place under the broiler for a moment to lightly brown the tops. Makes 6 1/2 doz.

*Beaten biscuits used to be beaten on old tree stumps in the backyards of early Kentucky settlers. If a kneader is not available, a rolling pin can be used to beat the dough.

Mathilde Rice, given to me by her daughter Dee Rice Amyx, Lexington, Kentucky

Southern Beaten Biscuits

2 c. all-purpose flour   1 T. lard, softened
1/2 t. salt   ice water

In a large mixing bowl stir together flour and salt. Then rub lard into flour with your hands. Add just enough ice water to make dough stiff. Knead dough several minutes. Wrap dough ball in a clean, dry tea towel and beat with a flat iron for 25 to 30 minutes. Cut dough into biscuit-sized pieces and prick with tines of a fork. Place on ungreased baking sheet. Bake at 350 degree F. for 35 to 40 minutes

Old-Fashioned Muffins and Biscuits, p. 22

Southern Beaten Biscuits

4 c. all-purpose flour   1 T. sugar
1/2 t. baking powder   1/3 c. shortening
1 t. salt   1 c. water or milk, more or less

Sift flour. Add baking powder, salt and sugar. Sift again. Cut in shortening with pastry blender or 2 knives. Add enough water or milk to make a stiff dough. Knead thoroughly. Run dough through a beaten biscuit machine or place on a wooden bread board and beat with a heavy mallet or the end of a rolling pin for 20 to 30 minutes or until dough blisters and is creamy smooth. Fold the dough over continuously during beating, keeping it in a small round ball. Roll 1/2" thick and cut with a small biscuit cutter. Prick top of each biscuit 3 times with a 3-tined fork. Place on a greased baking sheet. Bake in a 375 degree F. oven for approx. 25 minutes or until very lightly browned. Traditionally served with baked country ham. As a special treat for the children, shape any left-over dough into twists and bake.

Source unknown

Biscuits

2 c. all-purpose White Lily flour   1/2 t. salt
2 1/2 t. Clabber Girl   1/3 c. solid shortening
   baking powder   2/3 to 3/4 c. milk

Sift together flour, baking powder and salt. Cut in shortening until mixture resembles coarse cornmeal. Add milk and blend lightly with fork only until flour mixture is moistened and dough pulls away from sides of bowl. Turn out onto lightly floured board. Knead lightly approx. 10 times. Cut without twisting cutter. Bake at 475 degrees F. for 12 to 15 minutes. Makes 12, 2" biscuits.

Elizabeth Ross, White Lily flour package, Clabber Girl baking powder can

Biscuits

1 c. flour	3 T. shortening
1/2 t. salt	9 T. sweet milk
1 1/2 t. baking powder	

Sift dry ingredients. Cut shortening into flour. Make a well in the center of the flour and put milk into the well. Stir until the dough cleans the bowl, not over 1/2 minute. Knead 1/2 minute. Pat it out on a floured surface to approx. 1/2" or to desired thickness. Cut with 2" biscuit cutter. Bake at 425 degrees F. for 10 minutes or until golden brown.

We Make You Kindly Welcome, p. 3

Biscuits

2 c. White Lily plain	1 t. salt
all-purpose flour	1/4 c. shortening
1 T. baking powder	2/3 to 3/4 c. milk or buttermilk

Preheat oven to 500 degrees F. Measure flour into bowl by spooning into measuring cup and leveling off. Mix baking powder and salt with flour. Cut in shortening until like course crumbs. Blend in just enough milk with fork until dough leaves sides of bowl. Too much milk makes dough too sticky to handle; not enough milk makes biscuits dry. Knead gently on lightly floured surface 10 to 12 strokes. Roll dough about 1/2" thick. Cut without twisting cutter. Bake on ungreased baking sheet 1" apart for crusty biscuits; almost touching for soft sides at 500 degrees F. for 8 to 10 minutes. Serve at once. Note: For tender biscuits always handle dough gently and use as little extra flour for kneading and rolling as possible. Makes 12, 2" biscuits.

The White Lily Foods Company

Angel Biscuits

5 c. all-purpose flour	3 T. sugar
1 t. baking soda	3/4 c. vegetable shortening
1/2 t. salt	2 c. buttermilk
3 t. baking powder	1 yeast cake dissolved in
	1/2 c. lukewarm water

Sift dry ingredients. Cut in shortening until mixed. Add buttermilk and dissolved yeast. Work together with a large spoon until all the flour is moistened. Cover bowl and put in refrigerator and use as needed. When ready to use take out as much as needed, roll on floured board to 1/2" thick and cut out. Bake at 400 degrees F. on cookie sheet or shallow pan for 12 mintues until brown. Keeps several weeks in refrigerator. Makes 6 doz.

A Taste from Back Home, p. 39

Kentucky Angel Drop Biscuits

1 envelope yeast	1/2 t. baking soda
2 1/2 T. warm water	1/2 t. baking powder
2 1/2 c. flour or	1/2 c. shortening
1 1/4 c. 1/2 t. salt	1 c. buttermilk or
regular flour and	1 c. regular milk
1 1/4 c. whole wheat flour	with 1 T. white vinegar added
2 T. sugar	melted butter

Heat oven to 375 degrees F. Combine yeast and water and let stand. Stir together dry ingredients. Cut in shortening with pastry blender. Add yeast-water mixture. Stir in buttermilk with fork until all ingredients are moistened. Roll out 1/2" thick on floured board and cut. Place biscuits in 13"x9" pan with enough melted butter in it to cover the bottom. Brush tops of biscuits with melted butter. Bake 15 to 20 minutes until golden brown. Note: These biscuits are very close to those served in fast food places. Makes 1 doz.

The Courier-Journal Kentucky Cookbook, p. 240

Baking Powder Biscuits

1 c. flour	2 T. shortening
2 t. baking powder	milk
1/2 t. salt	

Mix ingredients together with enough milk so dough becomes sticky enough to follow the spoon around the bowl. Turn out on board or waxed paper and knead gently for a minute. Use very little flour on board or waxed paper. Flatten out to a thickness of 1/2 to 3/4". Cut with biscuit cutter and bake at 400 to 425 degrees F. for 15 minutes. Note: The secret of light, fluffy biscuits is to place biscuits close together on pan so they have no place to go but up.

Prairie Recipes and Kitchen Antiques, p. 35

Buttermilk Biscuits

2 1/2 c. flour	1 t. salt
2 t. baking powder	1/2 c. shortening, plus 2 T.
1/2 t. baking soda	3/4 c. buttermilk

Sift dry ingredients. Cut in shortening until it resembles coarse meal. Stir in milk. Knead lightly on floured board. Roll out 1/2" thick. Cut and place on lightly buttered pan. Bake at 375 degrees F. for 15 minutes.

Donna Gill Recommends, p. 39

Buttermilk Biscuits

2 c. White Lily self-rising flour	1/2 c. solid shortening
1 t. baking powder	1 c. buttermilk

Combine flour and baking powder. Cut in shortening until mixture resembles coarse meal. Add buttermilk and stir to form a soft dough. Turn dough onto floured surface and knead lightly, just enough to handle easily. Roll dough to 1/2" thickness. Cut with biscuit cutter. Bake at 450 degrees F. for 10 minutes or until lightly browned. Makes 1 doz.

Fountain Favorites, p. 3

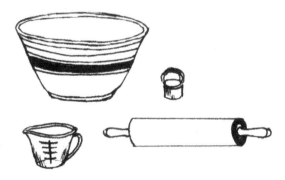

Buttermilk Biscuits

2 c. flour
2 t. baking powder
1/4 t. baking soda

1/2 t. salt
1/4 c. butter, chilled
3/4 to 7/8 c. buttermilk

Sift together dry ingredients into a mixing bowl. Cut in butter with knives or pastry blender until mixture resembles coarse meal. Make an indentation in center of mixture. Stir in buttermilk to a soft dough. Turn out onto a floured bread board and knead lightly one minute. Roll dough out to 1/2" thickness. Cut rounds with biscuit cutter. Place on ungreased cookie sheet. Bake at 450 degrees F. for 12 to 15 minutes.

Old-Fashioned Muffins and Biscuits, p. 22

Buttermilk Biscuits

2 c. buttermilk or
2 c. sweet milk
with 1 T. vinegar added
1/4 c. sugar
2 t. salt

1/4 c. melted shortening
1/2 t. soda
1 pkg. yeast
4 1/2 c. flour,
sifted before measuring

Scald milk, add sugar, salt, shortening and soda. When cooled to lukewarm, add yeast and stir well. Add flour and make a soft dough. Knead until smooth. Roll out and cut with biscuit cutter. Place in greased pan and brush tops with fat. Let rise in a warm place until they double in size. Bake in moderate oven for 15 to 20 minutes.

Southeastern REMC Electric Consumer, April, 1989

Cheese Biscuits

1 stick butter, softened
1 c. flour
1/4 t. cayenne pepper

1/2 c. nuts, chopped
1/2 t. caraway seed
1 c. sharp cheddar cheese, grated

Mix all ingredients well. Pinch off and roll into small balls and place on cookie sheet. Press with fork and bake at 325 degrees F. for 10 to 12 minutes. Makes 2 doz.

Cooking with Curtis Grace, Madelyn Kirkland, p. 15

Soda Biscuits

2 c. flour	2 t. baking powder
1/2 t. salt	3 T. shortening
3/4 t. sugar	1 c. buttermilk
1/2 t. soda	

Combine dry ingredients. Cut in shortening. Add milk to make a soft dough. Stir well. Roll out until dough is 3/4" thick. Cut with biscuit cutter and place 1" apart on a baking sheet. Bake at 475 degrees F. for 15 minutes. Makes 16 biscuits.

Source unknown

Nashville House Fried Biscuits

1 qt. warm milk	1/4 c. sugar
1 cake yeast	salt to taste
flour	1/2 c. lard, melted

Dissolve yeast in milk and add enough flour to make a soft batter. We used 6 c. of flour, sifted, at this point. Place in a warm place and let rise 1 hour. When it starts to show small bubbles of activity from the yeast division, add sugar, salt and melted lard that has cooled. Work in enough additional flour so dough will break immediately from spoon. Add approx. 3 more c. flour. Let rise another hour. Use your hands to make muffin-sized biscuits and let them rest on a board as you drop them, one by one, into deep hot fat. Be sure that the fat isn't hot enough to crust over the yeast dough before it has a chance to spring forth to capacity to make it light on the inside.

Note: This recipe comes from the Nashville House Restaurant in Nashville, IN, where they are served in a big basket with every meal.

Weisenberger Cookbook II, p. 104

Southern Raised Biscuits

2 pkg. yeast	1 T. baking powder
1/4 c. warm water	1/2 t. soda
2 c. buttermilk	1 1/4 t. salt
5 c. all-purpose flour	1 c. shortening
1/3 c. sugar	

Combine yeast and warm water. Let stand 5 minutes or until bubbly. Add yeast to buttermilk and set aside. Combine dry ingredients in large bowl. Cut in shortening. Add buttermilk mixture. Mix until dry ingredients are moistened. Knead lightly 3 to 4 times. Roll dough to 1/2" thickness. Cut out biscuits and place on lightly greased baking sheet. Cover and let rise 1 hour. Bake at 450 degrees F. for 10 to 12 minutes. Note: Biscuits may be made ahead and frozen. To freeze, bake 5 minutes. Cool. Wrap in aluminum foil and freeze. To serve, place biscuits on lightly greased baking sheet and thaw. Bake at 450 degrees F. for 7 to 10 minutes.

Mrs. William H. Riddell, Berea, Kentucky

Standard Biscuits

2 c. sifted enriched flour
2 t. baking powder
1/2 t. salt

3 to 4 T. shortening
2/3 to 3/4 c. milk

Sift flour with baking powder and salt. Cut in shortening until it resembles course cornmeal. Add milk all at once. Mix until dough follows fork around bowl. Turn onto lightly floured surface. Knead 1/2 minute. Roll out dough until it is 1/2" thick. Bake at 450 degrees F. for 12 to 15 minutes. Makes 16 medium biscuits.

Source unknown

Derby Breakfast Yeast Biscuits

1 pkg. or cake yeast
1 c. warm buttermilk or
   use powdered buttermilk mix
1/2 t. soda

1 t. salt
2 T. sugar
2 1/2 c. self-rising flour
1/2 c. shortening

Dissolve yeast in warm buttermilk. Set aside. Sift soda, salt, sugar and flour in a bowl. Cut in shortening. Add yeast mixture. Stir until blended. Knead and roll 1/2" thick. Cut biscuits and dip in melted butter. Place on greased pan. Let rise 1 hour. Bake at 400 degrees F. for 12 minutes.

Best of the Best from Kentucky; Kentucky Kitchens, p. 89

Buttered Bread Crumbs

4 T. butter

3/4 to 1 c. fresh bread crumbs, diced

Melt butter in saucepan and add crumbs. Continue stirring until lightly toasted and butter is absorbed. An excellent topping for most casserole dishes.

Welcome Back to Pleasant Hill, p. 34

Bourbon Sticky Buns

1 pkg. hot roll mix
3/4 c. scalded milk,
   cooled to lukewarm
1 egg
1/2 c. bourbon

2 3/4 c. brown sugar
1 c. pecans
1/4 c. butter, softened
2 t. cinnamon

Make dough according to pkg. directions, except use milk instead of water and add the egg. Grease 18 muffin cups. Into each cup measure 3/4 t. bourbon, 1 1/2 T. brown sugar and 3 to 4 pecans. Roll dough on lightly floured surface into a 12"x18" rectangle. Combine remaining bourbon, brown sugar, butter and cinnamon and spread on dough. Roll up jelly-roll fashion, beginning at the narrow end and cut roll into 18 slices. Place a slice in each muffin cup, cover pans and let rise approx. 30 minutes. Bake at 375 degrees F. for 18 to 20 minutes or until nicely browned. Cool on rack 5 minutes before turning out of pans. Serve warm.

A Taste from Back Home, p. 45

Bran Muffins

2 T. shortening
1/4 c. sugar
1 egg, well beaten
1 c. sour milk or cream
1 c. bran

1 1/2 c. flour
1 t. baking soda
1 t. baking powder
1/8 t. salt

Cream shortening and sugar together. Add egg, milk, bran, flour, baking soda, baking powder and salt. Mix well. Fill well-oiled muffin tins 2/3 full. If sour cream is used, omit 1 T. of the shortening. Bake in 425 degree F. oven approx. 40 minutes. Makes 1 doz.

The Household Searchlight Recipe Book, p. 40

Shaker Lemon Muffins

2 c. flour
1 T. baking powder
1/4 t. salt
1/2 c. sugar
2 eggs, beaten

3/4 c. milk
2 t. lemon juice
1 t. grated lemon peel
1/4 c. butter, melted

Combine dry ingredients in a mixing bowl. In separate bowl mix liquid ingredients. Stir liquid into dry mixture with a few quick strokes until just moistened. Spoon into greased muffin cups. Bake at 375 degrees F. for 15 to 20 minutes.

Old-Fashioned Muffins and Biscuits, p. 20

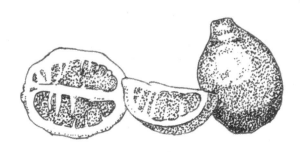

All-Bran Rolls

1 c. solid shortening	1 c. lukewarm water
1 c. all-bran cereal	2 eggs
1 c. boiling water	1 t. salt
1/2 c. sugar	6 c. sifted flour
2 pkg. yeast	

Mix first 4 ingredients and let cool. Dissolve yeast in water. Add yeast mixture to first mixture. Add beaten eggs, salt and flour gradually. Set in refrigerator. Chill overnight. This mixture will keep for several days. Bake in 400 degree F. oven for 15 minutes.

Cookbook of Treasurers, Jane Cobb, p. 75

All-Bran Rolls

1 c. shortening	1 1/2 t. salt
3/4 c. sugar, slight	2 yeast cakes
1 c. all-bran	1 c. lukewarm water
1 c. boiling water	6 1/2 c. sifted flour
2 eggs, beaten	

Mix shortening, sugar and bran in large bowl. Pour boiling water over it and set aside to cool. When cool, add beaten eggs, salt and yeast which has been dissolved in lukewarm water. Add flour gradually. Cover. Chill overnight. When ready to use, roll out and let rise. Bake in a 400 degree F. oven for 15 minutes. Makes 4 doz. rolls or 2 large loaves.

Favorite Recipes, Polly Noland, p. 68

Dinner Rolls

1 pkg. yeast	1/2 c. solid shortening
1/2 c. lukewarm water	2 c. hot water
6 T. sugar	6 c. flour
1 t. salt	1 stick margarine, melted

Dissolve yeast in 1/2 c. lukewarm water. Add sugar, salt and shortening to 2 c. hot water. Cool. Add flour to make soft dough. Add dissolved yeast and mix well. Cover. Let stand 1 hour at room temperature. Knead on floured board 5 minutes. Roll to 1/2" thickness. Cut with biscuit cutter. Dip in melted margarine and fold over. Put in roll pan. Let rise 1 hour. Bake at 450 degrees F. for 20 minutes.

Cookbook of Treasures, Evelyn Kennedy, p. 75

Carolyn Ingalls Icebox Rolls

1 cake compressed yeast	2 eggs, slightly beaten
1/2 c. lukewarm water	5 T. melted fat or liquid shortening
1/4 to 3/4 t. salt	1 c. warm water
1/2 c. sugar, or less	5 c. flour

Crumble yeast in bowl and add 1/2 c. water, salt, sugar and eggs. Beat. Add shortening and rest of warm water and beat 2 minutes. Add half of the flour and beat 3 minutes. Add rest of flour and mix well. Cover with waxed paper and cloth and place in refrigerator for 3 hours. Before baking, knead and shape into rolls. Let rise at room temperature. Bake at 425 degrees F. for 10 to 15 minutes.

Prairie Recipes and Kitchen Antiques, p. 33

Yeast Rolls

1 pkg. active dry yeast	1/2 t. salt
3/4 c. warm water,	1 egg
105 to 115 degrees F.	2 1/2 to 2 3/4 c. flour, if using
2 T. sugar	self-rising flour omit salt
2 T. vegetable oil	soft butter

Dissolve yeast in water in 2 1/2 qt. bowl. Add sugar, oil, salt and egg. Stir to dissolve sugar and salt. Stir in 1 c. of the flour until smooth. Cover with cloth and place on rack over bowl of hot water. Let rise 15 minutes. Grease a 9"x9"x2" square pan. Stir down batter and add 1 1/2 c. flour. Stir until mixed. Turn onto cloth-covered board. Knead 3 minutes. If dough is sticky, knead in 1/4 c. flour. Divide dough into 16 pieces. Quickly shape into balls. Arrange in pan and brush tops with butter. Cover with cloth and place on rack over bowl of hot water. Let rise 25 minutes. Bake 12 to 15 minutes in a 425 degree F. oven until light brown. Remove from pan to wire rack. Brush tops with soft butter. Serve warm.

Gold Medal Flour package, reprinted with the permission of General Mills, Inc.

Light Yeast Rolls

2 T. shortening, heaping	1 pkg. yeast in 1/4 c. lukewarm
1/2 c. sugar	water with a pinch of sugar

1 c. boiling water
1 c. cold water
1 egg, beaten

5 to 6 c. flour, or more if needed
melted butter

Put shortening and sugar in bowl. Pour 1 c. boiling water in bowl and melt shortening. Add 1 c. cold water. Add egg and yeast. Add flour. Let rise 1 hour. Make out into rolls with melted butter brushed over all. Let rise again. Cook at 350 degrees F. until done or golden brown.

Margaret Gwynne, Richmond, Kentucky

Whole Wheat Rolls

2 T. dry yeast
2 c. lukewarm water
1 egg
1/2 c. granulated sugar

1 t. salt
3 1/2 c. wheat flour
1 c. plus 1 T. shortening, melted
3 1/2 c. all-purpose flour

Dissolve yeast in lukewarm water. Add egg, sugar and salt. Add whole wheat flour. Mix in shortening. Add white flour and work into ball and let rise in warm place until double in bulk. Press down, cover with towel and let rise again until double in bulk. Roll out on floured board. Pull off small balls approx. 1" in size. Place 3 to a cup in greased muffin tins. Brush tops lightly with melted butter. Place in warm spot. Let rise until double in size. Bake at 400 degrees F. for 12 to 15 minutes or until brown. These freeze well to serve later.

Welcome Back to Pleasant Hill, p. 78

Salt-Rising Bread

1 c. milk	1 1/2 t. salt
1 T. sugar	1/4 c. cornmeal

Scald the milk in a small saucepan. Stir in sugar, salt and cornmeal. Pour mixture into a large 2 qt. glass or crockery jar or pitcher. Cover top and set in a pan of lukewarm water, 110 degrees F., for 6 to 8 hours until mixture ferments. Stir in the following in order given:

1 c. warm water	2 T. butter
1 T. sugar	2 1/4 c. flour, sifted

Beat the mixture until thoroughly mixed and place jar back in pan of lukewarm water. Allow to rise until mixture becomes spongy, light and bubbly. Then place in a large greased mixing bowl and gradually stir in 2 to 2 1/4 c. of flour, sifted, or enough to make the dough stiff for kneading. Knead the dough 3 to 5 minutes. Shape into 2 loaves and place in greased bread pans. Place in warm location and let rise to top of bread pans. Brush tops with butter. Bake in preheated 350 degree F. oven for 25 to 30 minutes. Cool on rack before slicing.

Old-Fashioned Bread Recipes, p. 20

Salt-Rising Bread

1 1/2 c. 1% milk	1 c. lukewarm water
1/2 c. coarse cornmeal	3 T. butter, melted and divided
1 T. sugar	4 1/2 to 5 1/2 c. unsifted
2 t. salt	all-purpose flour
	1 T. vegetable shortening

To make starter: Scald milk, remove from heat and stir in cornmeal, sugar and salt. Pour into a 1 qt. glass jar and cover loosely with plastic film. Set the jar on an electric heating pad covered with a terry bath towel. Pull towel up and around jar to hold in warmth, turn heating pad to low setting. If after an hour starter is less than lukewarm to the touch increase heat setting to medium. Leave covered starter on heating pad until foamy with a cracked surface and cheesy aroma which can take 6 to 24 hours. If after 24 hours these signs of fermentation are missing discard this batch and start over.

To make sponge: In mixing bowl combine water with 2 T. melted butter. Beat in 1 c. flour then beat in starter. Cover sponge with plastic film, place on heating pad set on low, cover with towel and let rise until doubled. Work in remaining flour, a cup at a time, to make a workable but slightly sticky dough. Turn onto lightly floured surface and knead until elastic and smooth, approx. 10 minutes.

Shape and bake: Grease 2 (8 1/2"x4 1/2"x3") loaf pans with shortening. Divide dough, shape into loaves and place in greased pans. Brush loaves with remaining melted butter, cover surface of loaves with plastic film and place on heating pad on low until doubled, 1 to 3 hours. Bake in preheated 400 degree F. oven for 10 minutes then reduce temperature to 350 degrees F. and bake 25 to 30 minutes or until browned and hollow sounding when tapped. Cool on rack. Makes 2 loaves.

From *One and Only Cook*, the column by Frances Price, R.D.

Salt-Rising Bread

2/3 c. milk	11 to 12 c. sifted enriched flour
1/2 c. freshly ground white cornmeal	1/4 c. shortening
	1 T. salt
2 c. warm water	3 T. sugar
1/4 t. baking soda	2 c. boiling water

Bring milk to boil. Add cornmeal. Beat thoroughly. Cover. Let stand in a warm place overnight. In the morning the mixture should be light, spongy and bubbly. If the mixture has not been kept warm enough and hasn't fermented enough, place container in hot water and let stand until mixture is full of bubbles, approx. 1 hour. To the 2 c. of warm water add soda and approx. 3 c. flour. It should be enough to make a thick batter. Add cornmeal mixture and beat well. Place in a pan of almost hot water and keep in a warm place approx. 1 hour or until very light and full of bubbles. Stir down. Add the shortening, salt and sugar to the boiling water. Let stand until lukewarm. Add to sponge and mix thoroughly. Add enough of the rest of the flour to make a stiff dough. Turn out on a lightly floured board. Knead approx. 10 minutes or until smooth and satiny. Divide into 3 parts. Form into balls. Let stand, covered, approx. 10 minutes. Shape into loaves and place in well-greased loaf pans approx. 9 1/2"x5 1/2". Brush lightly with melted butter. Let stand in a warm place approx. 1 1/2 to 2 hours or until doubled in size. Bake in a 400 degree F. oven 40 to 50 minutes. Brush tops of baked loaves with melted butter or fat. Makes 3 loaves.

Bess Hamilton, my Grandmother

Salt-Rising Bread

Starter:

3 medium potatoes	1 t. salt
3 T. cornmeal	4 c. boiling water
1 t. sugar	

Dough:

2 c. lukewarm water	1/8 t. salt
1 c. water	2 T. shortening, melted
1/8 t. baking soda	flour

Pare and slice potatoes. Add cornmeal, sugar, salt and boiling water in bowl. Wrap bowl in a heavy cloth. Cover and let stand in a warm place overnight. Remove potatoes and add milk, water, baking soda, salt and shortening to mixture. Add enough flour to make a dough just stiff enough to knead. Knead until smooth and elastic. Form into loaves. Allow approx. 1 lb. of dough for each loaf. Form each loaf into a ball and then into a smooth long roll just a little longer than the pan. Work quickly and lightly to form loaves. Place loaves in well-oiled or buttered pans. Cover and let rise until doubled in bulk. Bake at 400 degrees F. for approx. 45 minutes. Makes 3 loaves.

Prairie Recipes and Kitchen Antiques from the *Household Searchlight Recipe Book*, p. 43

Salt-Rising Bread

2 medium potatoes, peeled and grated	1 c. milk
2 T. cornmeal, heaping	1 T. solid shortening, heaping
2 T. sugar, heaping	2 t. baking powder
2 t. salt	1 t. baking soda
3 c. boiling water	flour, enough to make a stiff batter but not too stiff

Put potatoes, meal, sugar, salt and boiling water in a half gallon jar and keep warm overnight. The next day, strain the foam off the mixture, keep the liquid and discard the rest. Let the milk come just to a simmer before adding the shortening, baking powder and baking soda. Add the fermented liquid and mix. Put the mixture in a big bowl. Add enough flour to make a stiff batter which you can beat. Let rise in a warm place to double in size. Add more flour to make the dough a little stiffer. Shape into 3 loaves and let rise to double in size. Bake at 350 degrees F. for 1 hour.

Thelma's Treasures, p. 55

Salt-Rising Bread

Start early before you plan to make bread. Have an empty 3 lb. shortening or coffee can for convenience in mixing starter.

1 c. milk, scalded	1/8 t. soda
7 T. white cornmeal	1/2 t. granulated sugar
1/4 t. salt	

After scalding milk remove film and pour back and forth between can and pan to cool slightly. Pour milk into can and add the above ingredients. Cover and keep in a warm place until next morning. This batter will become light, puffy and full of bubbles.

1 c. warm water	1/8 t. soda
1/2 t. salt	2 1/2 c. flour

The next morning add second list of ingredients to can and mix well. Batter will be stiff. Allow to rise to top of can in a warm spot.

In a bowl have ready:

1/2 c. shortening	1 t. salt
6 c. flour	1 T. granulated sugar

Cut shortening into flour, salt and sugar in large mixing bowl. When starter mixture in can has risen to top, pour into mixture in bowl. Add 3/4 c. warm water and stir in well. Batter will become very stiff. Work dough with hands until smooth. When dough is ready, shape into 3 loaves. Place in ungreased 3"x7" loaf pans. Brush tops of loaves with soft butter. Allow to rise again in a warm place. Bake at 325 degrees F. for 5 to 10 minutes then increase oven to 350 degrees F. and bake for 45 minutes.

Welcome Back to Pleasant Hill, p. 55

Aunt Mary's Salt-Risin' Bread

Stage I:

Slice thin a mediumsized potato into a 7" bowl. Add:

1 t. sugar	pinch of salt
1/4 t. soda	

Fill bowl 1/4 full with boiling water. Thicken with 3/4 c. of cornmeal. Pour into a 1 qt. jar and seal. Set in a warm place to rise overnight. It should double in bulk to almost a full quart.

Stage II:

The next morning strain mixture into a 7" bowl. Add 3/4 c. flour to mixture to thicken. Add:

1/4 t. soda	1 t. sugar

Beat well. Leave in bowl, cover with a plate and set in warm place to rise for approx. 2 hours. Mixture will be bubbly.

Stage III:

Sift together 6 c. flour and a pinch of salt. Add lard the size of a large turkey egg (approx. 2 T.) and mix. Add to Stage II. Add water gradually 1/4 c. at a time to an approx. total of 1 1/2 c. water to make a firm dough. Knead until smooth. Divide dough into 2 oblong pans. Grease tops with lard. Cover and let rise until dough doubles in size, approx. 2 hours. Keep covered for 15 minutes of baking time. Total baking time 45 minutes in a 350 degree F. oven. The loaves will rise above tops of pans during last 15 minutes of baking.

Mrs. Lucian C. Adams, Orlando, Florida, formerly of Richmond, Kentucky

Mock Salt-Rising Bread

An old Southern recipe for cornmeal that is a good substitute for salt-rising bread and 10 times easier to make.

2 1/2 T. white cornmeal, water-ground if possible	1/2 t. salt
	1 egg, well beaten
1/4 c. white corn syrup, honey or sugar	2 c. flour, measured after sifting
	1 yeast cake
1 1/3 c. lukewarm milk	2 T. warm water
4 T. butter, margarine or lard, melted	

Mix the cornmeal with the corn syrup, honey or sugar. Add 2/3 c. of the warm milk, mixed with the melted butter, margarine or lard. Add salt. Put in a saucepan, place over a flame and let mixture come to a boil, stirring constantly to prevent lumping. Have the flame high at first until the mixture begins to boil and then reduce heat as low as possible. Let cook until mixture becomes a mush, 3 to 4 minutes, continuously stirring. Set aside and cool to lukewarm. To the cooled mush add the beaten egg, the remainder of the warm milk, the flour and the yeast cake dissolved in the warm water. Cover and let set in a warm room for about 1 hour. Then toss dough on a floured board and roll smooth, working as little extra flour into dough as possible. The dough is soft like biscuit dough, but it can be handled. To make this dough into 2 small loaves, divide the dough in half. Roll each half as nearly as possible the length and width of the loaf pan. Press dough into loaf pan well-greased with melted butter or margarine. Flatten the dough with the palm of the hand, making it cover the pan, then brush with melted fat. Let loaves rise 1 to 2 hours longer or until dough is light. Bake 25 minutes in a hot 400 degree F. oven, then reduce heat to 375 degrees F. and cook 25 minutes longer. Brush with melted margarine or butter but do not take from the oven for another 10 minutes. As soon as bread is taken from oven, turn out on a wire rack. Cool before serving, though some relish this bread while it is still warm. To toast, slice 1/2" thick and toast under broiler on the buttered side only. Makes 2 small loaves.

Out of Kentucky Kitchens, p. 77

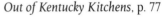
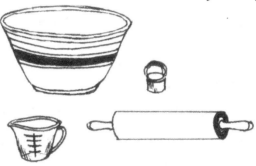

Party Shells

1 small egg	1 stick margarine
1 c. plus 2 T. flour	1/4 t. salt

Make the dough the day before making shells. You can make it up to 3 days before. Beat the egg, then mix it and all other ingredients together and chill. When ready to make them, take the dough out of the refrigerator and pinch off little balls and press into small ungreased pastry shell tins. Bake at 400 degrees F. for 10 to 12 minutes. You can use these shells for anything you want; lemon pies, chocolate tarts, chicken salad. Makes 36 shells.

Thelma's Treasures, p. 34

To Make Self-Rising Flour

1 c. flour   1/2 t. salt
1 1/2 t. baking powder

Mix together. Makes 1 c.

Weisenberger Cookbook II, p. 13

Salads & Salad Dressings

Ambrosia

1 qt. orange sections sliced out from pulp 1 c. bananas, sliced 1/2 c. pineapple bits	1/2 c. coconut 1/2 c. maraschino cherries 1/2 c. pecans, chopped 1 c. sugar

Mix all ingredients thoroughly. Chill. Serves 6.

Miss Daisy Entertains, p. 13

Kentucky Ambrosia

1 doz. oranges,
  peeled and sectioned
4 large grapefruit,
  peeled and sectioned
	1 can flaked coconut
	1 large can pineapple chunks,
	  drained
	1 pt. sour cream

Combine the fruits and coconut. Toss lightly with sour cream. Serves 8.

The Crowning Recipes of Kentucky, p. 78

Kentucky Ambrosia Salad

1 c. mandarin oranges,
  drained
1 c. pineapple tidbits,
  drained
3 bananas, sliced
	1 c. miniature marshmallows
	1 c. flaked coconut
	1 c. sour cream
	1 T. mayonnaise
	maraschino cherries, if desired

Any combination of fresh fruit can be used. Combine fruits. Mix sour cream and mayonnaise. Fold in fruit. Add coconut and marshmallows. Garnish with cherries. Ambrosia is a favorite dish with dinner or afterwards as a dessert. Use a big clear glass salad bowl. Recipe from Phyllis George Brown, former First Lady of Kentucky and Miss America, 1971.

The Crowning Recipes of Kentucky, p. 78

Tomato Aspic

1 envelope unflavored gelatin
1/2 c. cold tomato juice
1 1/2 c. hot tomato juice,
    boiling point

2 t. lemon juice
salt to taste
  dash Tabasco

Sprinkle gelatin over the cold tomato juice and stir until gelatin melts. Pour hot tomato juice into dissolved gelatin mixture and stir. Add lemon juice and seasonings. Pour into mold that has been rinsed in cold water. Chill until firm. Chopped or sliced olives or chopped celery may be added when aspic is cool before it jells. Unmold and serve on crisp lettuce leaves.

Welcome Back to Pleasant Hill, p. 9

Quick Tomato Aspic

1 12 oz. can V-8 juice or
    Bloody Mary mix
1 pkg. lemon flavored gelatin

1/2 c. water
1 T. vinegar

Heat V-8 juice to boiling. Pour over gelatin. Stir until gelatin is dissolved. Add water and vinegar. Pour into a 1 qt. mold. Chill until firm. Serve with cottage cheese. Also good on lettuce with mayonnaise.

Florence Ross, my Mother

Three Cheese Mold

1 1/2 t. gelatin
1/4 c. cold water
1/2 c. blue cheese, crumbled
1/2 c. cheddar cheese,
    shredded

1/2 c. cottage cheese
1/4 c. sour cream
1 1/2 t. onion, grated
1/2 t. Worcestershire sauce

Add the gelatin to cold water and heat. Beat blue, cheddar and cottage cheeses together and beat in sour cream. Add onion and Worcestershire sauce. Fold into gelatin and chill in a 2 c. mold. Serve with crackers.

Florence Ross, my Mother

Mother's Chicken or Turkey Salad

white chicken or turkey meat, cooked, cooled and cubed	slivered almonds, toasted
	salt and papper
	mayonnaise
celery, chopped	slaw dressing

Mix chicken with celery and almonds according to consistency desired. Salt and pepper to taste. Add enough mayonnaise to thoroughly moisten. Add just a small dollop of slaw dressing to give it its distinctive zip. Chill.

Florence Ross, my Mother

Coleslaw

2 lbs. cabbage, shredded	1/3 c. sugar
2/3 c. sour cream	1 T. salt
2/3 c. vinegar	1 1/2 T. raw carrots, chopped

Mix all together and chill. Serves 16 to 18.

Beaumont Inn Special Recipes, p. 19

Coleslaw

1 qt. cabbage, shredded	1/4 c. country dressing
1/4 c. carrot, shredded	(see salad dressings)
1/4 c. onion, chopped	1/4 c. mayonnaise
1/4 c. celery, chopped	1/2 to 3/4 t. salt
1/2 c. commercial slaw dressing	

Mix all together. If too dry, add more country dressing.

We Make You Kindly Welcome, p. 18

Kentucky Coleslaw with Boiled Mayonnaise

1 small head of green cabbage	1 to 2 T. sugar to taste
2 eggs, well beaten	1/4 c. water
1 T. flour, rounded	1/4 c. apple cider vinegar
1/2 t. dry mustard	1 T. butter or olive oil
1 t. salt or more to taste	3 T. sweet or sour cream

Shred cabbage very, very fine. There should be 2 c. Put in a bowl of ice water and let stand 20 minutes. Drain and pat dry in a towel. The dressing is made as follows: To the well-beaten eggs add flour, mustard, salt and sugar. Beat until smooth and creamy. Slowly add water mixed with vinegar. Pour into saucepan, add butter and set over a low flame, stirring constantly. Let cook until thick. The mixture will lump, but do not be discouraged. Remove pan from stove and beat and beat and beat the mixture until smooth once more. Add cream and correct the seasoning. Cool. Mix with the shredded cabbage. This slaw should be a moist one. This dressing is also good with sliced tomatoes, in potato salad or used with fresh fruits in frozen salads or aspics. Serves 4 to 6.

Out of Kentucky Kitchens, p. 166

Bauer's Hot Slaw

1 small head of cabbage	3/4 c. sugar
1 t. onion, finely chopped	2 t. salt
6 slices bacon, fried	1/4 t. white pepper
2 c. apple cider vinegar	dash garlic powder or garlic bud
1 c. water	

Slice cabbage finely as for sauerkraut. Add onion and stir. Fry bacon, drain and reserve grease. Crumble bacon and set aside. Combine bacon grease, vinegar, water, sugar, salt, pepper and garlic. Bring to a boil and stir until sugar dissolves. Pour over cabbage. Toss and top with bacon.

Kentucky Derby Museum Cookbook, p. 69

Cottage Cheese Mold

1 envelope gelatin	1/2 c. sugar
1/4 c. cold water	1/2 c. pecans, chopped
2 lbs. small curd cream	2 T. grated onion
style cottage cheese	1 green pepper, chopped, optional
8 oz. pkg. cream cheese	1 2 oz. bottle stuffed olives,
1/2 t. salt	reserve 10 for garnish

Soak gelatin in cold water. Using a pastry blender, cream together cottage cheese, cream cheese, salt and sugar. Dissolve soaked gelatin over hot water in a pan. Add nuts, onion, green pepper and chopped olives to gelatin. Add to cheese mixture and combine. Using a well-oiled 5 c. mold, arrange garnish in bottom and press cheese firmly into it. Refrigerate until firm and unmold.

Florence Ross, my Mother

Cranberry Mold

1 3 oz. pkg. strawberry	1 8 oz. can whole berry
or raspberry gelatin	cranberry sauce
1 c. boiling water	1 c. apples and/or celery, diced
3/4 c. pineapple juice	1/3 c. nuts, coarsely chopped

Dissolve gelatin in boiling water. Add pineapple juice and cranberry sauce. Chill until slightly thickened. Stir in remaining ingredients. Pour into a lightly-oiled 4 c. mold. Chill until firm.

Philadelphia Main Line Classics, Dru Huber Hammond, p. 117

Festive Cranberry Salad

1 3 oz. pkg. orange gelatin	1 16 oz. can whole berry
1 3 oz. pkg. raspberry gelatin	cranberry sauce
2 c. boiling water	1 14 oz. can crushed pineapple

Dissolve gelatin in boiling water. Add the cranberry sauce and crushed pineapple with the juice. Mix well. Put in individual molds or a 9"x9" dish. Chill until congealed.

Recipes from Miss Daisy's, p. 14

Cucumber-Potato Salad

3 c. new potatoes, cooked,
  peeled and cubed
3 eggs, hard-cooked and
  chopped
1 medium stalk celery, chopped
1/4 c. onion, chopped

1 small cucumber, pared,
  chopped and drained
2/3 c. mayonnaise
1 t. salt
1/4 t. pepper
1/2 t. dill weed

In a large mixing bowl, combine all ingredients. Toss lightly. Chill at least 3 hours before serving. Garnish with sliced hard-cooked eggs. Sprinkle with dill weed.

Note: I mix the dill weed with the salad before chilling. I think it improves the flavor.

Mary Lou Moore

Cucumbers and Onions

1 to 2 cucumbers, peeled
  and thinly sliced
1 medium onion, thinly sliced
1/2 c. cider vinegar

1/2 c. water
2 T. sugar
1/4 t. salt

Arrange cucumbers and onions in layers in a glass bowl. Mix vinegar, water, sugar and salt until sugar is dissolved. Pour over cucumbers and onions. Cover with glass lid or plastic wrap. Refrigerate and chill at least 2 hours.

Elizabeth Ross

Cucumbers in Sour Cream

1 large cucumber, peeled	1/2 T. onion, chopped
and thinly sliced	1/4 t. sugar
3/4 t. salt	1/8 t. white pepper
1/2 c. sour cream	parsley, minced
1 T. lemon juice	

Toss cucumbers with salt. Cover and refrigerate until well chilled. Combine sour cream, lemon juice, onion, sugar and pepper. Blend well. Reserve 1/4 c. of mixture for garnish. Combine cucumbers with remaining sour cream mixture. Refrigerate until well chilled, about 2 hours. To serve, arrange cucumber slices on a bed of salad greens. Top with small mound of reserved sour cream mixture and sprinkle with minced parsley. Serves 4.

Joyce LeCompte

Cucumbers in Sour Cream

1/2 pt. sour cream	1/2 medium sweet onion,
2 T. cider vinegar	thinly sliced
1/2 t. salt	2 medium cucumbers
1/2 t. dill seed	

Combine the first 5 ingredients and mix well. Peel cucumbers and slice thin. Add to sour cream and onion mixture. Refrigerate 3 to 4 hours before serving. Serves 4 to 6.

Florence Ross, my Mother

Cucumbers in Sour Cream

4 cucumbers, thinly sliced	1/4 c. lemon juice
1/2 medium white onion,	2 T. sugar
chopped fine	salt and pepper to taste
1 c. sour cream	

Combine all ingredients, mixing well. Chill for 1 hour before serving. Serves 6.

Speedwell Christian Church Cook Book, Edna M. Hord, p. 12

Frozen Fruit Salad

1 egg, separated	1 T. lemon juice
1 T. flour	1/2 c. heavy cream, whipped
1 T. sugar	1 can cocktail fruit or salad fruit,
1/4 t. salt	drained
1 c. apricot nectar or	1 banana, peeled and sliced
the syrup from canned fruit	1/4 c. orange sections

Combine egg yolk, flour, sugar and salt in top of a double boiler. Stir in the apricot nectar and lemon juice. Cook over hot water, stirring constantly, until mixture thickens. Let cool, then fold in whipped cream and stiffly beaten egg white. Last, fold in the drained canned fruit, banana and orange segments. Put into refrigerator trays and freeze until firm, 3 to 4 hours. To serve, slice and top with mayonnaise. Serves 6 to 8.

Cissy Gregg's Cook Book, vol. 1, p. 14,
The Courier Journal & Louisville Times Co., reprinted with permission

Frozen Fruit Salad

16 oz. can shredded pineapple	1 pt. whipping cream
16 oz. can peaches	1 c. mayonnaise
16 oz. can Royal Ann cherries	powdered sugar to taste
maraschino cherries, optional	

Drain fruit very well. Whip cream. Mix all ingredients and freeze.

Florence Ross, my Mother

Frozen Fruit Salad

1 T. unflavored gelatin,	1/2 c. mayonnaise
1 envelope	1 c. heavy cream, whipped
1/4 c. cold water	powdered sugar to taste, optional
2 c. fruit cocktail	

Soften gelatin in water, dissolve over hot water. Cool. Add fruit cocktail and syrup from can. Fold in mayonnaise and whipped cream. Pour into ice tray or molds and freeze.

Out of the Kitchen into the House, p. 6

Overnight Fruit Salad

1 c. seedless grapes, halved
1 c. white cherries, pitted
1 c. diced pineapple
6 marshmallows, cut in eighths
1/8 lb. cashew nuts, chopped

1 egg
1 T. sugar
2 T. light cream
juice of 1/2 lemon
1/2 c. heavy cream, whipped

Combine fruits, marshmallows and nuts. Beat egg until light and foamy. Add sugar gradually. Blend in light cream and lemon juice. Place egg mixture in a saucepan and cook over low heat or over hot water until the sauce is smooth and thickened, stirring constantly. Pour over combined fruits and mix lightly. Chill overnight in the refrigerator. Top with whipped cream. Serves 6.

Cissy Gregg's Cook Book, vol. 2, p. 8,
The Courier Journal & Louisville Times Co., reprinted with permission

Country Ham and Cottage Cheese Croquette Salad

2 c. creamed cottage cheese
2 T. chives
1 t. onion juice
1 t. Worcestershire sauce or
   more to taste

1 c. cooked ground ham
2 T. parsley, chopped
salt, pepper and Tabasco to taste
   chopped nuts

Mix all ingredients except nuts and shape into balls or croquettes. Roll in chopped nuts. We prefer pecans. Serve on lettuce with tart mayonnaise. A Kentucky specialty.

Out of Kentucky Kitchens, p. 170

Heavenly Hash

2 8 oz. pkgs. cream cheese
1 large can crushed pineapple,
  drained
3 1/2 T. pineapple juice

1/2 pt. whipping cream, whipped
1 medium-sized package miniature
  marshmallows
2 T. mayonnaise

Cream together cheese, pineapple and pineapple juice until light and fluffy. Fold in whipped cream, marshmallows and mayonnaise. Chill in refrigerator for 24 hours. Serves 8.

Cooking with Curtis Grace, p. 151

Kentucky Salad

1 medium can white cherries,
  chopped
1 small can crushed pineapple
juice from cherries and pineapple
1 pkg. lemon gelatin

2/3 c. mayonnaise
1 c. real cream, whipped
1 t. lemon juice
1/2 c. miniature marshmallows
nuts, if desired

Drain cherries and pineapple. Add enough water to the syrup to make a pt. of liquid for the gelatin. Dissolve gelatin thoroughly in boiling liquid. Let cook and thicken slightly. Add mayonnaise, whipped cream, lemon juice and marshmallows. Let thicken a little more. Fold in cherries, pineapple and nuts. Chill in refrigerator.

Speedwell Christian Church Cook Book, Edna M. Hord, p. 15

The Brown Hotel Kentucky Limestone Salad

1 head Kentucky limestone
  (Bibb) lettuce
1 oz. blue cheese, crumbled

1/2 oz. sweet red peppers
  cut in strips
toasted pecans

Wash and dry lettuce. Cut bottom off head and shingle leaves around 2 or 3 plates. Top with cheese, peppers and pecans. Serve with creamy raspberry dressing or raspberry vinaigrette. Serves 2 to 3.

Dining in Historic Kentucky, vol. 2, p. 135

Frozen Lemon/Pineapple Salad

1 pkg. lemon gelatin
1 c. hot water
8 oz. can crushed pineapple

1 qt. vanilla ice cream
1/2 c. nuts, chopped

Mix gelatin in hot water until dissolved. Add remaining ingredients and mix well. Keep frozen.

Verna Ross Bellamy

Lime Fluff

1 3 oz. pkg. lime gelatin
1 16 oz. carton cottage cheese

1 14 oz. can crushed pineapple,
   drained
1 6 oz. carton whipped topping

Sprinkle gelatin over cottage cheese in a large bowl. Mix and add pineapple and whipped topping. Mix thoroughly. Chill until served.

Recipes from Miss Daisy's, p. 94

Macaroni Salad

1 c. mayonnaise
2 T. vinegar
1 T. prepared mustard
1 t. salt
1/4 t. pepper

8 oz. elbow macaroni,
   cooked and drained
1 c. celery, chopped
1/4 c. onion, chopped

Combine first 5 ingredients. Stir in remaining ingredients. Cover and chill. Makes 5 c.

Elizabeth Ross

Netherland Salad

The long-popular Netherland Maurice Salad lives on as long as the magic of Maurice remains in memory. Maurice, Peter A. Mauridon, the one-time maitre d' of the Netherland Plaza, Cincinnati, created it and here is the original recipe. Make it and revel in the nostalgia for the days of leisurely lunches at the Netherland - a favorite thing to do for Kentuckians in town for pleasure or business.

Dressing:

3 T. mayonnaise, not salad dressing	1 t. Worcestershire sauce
	1 egg, hard-cooked and chopped
3 T. olive oil	1 t. chives, finely chopped
2 T. vinegar	

Salad:

3/4 head of crisp lettuce, cut julienne	1/3 c. julienned tomatoes, seeded
	1 T. chopped pickle
1/2 c. julienned chicken	tomato quarters and
1/2 c. julienned ham	hard-cooked egg slices for garnish

Note to new cooks: Julienne means ingredients cut in slender strips. Stir together mayonnaise, olive oil, vinegar and Worcestershire sauce. Add the egg and chives. In a 1 1/2 qt. salad bowl, combine the lettuce, chicken, ham, tomatoes and pickle. Immediately before serving add the dressing and toss to mix. Mound on 2 chilled dinner plates. Do not use lettuce leaves to serve on, put directly on plate. Garnish each with 2 tomato quarters and 2 slices of hard-cooked egg. Serves 2 as a luncheon salad.

Recipes Remembered, p. 181

Pea Salad

1 17 oz. can peas	1 T. green onion or chives, chopped
2 T. green pepper, chopped	1 T. pickle relish
1 t. pimiento, chopped	1 egg, hard-cooked and diced
2 T. celery, chopped	1 1/2 T. mayonnaise
2 T. sharp cheddar cheese, shredded	

Drain peas and set aside. Mix together next 6 ingredients. Add peas, egg and mayonnaise. Toss gently and chill thoroughly. Serves 4 to 6.

Florence Ross, my Mother

Country Pea Salad

1 can peas, drained	1/4 c. celery, minced
1/2 c. cheddar cheese, cubed	3 T. onion, minced
1/2 c. pecans, broken	2 eggs, hard-cooked and diced
1/2 c. mayonnaise	salt and pepper to taste

Combine all ingredients, toss lightly. Serve on a bed of lettuce. Serves 8.

The Crowning Recipes of Kentucky, p. 86

Pea and Cheese Salad

1 8 oz. can green peas, drained	1/4 c. onion, diced
1 c. sharp cheddar cheese, diced	1 t. salt
1 c. celery, diced	4 eggs, hard-cooked and diced
	1/2 c. mayonnaise

Combine all ingredients, toss lightly. Serves 6.

A Taste from Back Home, p. 76

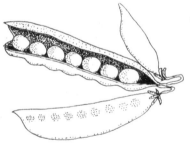

Green Pea and Cheese Salad

3/4 c. cooked peas	2 T. mayonnaise
1/4 c. cheddar cheese, diced	3/4 t. prepared mustard
1 T. onion, finely chopped	

Combine peas, cheese and onion. Toss with mayonnaise and mustard. Chill on lettuce cups. Serves 2.

Source unknown

Perfection Salad

1/4 c. cold water	1/4 c. vinegar
1 envelope unflavored gelatin	1 T. lemon juice
1 c. hot water	1/2 c. cabbage, finely chopped
1/4 c. sugar	1 c. celery, finely chopped
1/2 t. salt	1 pimiento, cut fine

Pour cold water in a bowl. Sprinkle gelatin on top of water. Add hot water, sugar and salt. Stir until dissolved. Add vinegar and lemon juice. When mixture begins to thicken, add remaining ingredients. Pour into a 5 c. mold and chill until firm.

Florence Ross, my Mother

Mayonnaise Potato Salad

3 c. (3 medium) potatoes, cooked, peeled and cubed	1 medium stalk celery, chopped
3 eggs, hard-cooked and chopped	1 T. prepared yellow mustard
1/4 c. onion, chopped	1 T. sweet pickle relish
2/3 c. mayonnaise	1 t. salt
	1/4 t. pepper

In a large mixing bowl, combine all ingredients. Toss lightly. Chill at least 3 hours before serving. Garnish with sliced hard-cooked eggs dusted with paprika.

Elizabeth Ross

7-Layer Salad

1 head lettuce, chopped	1 1/2 c. mayonnaise
1 c. celery, chopped	2 T. sugar
1 c. green pepper, chopped	2 1/2 c. cheddar cheese, shredded
1 1/2 c. red onion, chopped	8 slices bacon, cooked
1 c. frozen peas, cooked	crisp and crumbled

Arrange lettuce in bottom of deep bowl. In layers, add celery, peppers, onions, and peas. Do not toss! Spread mayonnaise evenly over layer of peas. Sprinkle with sugar and cheese. Cover and refrigerate at least 4 hours. Sprinkle bacon over salad and toss when ready to serve.

Diane Jackson

Marinated Slaw

1 medium head of cabbage	1 c. sugar
1 c. green pepper, chopped	1/2 c. cider vinegar
1 c. celery, chopped	1/2 c. oil
1 c. onion, chopped	1 1/2 t. salt

Mix all ingredients and let stand covered in refrigerator overnight.

Ruth Ross Ballard

Boyle County Stuffed Tomatoes

6 ripe summer tomatoes, peeled, scooped out and drained	green onions, chopped cucumber, seeded and diced
8 oz. cottage cheese	green olives, sliced
3 oz. cream cheese	salt and pepper to taste

Prepare tomatoes and set aside. Mix remaining ingredients together. Fill tomatoes with this mixture. Garnish with parsley or watercress. Serves 6.

Kentucky Derby Museum Cookbook, p. 70

Wilted Lettuce

lettuce	1 t. sugar
5 to 6 slices of bacon	black pepper
2 to 4 small green onions	radishes, sliced
1/4 c. vinegar	

Break the lettuce into pieces into a bowl. Cut the bacon in small snibbles and fry out crisp. Remove the bacon and then into the drippings chop the small onions, and add vinegar and sugar. Allow the vinegar to come to a boil; swish it around in the skillet so it gets mixed up with everything in the skillet and pour over the lettuce. Add freshly ground black pepper. Toss gently and sprinkle over the top the radish slices and the pieces of bacon.

Cissy Gregg's Cook Book, vol. 1, p. 12,
The Courier Journal & Louisville Times Co., reprinted with permission

Wilted Lettuce

1 head lettuce, broken up
4 to 5 slices bacon,
   fried and cut into small pieces
1 onion, chopped

4 T. vinegar
4 T. sugar
salt and pepper to taste
1 egg, hard-cooked

Break lettuce into small pieces. Fry bacon, reserving fat. Add bacon pieces to lettuce and chopped onion. Mix vinegar and sugar with hot bacon grease. Stir until sugar is dissolved. Pour over chopped lettuce, onion and bacon. Salt and pepper to taste. Garnish with sliced egg.

Sharing Our Best, Maggie Higgs, p. 26

Wilted Lettuce Salad

3 qts. Bibb lettuce,
   cleaned and dried
3 green onions, heads
   and tops, chopped fine
radishes, sliced, optional
1 t. sugar
1 t. salt

2 T. vinegar
5 slices bacon, crisply fried,
   crumbled
reserved bacon drippings
   from frying
2 eggs, hard-cooked and chopped

Place lettuce, onions, radishes, sugar and salt in bowl. Pour vinegar over all. Pour hot bacon grease over all and top with chopped eggs and crumbled bacon. Serve immediately.

Elizabeth Ross

Wilted Lettuce Salad

1 head lettuce or	3 T. sugar
2 bunches leaf lettuce	1/4 t. salt
6 slices bacon, diced	6 to 8 green onions, minced
1/4 c. vinegar	2 eggs, hard-cooked and chopped,
1/4 c. water	optional

Wash, remove core, drain and break up lettuce into bite-sized chunks or shred leaf lettuce with knife. Place in bowl. Cook bacon in skillet until crisp. Remove all but 1/4 c. bacon drippings from skillet, leaving fried bacon bits in skillet. Add remaining ingredients except egg. Bring to boil. Pour the hot salad dressing over lettuce and toss lightly. Sprinkle with chopped, cooked egg. Serve immediately after preparing. Serves 6 to 8.

Miriam B. Loo's Family Favorites Cookbook, p. 37

Blue Cheese Dressing

1/4 lb. blue cheese or	1/2 c. olive or salad oil
Roquefort cheese	3 T. vinegar
1/2 t. dry mustard	1 T. lemon juice
1/2 t. sugar	salt to taste
1/2 t. paprika	garlic pod

Put cheese in a bowl with mustard, sugar and paprika. Stir as you add oil, vinegar and lemon juice. Salt to taste. Rub salad bowl with garlic pod.

Florence Ross, my Mother

Blue Cheese Dressing

1/2 c. salad oil	2 T. vinegar
2 T. lemon juice	1 t. salt
1/2 t. dry mustard	1 t. sugar
1/4 t. paprika	1/2 t. Worcestershire sauce
1/4 c. blue cheese, crumbled	

Blend all ingredients well. Refrigerate and mix well before tossing salad.

We Make You Kindly Welcome, p. 64

Blue Cheese Dressing

1 1/4 lbs. blue cheese, crumbled	1/4 c. lemon juice
1 large can evaporated milk	1/4 c. thin French dressing
	2 qts. mayonnaise

Beat all ingredients together until light and smooth. Put in a jar and store in refrigerator. This recipe makes a large amount but will keep for weeks refrigerated.

Welcome Back to Pleasant Hill, p. 8

Bauer's Since 1870 Blue Cheese Dressing

1/2 lb. blue cheese, crumbled	3 1/2 c. mayonnaise
1 T. distilled white vinegar	1/4 c. milk
1 T. Worcestershire sauce	2 dashes red pepper sauce
1 T. olive or salad oil	

Mix all ingredients well. Allow to sit overnight before using. Makes 1 qt.

Dining in Historic Kentucky, vol. 1 , p. 117

Granny's Boiled Dressing

4 large eggs or 5 small ones, I generally just use 4	1 t. salt
1 c. sugar and 1/2 c. flour mixed together	1/2 t. mustard
shake of red pepper	1 c. vinegar
	1 c. water

Mix all ingredients and cook in double boiler until thickened. Add a pinch of baking powder when finished cooking. Beat and heat a few minutes longer.

Florence Ross, my Mother

Country Dressing

1 t. dry mustard	1/2 c. cold water
2 T. sugar	2 egg yolks
1/4 t. salt	1/4 c. vinegar
2 T. flour	2 T. butter

Dissolve mustard, sugar, salt and flour in water. Beat eggs and vinegar in top of double boiler. Add the dissolved ingredients. Cook and stir over boiling water until thick and smooth. Add butter. Use for chicken salad, coleslaw and country ham salad.

We Make You Kindly Welcome, p. 64

French Dressing

1 1/2 c. salad oil	3/4 c. vinegar
1 can tomato soup	1 t. dry mustard
2 T. Worcestershire sauce	1 t. salt
1/2 c. sugar	1 t. pepper

Mix thoroughly. Keep refrigerated. Great with lettuce, chopped bacon and croutons. Lasts indefinitely in the refrigerator.

The Crowning Recipes of Kentucky, p. 109

My Grandmother's French Dressing

1 can tomato soup	1 t. salt
3/4 c. vinegar or more to taste	1 T. Worcestershire sauce
1/2 t. paprika	1/2 t. black pepper
1 1/2 c. vegetable oil	1 t. mustard
1/2 c. sugar	onion juice and garlic, if desired

Put in bowl and beat until well blended. Keep in a qt. jar. Shake well before using.

Bess Hamilton, my Grandmother

Thin French Dressing

6 T. oil	2 t. lemon juice
2 T. vinegar	1 t. granulated sugar
1/4 t. salt	1/4 t. paprika
sliver of onion	

Put all ingredients in dressing bottle and shake well before using. This dressing will keep indefinitely in the refrigerator.

Welcome Back to Pleasant Hill, p. 8

My Mayonnaise

2 egg yolks	2 T. vinegar
1 t. salt	1 pt. vegetable oil
1 t. sugar	2 T. lemon juice
3/4 t. mustard	shake of red pepper and cayenne

Put yolks, salt, sugar, mustard and 1 T. vinegar in a bowl. Beat and add 1/2 c. oil very slowly. When this has thickened nicely, add rest of oil and vinegar and lemon juice, alternately. Add shake of pepper. At the last, add a generous T. of boiling water, 2 T. won't hurt it. I don't know what the water does, but it makes a nice dressing.

Florence Ross, my Mother

Brown Hotel Creamy Raspberry Dressing

4 oz. sour cream	3 oz. sugar
4 oz. raspberry vinegar	2 oz. bottled melba sauce

Pour sour cream in a bowl. Whisk in remaining ingredients and chill 1 hour before serving. Serves 4.

Dining in Historic Kentucky, vol. 2, p. 175

Roquefort Dressing

1/4 t. salt	3 oz. pkg. cream cheese
1/8 t. garlic powder	1/3 c. Roquefort or blue cheese
1/4 t. prepared mustard	1/2 c. mayonnaise
dash of Accent	1/2 c. light cream

Blend the seasonings with the cheeses. Add the mayonnaise alternately with the cream. Whip until smooth. Sour cream makes a wonderful addition. Also, lemon juice and Worcestershire sauce.

Florence Ross, my Mother

Kentucky Roquefort Dressing

1/4 lb. Roquefort or blue cheese	1/4 c. grapefruit juice
1/2 c. cream or evaporated milk	1 t. onion or garlic cloves,
1 c. mayonnaise	finely chopped

Blend cheese with cream or some of the mayonnaise and add remaining ingredients.

Mrs. Earle B. Combs, Sr.

Mrs. Chandler's Salad Dressing

1 onion, grated	juice of 1 lemon
2 T. sugar	1/2 c. vinegar
1 t. salt	1/2 c. salad oil
dash cayenne pepper	1/2 c. tomato catsup
1 clove garlic	

Combine all ingredients and beat with rotary beater. Serve cold over salads.

Mrs. Albert B. "Happy" Chandler,
by permission of her son, Albert B. "Ben" Chandler, Jr.

Poultry & Stuffings

Barbecued Chicken Breasts

1 c. vegetable oil	4 to 6 chicken breasts
1/2 c. vinegar	barbecue sauce, bottled
	or homemade

Mix oil and vinegar (this helps seal in juices). Pour over breasts in a Pyrex baking dish. Bake at 325 degrees F. for 30 minutes, turning occasionally. The breasts will be cooked and the juices sealed in so that the time on the grill will be for getting a nice barbecue coating and flavor. This method prevents over-charring and drying out of the meat.

Place chicken breasts, flesh side up, on grill. Barbecue over low indirect heat 10 to 15 minutes, brushing frequently with sauce. Turn chicken and barbecue another 10 to 15 minutes, basting with sauce.

Barbecue Sauce:

2 medium onions, chopped	2 T. Worcestershire sauce
3/4 c. catsup	1 t. salt
3/4 c. cold water	1 t. paprika
3 T. vinegar	1/4 t. black pepper

Mix all ingredients and cook slowly until mixture is well blended. Good for chicken, beef or pork.

Elizabeth Ross; *Cookbook of Treasurers*, Jean Hamilton, p. 24

Miss Jennie's Bluegrass Chicken

4- to 5-lb. hen	1 onion slice
1 lb. mushrooms	

Boil hen until tender. Skin and debone. Grind through fine blade of food grinder twice with mushrooms and onion. Make a medium cream sauce.

Sauce:

2 T. butter	1 c. rich milk or cream
2 T. flour	

Using 1 c. sauce to 3 c. chicken mixture, add:

1 T. butter	salt and pepper to taste
3 eggs, beaten	1 T. parsley, chopped

Pour into a greased mold, cover top with waxed paper or foil. Set in a pan of hot water and steam at 350 to 375 degrees F. for 1 1/2 hours. Serve with a mushroom sauce and small new potatoes. Serves 6.

Cabbage Patch Famous Kentucky Recipes, Miss Jennie Benedict, p. 61

Chicken A la King

1/4 c. green pepper, chopped	salt and pepper
1 c. mushrooms, sliced	1 egg yolk, beaten
1/4 c. butter	2 1/2 c. cooked chicken, diced
3 T. flour	2 T. pimientos, finely cut
2 c. milk	

Lightly brown green pepper and mushrooms in butter. Blend in flour. Add milk and season highly with salt and pepper. Cook until thick, stirring constantly. Stir part of the hot mixture into egg yolk and return to remaining hot mixture. Cook a minute until flavors are blended. Add chicken and pimientos. Serve in patty shells, on hot biscuits, toast points or chow mein noodles. Serves 6.

The Household Searchlight Recipe Book, p. 217; *Miss Daisy Entertains*, p. 105

Beaumont Inn Chicken Croquettes

Boil a 2 3/4 to 3 lb. young chicken until well done, about 1 hour. Cool. Remove skin, debone and grind. This should yield 2 c. of chicken.

2 c. ground chicken	1 t. salt
1 c. mashed potatoes, riced	1/4 t. white pepper
1 large egg	dash of Tabasco
4 oz. thick white sauce for croquettes, save the remainder to serve over croquettes (see Sauces)	2 eggs
	1/4 t. paprika
	cracker meal
4 T. onion juice	oil for frying
1 t. celery salt	parsley sprigs

Mix first 9 ingredients together well. Shape into croquettes 3 1/2" long and 1 1/2" in diameter. Should make 10 croquettes. Lightly beat eggs with paprika. Dredge the croquettes through this and roll in cracker meal. Lay the croquettes on a small tray covered with waxed paper. Chill for at least 1 hour in refrigerator. Can be rolled individually in waxed paper and frozen. Fry in deep fat in a basket fryer or iron skillet at 325 degrees F. for 4 minutes or until a deep golden brown. If frying from frozen it will take about 8 minutes. Either way, the croquettes will float when done. Serve 2 croquettes per serving with 2 T. of hot white sauce over them. Garnish with a dash of paprika and a sprig of parsley.

Beaumont Inn Special Recipes, p. 50

Chicken Croquettes

2 c. dry bread crumbs	1/2 c. celery, chopped
1 1/2 c. chicken broth	1/2 t. salt
4 c. cooked chicken	dash lemon juice
1 c. mushrooms	1/8 t. red pepper
1 t. onion, chopped	1 T. parsley, chopped
1/2 c. butter, melted	1 egg beaten with 2 T. water

Soak bread crumbs in broth. Grind chicken and mushrooms. Mix all ingredients together. Let cool. Shape into croquettes (2 oz. each) and chill. Dip into bread crumbs, then into beaten egg mixed with water or milk, then into bread crumbs again (this is the secret of good croquettes). Fry in deep fat. Serve with mushroom cream sauce (see Sauces).

We Make You Kindly Welcome, p. 300

Chicken Croquettes with Lemon

2 c. cooked chicken, chopped	1 T. lemon juice
1/2 t. salt	1 t. parsley, finely chopped
1/4 t. celery salt	1 c. thick white sauce
1/2 t. paprika	1 c. fine cracker or bread crumbs
1 t. onion juice	1 egg beaten with 1 T. water

Mix chicken together with all the ingredients except the fine cracker or bread crumbs and the egg. Chill in a shallow pan. Shape the mixture into 8 croquettes - the tepee type. Chill the formed croquettes. Just before frying, dip in crumbs, then in egg-water mixture, then in crumbs again. If using an electric fryer, place fat in fryer and turn dial to 350 degrees F. When signal light goes off, start frying. Fry until a light brown. Drain. Serve piping hot with lemon slices. Of course these can be done without an electric fryer by using a basket and a deep-fry thermometer or some bread cubes to give an idea of the temperature of the fat. The croquettes can be served with a rich white sauce or peas in cream sauce or with simple buttered peas.

Cissy Gregg's Cook Book, vol. 2, p. 12,
The Courier Journal & Louisville Times Co., reprinted with permission

Creme De Volaille

A Kentucky specialty for elegant occasions.

3 c. chicken, picked from boiled hen	3 eggs
1/2 can mushrooms, or 3/4 c., drained	1/16 t. red pepper
	1/4 t. white pepper
1 c. cream sauce	1/2 t. salt
1 full T. butter	1/2 t. parsley, minced very fine
	1 t. onion, minced fine

Grind chicken with the drained mushrooms. Mix with cream sauce (cream sauce should have 2 T. flour and 2 T. butter to 1 c. thin cream). Add the T. of butter and eggs. Beat very hard. Add the seasonings. Pour into a 1 qt. greased mold and steam 1 1/2 hours. To steam: Place mold in a pan of hot water in oven. Cover top with a layer of aluminum foil and tie string around to hold covering. Steam at 350 degrees F. Unmold on large platter and pour over with a mushroom sauce. Serves 6.

Cissy Gregg's Cook Book, vol. 1, p. 32,
The Courier Journal & Louisville Times Co., reprinted with permission

Creme De Volaille

4- to 5-lb. hen	1 c. canned mushrooms

Boil hen until tender. Cool in liquid in which it was cooked. Pick meat from bones. Grind in food chopper with mushrooms.

Cream sauce:

2 t. flour	1 c. milk or cream
2 T. butter	

Melt butter, blend in flour, gradually add milk. Stir constantly until smooth and thickened.

To 3 c. ground chicken, use 1 c. of cream sauce. Add an extra T. butter and 3 eggs to mixture and beat hard. Add a little lemon juice, salt and red pepper and pour into a greased mold. Cover mold with several layers of waxed paper and steam in a shallow pan with 1 1/2" water at 400 degrees F. for 1 1/2 hours. Serve with rich cream mushroom sauce.

Mrs. Earle B. Combs, Sr.

Creme De Volaille

3 c. cooked chicken, ground	1 c. cracker crumbs
1/2 c. fresh mushrooms, finely diced	1 t. melted butter
1 c. medium thick white sauce	2 t. salt
1 small onion, minced	1/3 t. red pepper
3 eggs, beaten	1 pimiento, chopped, optional
	3 to 4 sprigs parsley, chopped

Combine chicken and mushrooms with white sauce. Add remaining ingredients. Beat mixture hard. Pack firmly into a well-buttered mold. Place mold in a shallow pan filled with 1/2" water and steam at 400 degrees F. for 1 1/2 hours. Serve with additional white sauce to which peas, mushrooms and pimientos have been added or with mushroom cream sauce (see Sauces). In Kentucky, this dish is called "Cream Divoli" and is an old standby for bridge parties and luncheons.

Favorite Recipes, Mrs. T. J. Curtis, p. 45;
My Old Kentucky Homes Cookbook, p. 15; *We Make You Kindly Welcome*, p. 11

Fried Chicken

First comes selecting the bird. Be sure it is a young bird. The age given for a fryer is "not over 5 months old." It should have a flexible-tipped keel bone, be of tender flesh with a thin, waxy skin. In size, a 2 1/2 lb. (when dressed) fryer is best. To disjoint the chicken, cut it up so you have 2 drum sticks, 2 thighs, 2 to 3 breast pieces, 2 back pieces and 2 wings. Cut up so each piece has its portion of skin to prevent drying, to coat each piece to help keep in the juices and to assist in browning as well as add the crisp touch.

1. Seasoned flour may be used.
2. Seasoned flour and crumbs may be used in the proportion of 2 parts crumbs to 1 part flour.

Some people use stale bread rubbed though a sieve fastened over a large bowl. This takes more time and trouble than the flour way, but it gives a fine texture and crispness. Quick browning is desirable to prevent loss of juices.

3. Include basic seasoning - salt and pepper.

Fresh sweet fat should be used for frying and for flavor, some like to use part butter. To reuse fried chicken fat take very good care of it. Strain the fat poured off through a fine sieve, or cloth is even better, and store it in the refrigerator. Many cooks feel that the addition of the "once-fried" fat gives a better color than all fresh fat. The watchwords for frying chicken are low and slow.

1. Temperature of fat: For the initial browning of chicken in a skillet, the fat should be hot enough to sizzle a drop of water. A moderately-low temperature is important for the rest of the cooking.

2. Deep-fat fried chicken is the definition of the way we often fry chicken. For this, first coat the chicken. Heat a 2" layer of fat to a temperature of 350 degrees F. Lower the chicken slowly into the fat, placing the meatier side down. Cook the meaty dark pieces first, then the meaty white pieces. While the chicken is browning on all sides, keep fat temperature uniform at 325 degrees F. Cook slowly, uncovered, until the pieces are tender. To brown and cook tender it will take about 45 minutes in all. You can deep-fat brown the pieces as above, then lift the pieces from the fat and finish cooking in a covered skillet on top of the stove or in a slow oven. Either of these finishes is good for a large chicken.

Or chicken can be shallow fried: For this method, coat chicken and have only 1/2" deep sizzle-hot fat in the skillet. Fry meaty pieces first, slipping less meaty pieces between as chicken browns. Don't crowd the pieces. As soon as the chicken begins to brown, about 10 minutes, reduce heat, tightly cover and cook slowly until tender, from 30 to 60 minutes, depending on the size of the pieces. Again you can finish either on top of the stove or in the oven. Add 1 to 2 T. water before covering if pan cannot be tightly covered or if the bird is heavier than 3 lbs. Uncover last 15 minutes to recrisp skin, if desired.

Cissy Gregg's Cook Book, vol. 1, p. 24,
The Courier Journal & Louisville Times Co., reprinted with permission

Fried Chicken

chicken	pepper
salt	paprika
flour	vegetable oil

Put the chicken pieces in a large pot of water. Add 2 T. salt for every chicken you use. Soak chicken in the salt water overnight in the refrigerator. The next day, drain off water and pat chicken pieces dry. Mix the flour (enough to coat all of the chicken) with the pepper, paprika and a little bit of salt to taste. Coat each piece of chicken with this mixture. In an iron skillet, add the vegetable oil and heat until it sizzles. The oil should be even up with the chicken. Add a few pieces of chicken and turn heat down to medium. Cook the chicken 30 minutes or so on one side and flip it and cook it 30 minutes on the other side until it is evenly browned. Remove the pieces from the pan as they are done and drain on a paper towel.

Thelma's Treasures, p. 45

Fried Chicken

1 c. flour	8 to 10 pieces frying chicken
1 T. salt	shortening for pan frying
1/4 t. pepper	

Place flour and seasonings in a brown paper bag. Put chicken pieces in the bag and shake to coat with seasoned flour. Heat 1/2" shortening in heavy iron skillet. If shortening is hot enough, a drop of water placed in it will "pop." Place flour-covered chicken, meaty side down, in skillet. Do not place chicken pieces too close together so sides will brown nicely. Reduce heat and cook uncovered until golden brown. Turn pieces and fry until well done and tender, about 45 minutes altogether. Leave heavy pieces in a little longer than the smaller ones. Keep heat low and do not hurry the frying. Drain on paper towels before serving.

We Make You Kindly Welcome, p. 45; Elizabeth Ross

Fried Spring Chickens Kentucky Style

2 young spring chickens, weighing just 2 lbs. when dressed	salt and pepper
	flour in which to roll chickens
milk in which to soak chickens	2 lbs. lard, vegetable shortening or salad oil for frying

Disjoint the chickens, separating the legs and the breasts into 2 sections each, cutting off both wings and leaving backs intact. Place in a bowl and soak 20 to 30 minutes in milk. Drain but do not dry. Sprinkle with salt and pepper and roll in flour, or shake each piece of chicken in a bag in which 1 c. of flour has been placed - this is said to coat the chicken evenly. If you like an extra-crunchy jacket on your chicken, dip it in cream after it has been floured once, then dip again in flour and fry at once. Dip one piece at a time. Have the fat smoking hot in a deep iron chicken fryer or dutch oven (375 degrees F.). Put in a few pieces of chicken at a time and lower the flame. When the pieces are golden brown all over, remove them from the pan and put a few more pieces to fry until all have browned. It will take 1 lb. of lard or 2 c. of melted fat to fry each chicken, although there will be some left over when you are through. When all pieces are brown, pour off all but 2 T. of the fat. Return the chickens to the pot and cover, having a very low flame under the pot. Cook 20 to 30 minutes longer or until chickens seem done. Cut a piece to test. Serves 6.

Out of Kentucky Kitchens, p. 104, Nancy Lee Ross

Chicken Keene

1/3 c. butter	meat from 1 cooked hen, cubed
1/3 c. flour	1/2 lb. mushrooms, sliced
1 c. chicken broth	1 pimiento, in strips
1 1/2 c. milk or cream	1 green pepper, in strips
2 t. salt	sherry to taste
1/8 t. pepper	paprika

Melt butter in double boiler. Stir in flour slowly. Gradually add chicken broth, then milk or cream. Cook until thickened, stirring constantly. Season. Add cubed chicken, mushrooms, pimiento, green pepper and sherry. Serve in tart shells and sprinkle with paprika before serving.

Historic Kentucky Recipes, p. 86

Kentucky Pressed Chicken

Cook 2, 4 1/2- to 5-lb. stewing chickens until they are tender in water seasoned with a little celery, onion, bay leaf, 1/2 t. M.S.G. and red pepper. Simmer slowly until tender in broth to cover. Allow to cool in the broth. Remove meat from the bones. Keeping the dark and white meat separate, put the bones back in the broth and simmer longer to get a good strong chicken flavor. When ready to mold, strain broth and clarify - there should be more than a pint. Remove fat from stock and when it is possible, chill it so all the fat can be removed from the broth and any particles strained out. Taste to see if more seasonings are needed. If so, add now and not after clearing. For each qt., add 1 egg white which has been slightly beaten and mixed with 2 t. cold water. Add eggshell broken up into small pieces. Bring to boiling, stirring constantly, and boil 2 minutes. Let stand 20 minutes over very low heat. Strain again through a fine strainer, lined with double thickness of cheesecloth. The broth is now ready to be fortified with a little extra plain gelatin. Make up 2 pts. of broth and use 2 pkgs. of plain gelatin soaked in cold water and dissolved in the hot broth. When it is set, have the chicken cut up into medium-fine pieces, keeping the white and dark separate. Layer the meat in and pack gently. Fill with the gelatined broth and chill to become firm. Unmold on a platter and garnish, perhaps with halves of hard-cooked eggs with dabs of red caviar in the center.

Cissy Gregg's Cook Book, vol. 2, p. 12,
The Courier Journal & Louisville Times Co., reprinted with permission

Chicken Spaghetti

1 lb. thin spaghetti	2 large cans tomatoes
3- to 4-lb. hen, cooked and boned, reserve broth	2 to 3 bay leaves
	1 can mushrooms
2 to 3 green peppers, chopped	1 jar ripe olives
2 to 3 onions, chopped	1 jar stuffed olives
1 c. celery, chopped	1 lb. sharp cheese, diced
1/4 lb. margarine or butter for sauteing	

Cook spaghetti in chicken broth until barely tender. Drain. Saute peppers, onions and celery in margarine until soft but not brown. Add to spaghetti. Add tomatoes, bay leaves, mushrooms, olives, cheese and chicken pieces. Bake at 350 degrees for 45 minutes. Recipe can be halved. Serves 25.

Florence Ross, my Mother from Dovie Dudderer

Turkey Hash

4 c. medium sauce	1/2 c. cooked carrots, finely diced
3 c. turkey or chicken, cooked and diced	1/2 c. cooked celery, finely diced
	salt and pepper
1/2 c. cooked potatoes, finely diced	Parmesan cheese, for topping, optional

The medium white sauce is made on the basis of 2 T. butter or margarine and 2 T. flour per c. of milk. For this 4 c. of white sauce, use 8 T. butter or margarine and 8 T. flour for 4 c. milk. When the butter is melted and the flour blended in, the milk should be added gradually, and the cooking is done either over hot water in the top of a double boiler, or in a heavy saucepan. Either way, stir constantly so the sauce will be smooth like satin. When sauce has been completed, add the other ingredients and mix together gently. Place in a buttered casserole, a keep-hot dish or a chafing dish, and set in the oven at 350 degrees F. until thoroughly hot. If desired, sprinkle a little Parmesan cheese over the top of the hash before the final baking. This is enough for 10 servings with plenty of batter cakes.

Cissy Gregg's Cook Book, vol. 2, p. 12,
The Courier Journal & Louisville Times Co., reprinted with permission

Turkey Hash

1/2 c. onions, chopped	4 c. cooked, turkey, diced
1/2 lb. fresh mushrooms, sliced, optional	4 c. cooked potatoes, diced
8 T. butter	1/2 t. salt
1/2 c. flour	1/4 t. pepper
4 c. chicken or turkey stock	1/2 c. heavy cream, optional

In a heavy dutch oven saute onions and mushrooms in butter until soft. Stir in flour and cook over low heat until well blended. Slowly add stock, stirring constantly until thickened. Add turkey and potatoes, season and simmer 15 to 20 minutes. Add cream, if desired. Serve over griddle cakes or corn cakes. Left-over turkey gravy is a good addition to the hash. Serves 12 to 15.

Kentucky Derby Museum Cookbook, p. 100

Turkey or Chicken Hash

1 3/4 c. chicken broth
1 1/2 c. onion, chopped
1/8 t. black pepper
1/16 t. red pepper
3/4 t. salt

1/8 t. seasoned salt
1/2 c. flour shaken with
   1/4 c. cold water to make paste
3 1/2 c. cooked chicken or turkey,
   cubed
2 T. butter

Heat the broth and add seasonings. Taste for seasoning before adding the thickening. Shake flour and water together for thickening. Add this gradually to the broth. Add the turkey or chicken and then the butter. Cook to desired consistency. Serve over Indian griddle cakes.

We Make You Kindly Welcome, p. 11

Cooking Bag Roasted Turkey

1 Reynolds oven bag,
   turkey size
1 T. flour
2 stalks celery, sliced

1 medium onion, sliced
16- to 24-lb. turkey, thawed
2 T. vegetable oil

Preheat oven to 350 degrees F. Shake flour in oven bag. Place in roasting pan at least 2" deep. Add vegetables to bag. Remove neck and giblets from turkey. Rinse turkey and pat dry. Lightly stuff with your favorite stuffing recipe, if desired. Brush turkey with oil. Place turkey in bag. Close bag with nylon tie. Cut 6 1/2" slits in top. Insert meat thermometer through slit in bag into thickest part of inner thigh, not touching bone. Bake until meat thermometer reads 180 degrees F. 2 1/2 to 3 1/2 hours. Add 1/2 hour for stuffed turkey. Let stand in bag 15 minutes. If bag sticks to turkey, gently loosen bag from turkey before opening bag. Serves 16 to 24.

The Reynolds Metals Co.

Bread & Celery Stuffing

3 to 4 T. onion, chopped
1 c. celery, chopped
butter or margarine

1/4 t. salt
1/4 t. pepper
1/2 t. poultry seasoning

4 c. dry bread crumbs
(7 medium slices cut
into 1/2" cubes)

1/4 t. ground sage, or less
4 to 6 T. water or chicken broth

Cook onion and celery in butter until brown. Combine with bread and seasonings. Toss with enough liquid to moisten. Use to stuff fowl or pork chops.

Source unknown

Cornbread Stuffing

2 c. cornmeal, medium-ground
2 T. baking powder
1/2 c. flour
1 t. baking soda
1 t. salt
2 c. buttermilk

1 egg
2 c. celery, chopped
1 1/2 c. onion, chopped
pinch of sage
stock and water

Mix first 7 ingredients to make cornbread. Cook in a 400 degree F. oven until done. Break into pieces and add celery, onion and sage. To make stock, cook giblets in water. Cook livers separately and discard liver stock; it will taste better. Add some stock from turkey pan to giblet stock for more flavorful dressing. Save giblets for gravy. If necessary, add some water to stock and pour over corn bread mixture until it is a little soupy. Stuff bird or bake in 350 degree F. oven until brown on top.

Ava Lanier, Murrells Inlet, South Carolina

Cornbread Stuffing

1 c. celery, chopped	1 t. salt, or to taste
3/4 c. onion, finely chopped	1/2 t. pepper, or to taste
1/2 c. butter or margarine	1 t. dried sage or poultry seasoning
3 c. day-old corn bread crumbs	1 egg, well beaten
2 c. day-old dry white bread, cubed	1 t. baking powder
	1 3/4 to 2 c. chicken broth or giblet stock, warmed

In a small skillet, saute the celery and onion in the butter until tender and golden. Do not brown. Combine this mixture with breads, salt, pepper and sage in a large mixing bowl. Mix together gently but thoroughly. Add egg and stir lightly. Blend in baking powder and add enough chicken broth to moisten, but keep the mixture crumbly. To make dressing balls, shape the dressing, using cupped hands, into small compact balls. Place on a greased baking sheet. Bake at 400 degrees F. for 10 minutes or until crispy and browned. Arrange on platter around hen or turkey. To stuff, follow directions on turkey package or bake in a casserole at 350 degrees F. until brown for 20 to 30 minutes. Makes enough for a 10 lb. bird.

Weisenberger Cookbook II, p. 155, Elizabeth Ross

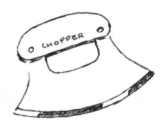

Dressing Balls

2 1/2 T. celery, chopped
2 t. parsley, chopped
1 small onion, chopped
3/4 stick butter
6 1/2 c. stale bread crumbs
chicken broth

1 egg, beaten
black pepper
poultry seasoning
salt
seasoning salt

Saute celery, parsley and onion in butter. Add bread crumbs. Add chicken broth until consistency is right for molding mixture into 2" balls. Stir in egg and add seasonings to taste. Bake at 350 degrees F. for 20 minutes. Serve immediately. Makes 10.

Historic Kentucky Recipes, Ruth Payne, p. 19; *We Make You Kindly Welcome*, p. 46

Southern Bread Dressing

3 c. cornbread,
  broken in pieces
2 c. white bread,
  broken in pieces

1/3 T. ground sage
1/4 t. black pepper
2 c. rich chicken stock
1/2 c. onion, minced

Mix all ingredients together. Place in a baking pan and bake at 350 degrees F. for 35 minutes. This is the dressing the Northerners wonder how the Southerners make and the Southerners wonder why the Northerners don't know how.

Look No Further, p. 156

Moist Cornmeal Dressing

1 c. cornmeal
2 c. cold stock
1/3 c. mayonnaise
1 c. celery, chopped
1 t. salt

1 1/4 t. poultry seasoning
1/2 c. onion, chopped
1/4 t. pepper
5 c. toasted bread cubes
2 eggs, beaten

Combine meal and stock. Cook until thick, then combine with the other ingredients. Bake at 325 degrees F. for 50 to 60 minutes.

A Taste from Back Home, p. 40

Quick Cornbread Stuffing Balls

1 6 oz. box cornbread
  stuffing mix
1 2/3 c. water less 2 T.
  with 1 chicken bouillon
  cube added or equivalent
  amount of chicken broth
  skimmed of fat

1 small onion, finely chopped
1 stalk celery, finely chopped
1/2 stick margarine

Prepare stuffing mix according to package directions for saucepan cooking, using stock. Saute onions and celery in margarine until soft but not browned. Fold into cooling stuffing mix. Combine well. Let cool to room temperature or until easily handled; can be chilled longer. Form into egg-sized balls and bake at 400 degrees F. for 25 minutes or until nicely browned and crusty on the outside. Can be made ahead, frozen and used as needed. Makes 1 doz.

Elizabeth Ross

Country
Ham
&
Pork

Country Ham

Soak ham overnight. Scrub rind. Place ham in pot large enough to hold ham. Completely cover the ham with water. Add 1 c. sugar and a handful of allspice. Simmer on stove using 2 burners if necessary to heat the pot. Cook 20 minutes per lb. or until meat draws away from bone. When done, let the ham cool in same water. When ham is cool, skin, leaving a nice layer of fat. Rub fat with brown sugar. Score fat as desired and dot with cloves. Brown in oven.

The Crowning Recipes of Kentucky, p. 204

Country Ham

Before the ham is cooked, hang it in a cool, dry place. Do not store a country ham in the refrigerator. A garage or basement is a good place to hang a ham because it will drip moisture and continue to mold until you prepare it for cooking.

To prepare the country ham for cooking, scrub it in warm water with a stiff brush to remove mold, rinse it well. Cut off the hock which can be used later for seasoning other dishes. Soak the ham 12 to 24 hours. This will help remove some of the salt and add moisture back to the cured ham. Discard this water after you finish soaking the ham.

To boil or simmer your country ham, place it in a large roaster, skin side up. Cover 2/3 of the ham with fresh, cold water. Add 1/2 c. vinegar to the water. Place cover on the roaster. Put the ham on the stove and bring to a boil, then turn the heat down to a simmer. Allow the ham to simmer for 15 to 20 minutes per lb. or until a meat thermometer reads 160 degrees F. This will take 4 to 6 hours, depending on the size of the ham. You can also tell that the ham is done when the large bone in the butt end of the ham becomes loose and protrudes. Add water if necessary during the cooking process to keep the ham 2/3 covered. Allow the ham to cool in the cooking water. When it has cooled, pour off the water and carefully remove the skin and trim away the excess fat. If desired, the bone can be removed at this time. Place the ham on a rack in a shallow roasting pan. Score the fat in a diamond pattern and stud with cloves. Pat 1 c. dark brown sugar on ham. Place the ham in a 350 degree F. oven and bake for 30 minutes.

Ham should be served only after it has cooled to room temperature. Always cut slices as thinly as possible.
After ham is cooked, it should be tightly wrapped in plastic wrap and refrigerated. It will keep in the refrigerator up to 6 weeks. Country ham can be frozen, but the flavor is not as good afterward.

Finchville Farms County Hams, Finchville, Kentucky

Baked Country Ham

Soak ham overnight. Put ham in 6 to 8 c. water in roast pan. Cook in 350 degree F. oven 15 minutes per pound if ham weighs 16 lbs. Cook it 4 hours. Stick a fork or knife in ham to the bone to be sure ham is done. Remove ham from oven and place on pan to bake. Trim and remove skin. Cover with brown sugar and sprinkle with cracker crumbs. Add cloves, if desired. Bake until brown. Take out and place on large meat dish. Wrap and place in refrigerator until time to slice. It will slice better if taken out of refrigerator 2 to 3 hours before slicing.

Cookbook of Treasures, Jane Cobb, p. 36

Baked Country Ham

Soak ham overnight in cold water. Trim dark places and excess fat. Place ham in roaster. Partly cover with cold water to which has been added 1 c. brown sugar, 1/2 c. vinegar, 1 whole onion, 1 whole apple and 1 handful of whole cloves. Heat quickly until water starts to boil briskly. Cut down heat to 325 degrees F. and cook until tender, about 15 minutes per pound. Let set in water until cool. Put on tray and skin, score and baste with 1 c. bread crumbs and 1/2 c. brown sugar. Put 1 whole clove in each scored section. Place in slow oven and brown. Meat thermometer should register 158 degrees F. when ham is done. Baked ham should be boned while warm. Dissolve 1 pkg. of Knox gelatin in 1/4 c. cold water. Add 1 1/2 c. hot ham liquor, 3 T. meal and 1/2 c. brown sugar. Fill crevices left inside of ham after boning, then tie securely and place in cloth or aluminum foil. Place in refrigerator overnight to cool. Slice in even slices on a meat slicer. Portion carefully, 2 1/2 oz. each, and place between layers of aluminum foil or oiled paper until serving time. Never slice baked ham longer than 1 day ahead of serving time. Serve cold, never reheat baked country ham.

Recipes from Kentucky State Resort Parks, p. 69

Baked Country Ham

Trim ham and soak it in hot water for a while. Weigh it. Wrap in heavy duty wrap, skin side up. Cook 22 minutes per pound. Cook 20 minutes at 450 degrees F., then turn back to 350 degrees F. and start timing. Place ham on rack. Add enough water to keep from smoking. After it cools, take skin off and put brown sugar on top. Put back in stove until it melts and goes through ham. To figure time - take your pounds times 22 and divide by 60. Wrap ham in aluminum foil.

Speedwell Christian Church Cook Book, Glenda Maupin, p. 22

Cooking Country Ham

Soak ham overnight. Put ham in covered roaster with 7 c. water for whole ham or 5 c. water for 1/2 ham. Preheat oven to 375 degrees F. Put in ham and turn oven to 500 degrees F. Cook for 25 minutes and turn oven off. Leave 3 hours. Do not open door. Turn oven on again to 500 degrees F. and cook for 20 minutes. Turn oven off and leave unopened for 5 hours. Do not open door any time during this 8 hour and 45 minute cooking time. When ham is cool, remove skin and most of fat. Trim all undesirable bits, etc. Score fat side. Add glaze made of brown sugar, mustard and cloves. Brown, fat side under broiler, but place ham on bottom rack for this - don't get too near the broiler.

Cookbook of Treasures, Connie Congleton, p. 36

How to Cook a Country Ham

Scrub a large ham, removing all mold and dirt. Place it in a large container. A lard can is recommended. Cover ham with water and heat to a slow, rolling boil slowly, for 30 minutes. Secure lid on can. Remove from heat and place on floor on a pallet composed of a blanket, heavy quilt and many layers of newspapers. Wrap can in newspaper then cover with blanket and let it set. After 24 hours, lift ham out of can - water will still be very hot. Remove skin and bones while it is hot. Make 1 c. of paste from sweet pickle juice, meal, brown sugar, ground cloves and ground mustard and spread on top of ham. With fat side up, bake at 300 degrees F. for 20 minutes and score and decorate with whole cloves. Your ham remains moist and is not dried out using this recipe.

Best of the Best from Kentucky, Country Cookbook, p. 136

Kentucky Country Ham

The best way to cook old hams is to boil them. Not having a large boiler, we cleaned our copper clothes-boiler and used it successfully. Put the ham into the boiler half filled with water. Cover and set on top of the stove where 2 burners can be turned on under it. When the water boils, turn the burners very low and let the ham simmer 15 to 20 minutes per pound, depending on the age and the hardness of the meat. Add more water if necessary, but never fill the boiler more than half full. Turn the ham from side to side every so often. To test it, pull out the tiny end bones with your fingers. When you can do that, the ham is ready to be taken off the stove. Another method of testing is to stick the ham through to the bone with a long-pronged fork. When it sticks tender, it is done. Remove ham from boiler. Just before serving, place the ham in a flat pan with 1 1/2" sides, trim off the top skin and enough of the fat to make a smooth surface. With a sharp knife mark the fat into squares, being careful not to cut through to the meat. Insert a whole clove in each square, dust surface with powdered cloves, then spread a thin layer of prepared mustard over this. Next, pat a c. of soft, medium brown sugar over the mustard. In some parts of Kentucky, a T. of water-ground cornmeal is previously mixed with the sugar, but this is not essential. Place the ham in the grill or broiler, then light the broiler and close the door. Let the ham remain until the sugar bubbles and the whole surface seems glazed, but check now and then to see that it does not burn. Remove the ham to a platter. When sliced, the meat will be of dark reddish-brown color, flecked with white.

Out of Kentucky Kitchens, p. 130

Kentucky Country Ham

Old Kentucky hams should weight 18 to 20 lbs. and have been aged from 1 1/2 to 2 years. When buying country hams, be sure they have been smoked and not cured by the quick method of liquid smoke preparation. Uncooked country hams should never be placed in a refrigerator, but should be hung in a cool, dry place.

Recipes from Kentucky State Resort Parks, p. 68

Old Kentucky Ham

Scrub ham well. Soak at least overnight in water to cover. If possible, a large ham should be soaked 3 to 4 days with the water changed every day. Place the soaked ham in a large roaster or anything that will allow cold water to cover the ham. Add 2 c. brown sugar and 1 c. vinegar to water. Cover and simmer slowly, 20 minutes to the pound. Never boil an old ham. It is hard to stand firmly by any definite timing for these hams since all are cured slightly differently. The ham should be tender and poking it with a fork is the only way I know to find out. Turn off the flame and let the ham bathe in its own juice overnight. Next morning, remove ham from liquid. Remove skin and fat. Glaze top with fine bread crumbs and brown sugar mixed together. Do this by patting mixture over top of ham, then browning in 375 to 400 degree F. oven until crust forms over top. Wine can be used for basting.

Cissy Gregg's Cook Book, vol. 1, p. 32,
The Courier Journal & Louisville Times Co., reprinted with permission

Old Kentucky Ham

Scrub ham in cold water. Soak at least 15 hours if over 20 lbs. Soak 2 or 3 days, changing water once and adding 1/2 c. vinegar. Place soaked ham in a large roaster or anything large enough to let ham be completely submerged. Fill with water. Add 2 c. brown sugar and 1 c. vinegar. Cover and simmer slowly 20 minutes per pound. Never allow old ham to boil. Turn off heat and let set overnight. To glaze, remove skin from fat side. Top with brown sugar and cloves sprinkled with meal on top.

Florence Ross, my Mother

Southern County Ham

| 1 c. brown sugar | country ham |
| 1 c. cider vinegar | pepper |

Dissolve brown sugar and cider vinegar in large roaster. Place ham in roaster and fill with water until 3" from top. Cover and bake at 400 degrees F. Reduce heat to 275 degrees F. when water boils and cook 20 minutes per lb. of ham. Allow ham to remain in roaster until completely cooled. Trim off skin and rub with brown sugar and pepper. Heat under broiler before serving.

A Taste from Back Home, p. 141

Sugar Cure for Hams

1 c. brown sugar	1 T. red pepper
1 pt. salt	2 T. black pepper

Combine all ingredients. Rub meat with mixture until it sweats. Wrap well in cloth and sack it with hock down to cook. Put in a container large enough to cover all the meat with cold water. Soak overnight. The next day, take out of water and trim off part of fat and all of the molded parts - it should be clean. Put ham in roaster with about 1/2 gal. of water. Cook at 375 degrees F. in roaster with cover on or a pan large enough to hold it and cover it with heavy duty foil wrap. Cook for 3 1/2 to 4 hours depending on size. Check for doneness with an ice pick. It should come out easily.

Ruth Ross Ballard

Country Ham and Angel Biscuits

5 c. flour, unsifted	1 c. shortening
1/4 c. sugar	1 pkg. dry yeast
3 t. baking powder	2 T. warm water
1 t. salt	2 c. buttermilk
1 t. soda	2 to 3 lbs. cooked country ham, thinly sliced

Sift dry ingredients together. Cut in shortening. Dissolve the yeast in the warm water and add with buttermilk to dry mixture. Mix well. Turn out on lightly floured board, add more flour if necessary, and roll to 1/4" thickness. Cut with 1 3/4" biscuit cutter and place on greased cookie sheet. Bake at 400 degrees F. for 10 to 15 minutes or until done. Serve with sliced ham.

Florence Ross, my Mother

Country Ham Biscuits

1 c. country ham, ground   bite-size biscuits
4 T. butter

Mix country ham with butter to produce a smooth consistency. Make biscuits, cutting them about the size of a 50-cent piece. Let them cool and cut them open. Fill biscuits with country ham mixture. Before serving, heat at 425 degrees F. for 5 minutes.

Beaumont Inn Special Recipes, p. 134; *We Make You Kindly Welcome*, p. 14

Fried Country Ham (Trigg County way)

Cut a large country ham into 1/4" thick steaks. If meat is thin enough, the steaks will not have to be parboiled, otherwise they will need some preliminary cooking. Put just enough ham fat into the skillet to keep the meat from sticking. Have the skillet very hot. Add the ham steak or steaks on both sides. Add a c. of coffee or water and when the mixture begins to boil put a top on the skillet, lower the heat and let them simmer for 15 to 20 minutes or until meat sticks tender when pierced with a fork. Most of the gravy will have cooked away but enough should be left to moisten the ham. This gravy is often reddish-brown in color.

Out of Kentucky Kitchens, p. 131

Fried Country Ham

Cut a large country ham into 1/4" steaks. Have skillet very hot. Sear ham steaks until brown on both sides. Reduce heat, add c. of hot water and let simmer for 15 minutes or until tender. The gravy is reddish-brown in color. For a quick a la carte service, have country ham cut and portioned ready in deep freeze. The ham slices can be thawed in warm water in 5 minutes, if necessary.

Recipes from Kentucky State Resort Parks, p. 69

Fried Country Ham with Red-Eye Gravy

Ham should be cut in slices 1/4" thick. Trim off rind and cut gashes in fat to keep ham from curling. Put the slice of ham in a hot skillet (300 degrees F.). Brown quickly on one side, turn and brown the other side. Repeat until the fat is translucent. Do not overcook. It will cause the ham to be tough and dry. If the ham is too salty for your taste, soak the slices in milk or water for 30 minutes before cooking. After the ham is fried, pour off most of the grease. Add a small amount of water and let simmer for a few minutes. Pour gravy over ham or biscuits and serve hot.

Finchville Farms County Hams, Finchville, Kentucky

Fried Country Ham with Red-Eye Gravy

4 slices country ham,   1 c. coffee, freshly brewed
    cut 1/4" thick

Soak ham slices in milk for at least 30 minutes before cooking. This seems to take out some of the salt. Trim rind and excess fat from ham and cut into small pieces. Place fat in a large, heavy ungreased iron skillet. Stirring often, fry over moderate heat until pieces are crisp and have rendered all their fat. Discard fat and add ham slices. Add 1 c. of water and simmer gently until water is gone. Turn the slices and regulate heat so they color richly and evenly without burning. Transfer ham to heated platter. Pour the coffee into the skillet. Bring to a boil scraping in the brown bits that cling to the bottom of the skillet. Boil briskly, uncovered, until gravy turns red, then pour over ham. If you prefer, pour gravy into a gravy boat to be spooned over ham and hot biscuits. Serve at once.

Note: 1 t. brown sugar may be added while stirring gravy, if desired.

Elizabeth Ross

Frying Kentucky Country Ham

Ham should be cut in slices 1/4" thick. Trim off rind, also trim the dark edge from the meat side of the slice. Cut off the fat in a clean skillet and render. After all the grease has been cooked out of the fat, remove the fat from the skillet. Put the slice of ham in the hot skillet, brown quickly on one side, turn and brown on the other side. Repeat until done. Caution: If cooked too long, it will become hard and dry. If the ham is too salty for your taste, you can soak the slices in milk and sweet syrup or just water for 15 to 30 minutes. To make red-eye gravy after the ham is cooked, pour off most of the grease and leave residue from ham in skillet to brown. When sufficiently browned, add small amount of water. It may be spooned over the ham, hot biscuits or grits.

Historic Kentucky Recipes, Claudia Sanders Dinner House, p. 95

Doe Run Inn Country Ham Balls

2 lbs. country ham, ground	2 eggs
1 lb. sausage, uncooked	milk
1 c. dry bread crumbs	

Sauce:

2 c. brown sugar	1 c. white vinegar
1 c. water	1 T. prepared mustard

Mix sauce ingredients together and bring to boil for a few minutes. Mix together ham, sausage and bread crumbs. Add eggs and enough milk to moisten. Make into small balls. Place in a casserole. Cover with 1/2 of the sauce and bake at 350 degrees F. until firm for 25 to 30 minutes. Serve with remaining sauce.

Cookbook of Treasures, Ruth Congleton, p. 3

Country Ham Cocktail Balls

4 c. country ham, ground	2 eggs
1 c. dried bread crumbs	1/2 c. milk

Sauce:

1/2 c. vinegar	1 c. brown sugar
1/2 c. water	2 t. mustard

Mix first 4 ingredients. Form into small meat balls. Place in baking dish. Mix ingredients for sauce and pour over meat balls. Bake at 350 degrees F. until brown.

Froelich's Country Hams, Philpot, Kentucky

Country Ham Salad

2 c. country ham, ground	1/2 c. pickle relish
3 eggs, boiled and chopped	1/2 c. mayonnaise
1 c. celery, finely chopped	

Mix all ingredients together and refrigerate. Serve on bread or with crackers.

Finchville Farms Country Hams, Finchville, Kentucky

Scalloped Ham and Potatoes

Use a 1 1/2" slice of uncooked ham or shoulder. Sear ham in a lightly greased hot skillet. Place ham in a deep casserole. Add 2 c. raw, sliced potatoes. Dust with pepper. Add enough milk to cover potatoes. Put lid on casserole and bake in moderate oven at 350 degrees F. for 1 hour. Uncover and reduce heat to 300 degrees F. and bake 15 minutes longer.

Source unknown

Pan-Grilled Pork Chops

1 large garlic clove, crushed	1/2 t. ground pepper
1 t. thyme leaf, crumbled	1 t. lemon juice
1 t. seasoned salt	10 nice pork chops, thinly cut

Thoroughly mix garlic, thyme, seasoned salt, pepper and lemon juice to make a paste. Spread on both sides of each chop. Chill. Heat a large iron skillet and add 1 T. shortening. Cook chops 4 minutes on each side. Place on warm platter. Add 1/2 c. water to the pan and mix with browned crumbs. Boil down to make gravy.

Source unknown

Breaded Pork Tenderloin

Slice off the tenderloin and hit with a meat cleaver to flatten. Dip each piece into 1 egg beaten with a T. of water, then into bread crumbs. Fry until browned, seasoning with salt and pepper. Pork chops are nice cooked the same way.

Kirksville Historical Cookbook, p. 59

Pork Tenderloins and Cream Gravy

Saute pork tenderloins in shortening and remove from pan. Keep warm. To make gravy, use 2 T. drippings and 2 T. flour to 2 c. milk. Heat drippings and sprinkle in the flour. Stir with wire whisk constantly and quickly and simmer until very smooth and bubbly.   Remove pan from heat and stir in 2 c. milk, again stirring quickly with wire whisk to prevent lumps. Return to heat. Cook and stir until smooth. Season with salt and pepper.

We Make You Kindly Welcome, p. 30

Barbecued Spareribs

2 sides of spareribs	2 T. vinegar
1/2 c. catsup	1 t. salt
1 c. water	1 T. sugar
1/2 t. chili powder	1 t. dry mustard
1 1/2 T. Worcestershire sauce	2 medium onions

Have spareribs cut into serving pieces. Combine remaining ingredients except onions for sauce. Place a layer of ribs in roasting pan. Slice onions over them and cover with half of the sauce. Repeat layers. Cover pan and bake at 325 degrees F. for 2 hours. Uncover the last 30 minutes for the ribs to brown off.

Cissy Gregg's Cook Book, vol. 1, p. 22,
The Courier Journal & Louisville Times Co., reprinted with permission

Finger Lickin' Spareribs

6 lbs. country-style spareribs	1/2 c. water
1/2 c. sherry	

Sauce:

1 t. chili powder	1/4 c. vinegar
1 t. celery seed	1/4 c. Worcestershire sauce
2 c. water	1/4 lemon, sliced thin
1/2 c. onion, chopped	1/8 t. pepper
1 t. salt	1/2 c. brown sugar
1 c. catsup	

In a large frying pan, brown spareribs. Add sherry and water and cook, covered, for 1 hour. In another pan, combine all sauce ingredients and cook for an hour. Let ribs cool in liquid long enough to skim off fat. Remove ribs and drain. Lay drained ribs in large casserole, cover with sauce and bake 1 hour at 300 degrees F.

Historic Kentucky Recipes, p. 82

Spareribs and Sauerkraut

Use a heavy-bottomed saucepan with a tightly fitting lid. Place in bottom, with skin side up, some sugar cured ham rinds or a couple of slices of uncooked bacon. Spread some sliced onion over the bacon. Put a layer of sliced apples over onions, if desired. Next, put in a layer of undrained kraut seasoned with a pinch of dill. Add a layer of spareribs (or metts or hot dogs), then a layer of kraut until pan is nicely filled. Add no water. Fasten lid on as tightly as possible. This will prevent the escape of steam so food will cook in its own moisture. Cook for 2 1/2 hours or until ribs are tender.

Elizabeth Ross

Fish
&
Seafood

Crappie Fish

Filet fish. Salt, then dip each filet into buttermilk and then into cornmeal. Fry in hot fat in an iron skillet until golden brown. Serve hot.

My Old Kentucky Homes Cookbook
from Jim's Seafood Restaurant, Frankfort, Kentucky, p. 23

Fried Fish Filet

1 fish filet per person	flour or cornmeal with
eggs, slightly beaten	salt and pepper
	cooking oil

Cut filet into serving size pieces. Wash and dry. Dip into egg, then into seasoned flour. Pour cooking oil into fry pan at least 1/2" deep. Heat to smoking stage. Drop floured fish into hot fat. Brown on both sides.

Fort Lauderdale Recipes, Recipes Selection Committee, p. 196

Southern Fried Fish

white cornmeal	vegetable oil or solid shortening
salt and pepper	for frying
pan fish, fileted and cleaned	large heavy skillet,
milk or beaten egg, optional	preferably cast iron

Pour cornmeal onto large piece of waxed paper. Salt and pepper cornmeal liberally and mix well. If desired, dip filets in milk or beaten egg and then cover well on both sides with cornmeal mix. Fry in 1/4" to 1/2" preheated oil on medium-high heat. Fry about 5 to 6 minutes on each side, turning once, until golden brown. Drain on paper towels. Serve hot with coleslaw and hushpuppies.

Elizabeth Ross

Southern Pan-Fried Fish

pan fish, fileted and cleaned	salted white cornmeal
black pepper	oil for frying

After the fish are cleaned and ready to fry, pepper them real well, then meal each piece separately. Fry, turning once, in electric skillet with enough oil to come about half way up the fish. Cook at 380 degrees F.

Ruth Ross Ballard

Fried Oysters

1 qt. oysters, shucked	1/16 t. ground thyme
1 c. flour	2 eggs beaten with 3 T. water
salt and pepper to taste	1 c. cornmeal

Drain oysters and reserve liquid. Pat dry between paper towels. Combine flour with seasonings and dredge in this combination, in the egg mixture and then in the cornmeal, to coat thoroughly. Drop into oil that has been heated to 375 degrees F. Fry until golden brown. Drain on absorbent paper and remove to hot platter. Mix reserved oyster liquid with any remaining egg and cornmeal. Drop mixture by spoonfuls into hot oil and fry to a golden brown. Serve along with the oysters for added interest. Serves 4 to 6.

The Shaker Cookbook, p. 57

Louisville Rolled Oysters

A Louisville invention that is associated with Mazzoni Oysters.

1/2 c. flour	18 medium sized oysters, drained
1 t. baking powder	1 c. white cornmeal or cracker meal,
1/4 t. salt	enough in which to roll
1 egg, well-beaten	batter-coated oysters
1/4 c. milk or more if needed	lard or vegetable shortening
	for frying

Sift the flour, baking powder and salt together. Beat the egg and milk and add to flour mixture. It should be stiff, but if too stiff to coat the oysters, add a little more milk. Beat smooth. Put all the oysters in this and coat them well. Take 3 batter-coated oysters at a time and form them in the hand into a croquette. Quickly roll the croquette in the meal, covering completely. The trick is to prevent the individual oysters from escaping the roll and separating when fried. It helps to coat them a second time, putting the rolled croquettes back once more into the batter or cracker meal. The 6 rolled oysters are now ready for frying. They can be made up in the morning, refrigerated and fried in the evening. When ready to fry, treat the oysters like donuts. Have a pan of deep lard on the stove. Heat to 375 degrees F., put the oysters in a basket and lower them into the fat. Do not cook too quickly as they should be cooked through. Lower the heat as soon as they hit the fat. They should cook on both sides at once if enough fat is in the pan. If not, cook on one side, turn with pancake turner and cook on the other. This will take 3 to 4 minutes all together. Drain on absorbent paper. Cook only 3 of these oysters at a time and leave space around them so they can brown evenly. Serve hot. Serves 6.

The Courier-Journal Kentucky Cookbook, p. 136

Oyster Casserole

1 can oysters, drained	1/3 c. butter, melted
1 t. onion, grated	3/4 c. light cream or milk
2 c. cracker crumbs	

Drain oysters and retain juice. Combine crackers with onions and add melted butter. Arrange oysters in buttered 8" pan. Top with 1/2 c. cracker crumbs. Preheat. Add 1/4 oyster juice to milk. Pour over entire top. Bake at 425 degrees F. for 20 minutes.

Speedwell Christian Church Cook Book, Mae Baker, p. 23

Scalloped Oysters

1/2 c. bread crumbs	2 T. oyster liquid
1 c. cracker crumbs	1 T. cream or milk
1/2 c. butter, melted	salt, pepper and nutmeg
1 pt. oysters, drained, reserving liquid	

Mix together bread crumbs, cracker crumbs and butter. Mix together oyster liquid and cream. Butter a small baking dish and spread the bottom with 1/3 of the buttered crumbs. Distribute half of the oysters over the crumbs, and sprinkle with salt, pepper, ever so little nutmeg, and 1/2 of the oyster liquid/cream mixture. Add more crumbs, the remaining oysters, seasonings and liquid. Lastly, top with remaining crumbs. Bake 30 minutes in preheated 450 degree F. oven. Warning: Should you want to double or triple this recipe, never have more than 2 layers of oysters or the middle might be underdone. Use a larger shallow dish. Take it easy with the nutmeg. Serves 4.

Bentley Farm Cookbook, p. 116

Scalloped Oysters

1 1/2 c. cracker crumbs	salt and pepper to taste
1 pt. oysters, drained, reserving liquid	6 T. cream and oyster liquid
	1/2 c. butter, melted

Grease a baking dish and cover with 1/3 of the crumbs. Cover with 1/2 of the oysters and season. Add 1/2 oyster liquid and cream. Repeat. Cover the top with remaining crumbs. Pour melted butter over all. Bake at 400 degrees F. for 30 minutes. Serves 6.

Cookbook of Treasures, Virgie S. Young, p. 42, Lucille Vann

Scalloped Oysters

1/4 c. stale bread crumbs	2 T. milk or cream
3/4 c. cracker crumbs	1 t. salt
1/4 c. butter, melted	1/2 t. black pepper
1 pt. oysters, drained	dash of Tabasco sauce
1/4 c. oyster liquor	trace of mace or sherry

Mix crumbs and butter and put a layer in buttered baking dish. Add a layer of oysters, then 1/2 of seasonings and liquid. Repeat. Never allow more than 2 layers of oysters. Cover with remaining crumbs. Bake at 325 degrees F. for 30 minutes. Serves 4.

Cooking with Curtis Grace, p. 140

Scalloped Oysters

1 pt. oysters	1/2 t. salt
2 c. cracker crumbs,	dash pepper
medium course	3/4 c. cream
1/2 c. butter or	1/4 c. oyster liquor
margarine, melted	1/4 t. Worcestershire sauce

Drain oysters, saving liquor. Combine crumbs, butter, salt and pepper. Spread 1/3 of the buttered crumbs in a greased 8" round pie plate. Cover with half the oysters. Put another layer of crumbs, using 1/3 amount again. Add remaining oysters. Combine cream, oyster liquor and Worcestershire sauce. Pour over oysters. Top with last of crumbs. Bake at 350 degrees F. for 40 minutes. Serves 4.

Out of the Kitchen into the House, p. 46

Scalloped Oysters

1 pt. oysters	6 T. cream and oyster liquor
1 1/2 c. coarse cracker crumbs	1/2 c. butter, melted
salt and pepper	

Pick over oysters and drain, reserving liquor. Grease baking dish and cover with 1/3 of the cracker crumbs. Cover with 1/2 of the oysters and season. Add 1/2 of the cream and oyster liquor. Repeat. Cover top with remaining crumbs. Pour melted butter over all. Bake at 400 degrees F. for 30 minutes. Serves 6.

We Make You Kindly Welcome, p. 47

Beef, Variety Meats & Sauces

Country Meat Loaf

1 egg
1 1/2 lbs. ground beef
1/2 c. onion, finely chopped
1 1/2 t. salt
1/4 t. pepper

2 T. celery, diced
2 T. green pepper, diced
1 c. tomato juice
3/4 c. oatmeal

Beat egg slightly. Add beef, onion, salt, pepper, celery, green pepper. Toss with a fork until blended. For a light loaf avoid packing the ingredients during mixing. Lightly stir in tomato juice, then oatmeal. Shape into a loaf and put in aluminum foil on rack in pan. Be sure to spread foil so that fat runs away from loaf. Bake at 350 degrees F. for 1 1/2 hours. Let stand 5 minutes before slicing. Serves 8.

We Make You Kindly Welcome, p. 12

Flatwoods Meat Loaf

2 medium onions, chopped
2 medium potatoes,
  peeled and cubed
1 rib celery, chopped
2 slices bread,
  softened in 1/2 c. milk
2 eggs

2 T. Worcestershire sauce
1 8 oz. can tomato sauce
2 lbs. ground beef
2 pork chops, ground
salt and pepper to taste
2 strips bacon

Cook onions, potatoes and celery in a little water. Drain and mash. Mix with the soaked bread, eggs, Worcestershire sauce and half of the tomato sauce. Add beef and pork. Add salt and pepper and blend well. Pack mixture into loaf pan. Cover with strips of bacon and pour remaining tomato sauce over top. Bake, uncovered, at 350 degrees F. for 1 1/2 hours.

Florence Ross, my Mother

Country Fried Steak

1 1/2 lbs. round steak,	3 T. oil
tenderized	1 T. flour
flour to dredge meat in	1 c. water
salt and pepper	1 t. onion flakes

Dredge steak in flour seasoned with salt and pepper. After it is browned on both sides in oil, remove from pan and add 1 T. flour to the drippings in pan. Slowly stir in water to form a gravy. Add onion flakes. Return the meat to the skillet and cover. Simmer 1 1/2 hours. Serves 6.

The Crowning Recipes of Kentucky, p. 164

Country Fried Steak

1 1/2 lbs. round steak, 1" thick	2 T. shortening
1/2 t. salt	1 small onion, sliced
dash of pepper	2 T. flour
1/4 c. flour	2 c. water

Cut steak in serving slices. Season with salt and pepper. Pour in flour and brown in hot shortening. Add onion. Stir 2 T. flour into drippings. Add water to make gravy. Cover and simmer gently 2 to 2 1/2 hours.

Historic Kentucky Recipes, p. 81

Country Fried Steak

1/4 c. flour	bacon drippings or shortening
1 1/2 t. salt	for frying
1/4 t. pepper	1 to 2 T. flour
1 1/2 lbs. round steak,	2 c. milk
cut 1/2" thick in squares	

Pound flour and seasonings into steak. Fry in 3 T. very hot drippings until brown on each side. Place on warm plate. Add 1 to 2 T. flour to drippings and blend. Add milk and stir until smooth. Taste for seasonings, it may need more salt. Serves 4.

Elizabeth Ross

Oven Fried Steak

1 round steak, cut into pieces 3/4" thick 1/3 c. flour	1 1/3 t. salt 3 shakes black pepper 2 1/2 c. boiling water

Trim fat from steaks. Put flour, salt and pepper in a paper bag. Shake once. Add steak and shake until coated. Spray large skillet 5 times with vegetable oil spray. Brown steaks on both sides. Place steaks in warm pan to go in oven. Into drippings left in skillet, add any leftover flour, salt and pepper mixture. Mix and blend thoroughly. Add 2 1/2 c. boiling water to make a very thin gravy. Gravy should cover bottom of pan about 3/4". Pour gravy in pan on top of steaks. Cover well with aluminum foil to keep steam in. A covered casserole works best for home use. Steaks must not be allowed to get dry! Cook, covered, at 350 degrees F. for 1 to 1 1/4 hours. If it gets too dry, add hot water while cooking. Recipe from Bales Restaurant, Richmond, Kentucky.

Cookbook of Treasures, p. 43

Jockey Club Steaks

This is the way you would be served club steaks at the famous Jockey Club Restaurant at Churchill Downs, home of the Kentucky Derby.

2 T. butter 1 garlic pod	4 club steaks cut 1" thick salt and pepper to taste

Melt butter in skillet. Add garlic. Sprinkle steaks with pepper. Saute in butter for 4 to 6 minutes, depending on how well done you like your steaks, letting first one side brown, then the other. Salt as soon as meat is brown. Remove garlic. Serve meat at once while very hot. Henry Bain sauce often accompanies these steaks in Louisville. Serves 4.

Out of Kentucky Kitchens, p. 116

Iron Pot Beef

An old Kentucky recipe for beef a la mode.

4-lb. pot roast (top round)	1 blade mace
1/2 t. black pepper	1/2 t. mixed herbs
1/4 c. mild vinegar	(marjoram, thyme, basil)
3/4 c. red wine	1/2 lemon, sliced thin
1 garlic pod, sliced	flour for dusting roast
1 onion, sliced	fat for browning roast
2 bay leaves	salt
4 cloves	water-wine mixed to make 2 c.
2 allspice berries	4 carrots
	2 onions

Rub roast with black pepper and put in a bowl. Let stand overnight with the vinegar, red wine, garlic, onion, bay leaves, spices, mixed herbs and lemon. This must soak at least 24 hours, 2 to 3 days would be even better. Turn the roast occasionally so that marinade goes through it. To cook roast, dust with flour and brown in fat. Pour off excess grease and salt the meat well. Add the marinade in which meat was soaked and enough water and wine mixed to make 2 c. Add carrots and onions. Cover and simmer slowly until meat is done, about 4 hours. More water may have to be added from time to time. If desired, 30 minutes before serving add 4 whole onions and 4 whole carrots. Serve on a platter surrounded with vegetables and pass the gravy separately. Do not prepare this recipe for a small family as a small roast is not satisfactory prepared this way. The meat is delicious sliced cold. Serves 8.

Out of Kentucky Kitchens, p. 116

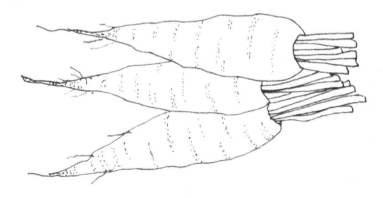

Pot Roast of Beef

4- to 5-lb. chuck roast	4 peppercorns
1 large onion, chopped	1 12 oz. can mixed vegetable juices
1 clove garlic	6 potatoes, pared and halved
1 bay leaf	6 carrots, scraped and halved
2 t. salt	and quartered

Brown meat in its own fat in Dutch oven. Add all remaining ingredients except vegetables. Cover tightly and simmer 2 hours. Lay vegetables around meat and cover. Simmer 30 minutes longer or until vegetables are tender. Remove meat and vegetables to heated platter. Strain broth into a 4 c. measure, pressing onion through a sieve. Let stand until fat rises to top and skim off. Return 2 T. fat to pot and blend in 2 T. flour. Add water to broth to make 2 c. Stir into flour mixture. Cook, stirring constantly until mixture has thickened. Boil 1 minute. Serves 6.

Florence Ross, my Mother

Beef Stew

1 1/2 lbs. beef stew meat, cubed	1 t. marjoram or thyme
1/4 c. flour	12 small onions, peeled
1 1/2 t. salt	1/2 lb. turnips, peeled and cubed
1/4 t. pepper	2 large carrots, cut in chunks
3 T. oil	2 medium potatoes, peeled and quartered
water	1 c. cut green beans, optional

Coat meat in flour seasoned with salt and pepper. Brown meat in hot oil. Add water just to cover (3 c.) and marjoram or thyme. Bring to a boil. Reduce heat and cover. Simmer 1 hour or until meat is tender. Add remaining ingredients except beans. Cover and simmer another 45 minutes. Add beans, if desired, and cook 10 minutes more. Serve generously.

Florence Ross, my Mother

Johnnie Marzetti

8 oz. broad noodles or macaroni, cooked to just tender, drained	1 can tomato puree
	salt and pepper to taste
	1/4 t. basil
2 T. butter or margarine	1 bay leaf
1 lb. round steak, ground	1 c. water
3 stalks celery, diced	1/2 c. cheddar cheese plus
2 medium onions, chopped	extra for topping, grated
1 green pepper, chopped	1/2 c. bread crumbs

Place noodles in greased baking dish. Melt fat in skillet. Add meat, celery, onion and green pepper. Cook 10 minutes, stirring to prevent sticking. Add tomato puree, salt, pepper, basil, bay leaf and water. Simmer 5 minutes. Add cheese and mix with noodles and sprinkle with cheese and bread crumbs. Bake until top browns in a moderate 350 to 375 degree F. oven for 20 to 30 minutes.

Out of Kentucky Kitchens, p. 117

It is said that the first cheeseburger was served in 1934 at Kaelin's Restaurant in Louisville.

Chicken Livers on Toast with Mushroom Sauce

Saute chicken livers in butter. Do not overcook. Season with salt and coarse black pepper. Serve on toasted homemade bread. Top with mushroom sauce (see Sauces).

We Make You Kindly Welcome, p. 29

Creamed Chicken Livers

4 slices bacon	1 T. onions, chopped
2 T. flour	1 can cream of mushroom soup
dash of pepper	1/4 c. water
1/2 lb. chicken livers	1 c. cooked rice, hot

Fry bacon in skillet until crisp. Remove from skillet. Drain, reserving drippings. Combine flour with pepper. Coat livers with flour mixture. Brown livers and onion in 2 T. reserved bacon drippings. Cover. Cook over low heat for 8 to 10 minutes. Blend soup with water. Stir into liver mixture. Heat through. Spoon over rice. Top with bacon strips. Serves 2.

Miss Daisy Entertains, p. 109

Frog Legs

12 frog legs	1/4 c. milk
salt and pepper	1 c. all-purpose flour
2 eggs	

If frozen, thaw frog legs. Salt and pepper. Beat together eggs and milk. Dip frog legs in batter and then in flour. Dip and flour again. Fill heavy skillet 1/2" up the side with grease. Heat. Fry legs until golden brown and tender. Serve hot.

My Old Kentucky Homes Cookbook from Jim's Seafood Restaurant, Frankfort, Kentucky, p. 23

Fried Frog's Legs

12 jumbo legs or	flour or bread, cracker or cornmeal
24 small ones	crumbs with salt and pepper
1 egg, beaten	oil and butter

Wash legs well. Dip into beaten egg and then into crumbs. Have 1/2" oil in bottom of fry pan. When hot put in legs. Brown on one side. Turn, put pat of butter into oil and brown. Drain on paper towel and serve at once. Serves 4.

Fort Lauderdale Recipes, Recipe Selection Committee, p. 194

La Taberna Lamb Fries

lamb fries	cracker meal
1 egg, beaten	deep fat for frying
1 c. milk	

Slice lamb fries 1/4" thick. Slicing will be easier if they are partially frozen. Combine egg and milk. Dip lamb fry slices in this batter, then roll in cracker meal. Fry in deep fat at 300 degrees F. until golden brown. "Lamb fries" is the local euphemism for the testes of young sheep, a delicacy of long tradition in Kentucky.

Dining in Historic Kentucky, vol. 1, p. 140;
My Old Kentucky Homes Cookbook, Hall's on the River, Boonesborough, p. 23

Liver and Onions

Pan-fry bacon (1 to 2 slices for each slice of liver). Peel and slice a large sweet onion (a Vidalia, if possible) crosswise. Remove bacon from skillet and drain on paper towel. Pan fry onion slices in the bacon drippings. Brown evenly. Push to one side and fry the liver (calves' liver, if possible). Season the onions with salt and pepper. Serve with the liver and bacon strips. If you do not wish to serve liver with onions, dip liver slices in flour seasoned with salt and pepper and fry in bacon fat. You can make cream gravy to go with this.

Elizabeth Ross

Sweetbreads Financiere

2 strips bacon, diced	1 lb. veal sweetbreads
1 T. butter	1 celery stalk, chopped
1/2 medium onion, chopped	1/2 medium onion, chopped
1 clove garlic, minced	1 bay leaf
1/2 c. mushrooms, sliced	pinch of thyme
3/4 c. dry sherry	1 lemon, halved
3/4 c. beef stock or consomme	flour
2 T. catsup	salt and pepper
1 T. Maggi seasoning	1/4 c. butter, melted

Cook bacon over medium heat until it begins to brown. Add butter, onion and garlic and saute until onion is translucent. Add mushrooms. When mushrooms are slightly brown, add sherry, beef stock, catsup and Maggi seasoning. Bring to simmer. Set aside. Place sweetbreads in boiling salted water to cover along with celery, remaining onion, bay leaf and thyme. Add juice of 1/2 lemon plus squeezed lemon half. Poach gently 20 minutes. Drain and cool slightly. Remove all fat and membranes from sweetbreads. Transfer to plate, cover with another plate and place weight on top. Allow to stand for at least 1 hour (sweetbreads should be about 1" thick). Slice in half. Roll sweetbreads in flour seasoned with salt and pepper to taste and saute in butter until lightly browned. Transfer to sauce, add juice of remaining 1/2 lemon and cook until sauce is reduced by 1/2. Serve at once. Serves 4.

Chef John T. Elliott, The Ballard Store, Solvang, California

Louisville Sweetbreads with Bacon

Sweetbreads are precooked and this makes them easy to handle for last-minute fixing. In buying sweetbreads, keep in mind that they are perishable meat and must be kept chilled or frozen by your meat man and by you once they are purchased. Drop the sweetbreads into boiling salted water to which a little lemon juice or vinegar has been added. The lemon juice or vinegar is supposed to keep them white. Cover the saucepan and simmer for 15 minutes. Chill the sweetbreads as soon as they are done by placing them in the refrigerator or for extra-quick chilling, put them in cold water before sending them to the refrigerator. If not using at once, put them in a covered dish or wrap in cooking foil and keep them in the coldest part of the refrigerator. When the sweetbreads are cold, lift off the thin membranes that cover them. If you prefer, hold them under running cold water and slip off the membranes with your fingers. Remove any dark veins with a sharp knife, being very careful not to break the sweetbreads. Now they are ready for the final touch.

8 precooked sweetbreads	1 c. bouillon
8 slices bacon	1 T. catchup
flour for dusting	1 t. Worcestershire sauce
butter or margarine	

Wrap each sweetbread in a slice of bacon and skewer it with a toothpick. Dust the tops with flour and put 2 dots of butter or margarine on each. Place in a pan. Mix bouillon with catchup and Worcestershire sauce and pour around them. Either broil under a gentle flame until the bacon is crisp and the sweetbreads have taken on a good color, basting frequently with the bouillon mixture, or place in a 400 degree F. oven until the same degree of brownness is obtained, again basting frequently. Have ready the same number of toast slices. Mount each sweetbread on its piece of toast and spoon any juice left in the pan over the top.

Cissy Gregg's Cook Book, vol, 1, p. 22
The Courier Journal & Louisville Times Co., reprinted with permission

Shaker Sweetbreads

1 pair sweetbreads	1 T. lemon juice
water to cover	1/2 t. salt
1/2 t. salt	1/16 t. pepper
1 t. lemon juice	2 egg yolks
2 T. butter	1 T. parsley, minced
2 T. flour	6 toast rounds or rusk

Parcook sweetbreads in 3 to 4 c. water to which salt and lemon juice have been added. Drain, reserving broth. Carefully trim any fat and all membranes. Cut into 1/2" squares. Melt butter and blend in flour to form a roux. Add 2 c. of the broth, lemon juice, salt and pepper. Cook gently to form a veloute (white sauce). Beat egg yolks until frothy and pour in a little of the hot veloute. Beat the yolk mixture into the remaining sauce, add sweetbreads and heat to 160 degrees F. until sauce thickens. Serve on rounds or points of toast, in a pastry shell or over rice. Sprinkle with parsley. Serve immediately with an accompaniment of green peas.

The Shaker Cookbook, p. 49

Cream Sauce

2 T. butter
2 T. all-purpose flour
1/2 t. salt

1/8 t. pepper
1 c. milk

In heavy saucepan, melt butter over low heat. With wooden spoon, blend in flour and seasonings. Stir constantly until smooth and bubbly. Remove from heat. Add milk gradually and return to heat stirring all the while. Bring to a boil for 1 minute. Makes 1 c.

Welcome Back to Pleasant Hill, p. 34

Brown Crumb Gravy (Cream Gravy)

2 T. fat and brown crumbs
   from pan in which chicken
   was fried

1 T. flour
1 c. milk, 2% milk will work fine
salt and pepper to taste

After removing chicken to a serving platter, pour off all but 2 T. of fat. Save all the brown crumbs and drippings. Return pan to low heat and sprinkle flour over drippings. Stir constantly until brown, about 2 minutes. Add milk slowly, stirring to prevent lumping. Add salt and pepper to taste. Do not cook too thick, only about 2 minutes. Serve hot.

Out of Kentucky Kitchens, p. 105

Milk or Cream Gravy

3 T. oil or fat with scrappies   2 c. milk, hot is best
   (pan drippings from frying)   1/2 t. salt
3 T. all-purpose flour   1/8 to 1/4 t. pepper

Save fat from fried chicken, country fried steak or pork chops. Pour 3 T. back into hot skillet. Stir in flour and blend well. Cook and stir until lightly browned. I use the seasoned flour from making fried chicken, etc. Over medium heat, gradually add milk, stirring constantly, until thick and bubbly. Stir in salt and pepper. This gravy goes with everything.

Elizabeth Ross

Pan or Milk Gravy

1/4 c. Wondra flour   1 c. cold water and 1 c. cold milk,
1/2 c. drippings   mixed
   (left in heavy skillet   1 t. salt
   from pork or chicken frying)   1/2 t. pepper

Add flour to drippings in skillet and stir constantly until mixture is bubbly. Stir in cold milk and water. Heat to boiling, stirring constantly. Boil and stir 1 minute. Add salt and pepper.

Mrs. Elaine Taylor, Guilford, Indiana,
served with the fried chicken dinner at the Fire Department Festival

Turkey Gravy

Remove the turkey from the roasting pan. Scrape up the brown pieces and mix with the broth in the pan. Pour 1 c. of the liquid into a saucepan. This will make 1 qt. of gravy. Let the broth come to a boil. In the meantime, in a bowl mix 3 T. of flour with a little water and make a paste. Add 2 c. of water to the paste and stir it well. Add this to the broth. Let it all cook until thick, stirring constantly. Season if necessary, but the broth should have enough flavor on its own.

Thelma's Treasures, p. 43

Henry Bain Sauce

1 14 oz. bottle catsup
1 12 oz. bottle chili sauce
1 10 oz. bottle A-1 steak sauce

1 10 oz. bottle Worcestershire sauce
1 8 oz. jar Major Grey's chutney
2 T. Tabasco sauce

Combine all ingredients. Mix well and pour into bottles. Sauce will keep for months stored in the refrigerator. Serve with steak or pot roast.

Cabbage Patch Famous Kentucky Recipes, p. 55

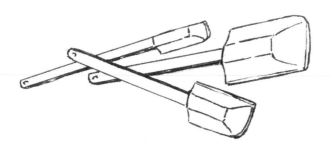

Henry Bain Sauce

Henry Bain went to work for the Pendennis Club in 1881 and was head waiter when he created his famous sauce. This is a modified version obtained by Cissy Gregg from Livingston Whaley, another well-known Louisville waiter. This sauce will keep indefinitely refrigerated and it is good on ham, steak or French fried potatoes. Thinned with oil and vinegar it snuggles up to Bibb lettuce. The ingredients are not expensive.

1 12 oz. bottle chili sauce
1 14 oz. bottle catsup
1 11 oz. bottle A-1 sauce
1 10 oz. bottle Worcestershire Sauce

1 1 lb. 1 oz. bottle chutney
Tabasco or hot pepper sauce
watercress, chopped, as desired

Mix together and add the hot sauce according to taste. It takes more than you think. If the chutney comes with large pieces of mangoes or other chutney fruit in it, chop finely. Chopped watercress may be added as you like.

Cissy Gregg's Cook Book, vol. 1, p. 32,
The Courier Journal & Louisville Times Co., reprinted with permission

Henry Bain Sauce

12 oz. bottle chili sauce	10 oz. bottle Worcestershire sauce
14 oz. bottle ketchup	1lb. bottle chutney
11 oz. bottle A-1 sauce	Tabasco to taste

Combine all ingredients and put into blender. Blend until smooth. This sauce is delicious served over cream cheese as an appetizer spread over assorted crackers. It also makes a great steak sauce.

Donna Gill Recommends, p. 36

Horseradish Cocktail Sauce

1/2 c. horseradish	juice of 1 lemon
3/4 c. chili sauce	onion to taste, grated

Combine all ingredients and chill.

Thomas' F & N Steakhouse, Dayton, Kentucky

Inverness Sauce (Wedgewood Farm)

A marinade for steaks, pork or lamb on the grill.

2 cloves garlic, minced	2 T. catsup
1/2 c. oil or olive oil	1 T. vinegar
3 T. soy sauce	1/2 t. fresh ground pepper

Mix all ingredients well. Pour over meat. Cover and refrigerate overnight for best flavor; 2 to 3 hours of marinating will do in a pinch. Makes 1 c.

The Kentucky Derby Museum Cookbook, p. 174

Mushroom Sauce

1 1/2 c. mushrooms,
   stems and pieces, drained
1/4 c. butter

1/4 c. flour
1 1/2 c. water
1/4 c. sherry to taste

Saute mushrooms slowly in the butter. Add flour slowly. Add the juice of the mushrooms, water and sherry. This sauce is excellent with veal cutlets or broiled chicken livers.

We Make You Kindly Welcome, p. 29

Mushroom Cream Sauce

3 T. butter
1/4 c. flour
salt and pepper to taste
dash paprika

1 1/2 c. warm milk
1 1/2 c. canned unsweetened
   condensed milk
mushroom buttons, sliced (if using
   fresh, brown lightly in butter)

Melt butter in top of double boiler. Add flour, salt, pepper and paprika while stirring with a wire whisk until blended and smooth. Add milk slowly, stirring constantly to prevent lumps. Cook until smooth and thickened, stirring constantly. Add mushrooms. Serve with Creme de Volaille or chicken croquettes.

We Make You Kindly Welcome, p. 59

Thick Sauce for Croquettes

3 T. butter or margarine   1 t. salt
1/3 c. all-purpose flour   1/4 t. paprika
1 c. milk

Melt butter in top of double boiler. Blend in flour until smooth. Gradually add milk, stirring constantly. Add seasonings. Cook slowly until sauce is thick and smooth.

Beaumont Inn Special Recipes, p. 38

Vegetables

Asparagus

Asparagus, aristocrats of vegetables and often served at Derby parties, is a member of the lily family. Thought to have its origin in the Mediterranean, it was highly prized by the ancient Greeks and Romans, both as a food and for medical properties it was believed to possess. It is a perennial with fleshy roots and fernlike, feathery foliage growing about 3 feet tall. The part eaten is the tender young stem. The two types of asparagus available are the white or French variety and the more familiar green variety. Fresh asparagus is usually available from February to early summer. It is sold loose or in bundles and can be thick or thin, light or dark green or green and purple. Size does not affect the quality but it is a matter of choice. Some prefer the thinner, other the fatter. Use asparagus with fresh green stalks tightly budded at the tips. When it begins to blossom it loses its flavor. Also, try to pick stalks with the least number of tough white ends. For uniform cooking, choose stalks of even size. Asparagus is very perishable but will keep in the crisper drawer of the refrigerator or upright in about an inch of water. Needless to say, it is best eaten fresh. Use 2 lbs. for 4 servings.

Source unknown

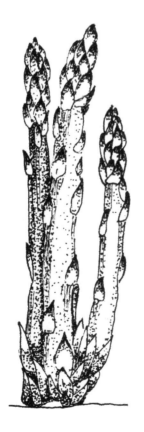

To Cook Fresh Asparagus

Place trimmed asparagus in a large skillet. Add water and boil until spears bend when picked up with a fork, about 5 minutes should be enough. To microwave, place spears in a flat microwave dish with tips toward the outside. Add about 1/4 c. water and cover with plastic wrap. Microwave on high 5 to 7 minutes. Let stand 3 to 5 minutes and serve hot.

Elizabeth Ross

Asparagus Au Gratin

2 lbs. fresh asparagus	3/4 c. American cheese, grated
1/2 c. asparagus cooking water	1 scant c. soft bread crumbs
1 c. milk	1 1/2 T. butter, melted
2 T. butter	paprika
2 T. flour	

Wash asparagus thoroughly and cut into 1" pieces. Cook tougher portions in a small amount of slightly salted water until almost tender. Add remaining pieces and continue cooking 5 to 8 minutes. Drain. Make a cream sauce using asparagus cooking water, milk, butter and flour. When the sauce has thickened, stir in grated cheese. Stir until cheese has melted. Combine the sauce and well-drained asparagus, stirring very gently. Pour into a buttered baking dish. Sprinkle the entire surface with bread crumbs. Sprinkle with melted butter and then a little paprika. Place the dish under the flame of the broiling oven until crumbs are delicately browned. Serve immediately.

The Gold Cookbook, p. 601

Asparagus and Eggs Au Gratin

1 c. cracker crumbs	4 eggs, hard-cooked
1 c. American cheese, grated	2 c. cooked asparagus
1 1/2 c. cream sauce	salt and pepper to taste

Sprinkle about one-half of the crumbs in bottom of casserole. Mix grated cheese with well seasoned cream sauce. Place alternate layers of sliced hard-cooked eggs, asparagus and sauce in dish. Sprinkle salt and pepper on each layer and cover the top with crumbs. Bake in moderate 350 degree F. oven for 20 minutes.

Historic Kentucky Recipes, p. 164

Baked Asparagus

2 c. fresh asparagus cut into 1" lengths	1/2 c. slivered almonds
	1/2 lb. cheddar cheese, grated
2 eggs, hard-cooked and sliced	1 can cream of mushroom soup
	1 c. Ritz cracker crumbs

Preheat oven to 350 degrees F. Layer asparagus, eggs, almonds and cheese in a greased baking dish. Cover with soup. Sprinkle with crumbs. Bake 35 minutes until thick and bubbly. Makes 4 to 5 servings.

Miss Daisy Entertains, p. 119

Asparagus Casserole

1 t. butter	salt and pepper to taste
2 T. flour	2 lbs. fresh asparagus cut
1 1/2 c. milk	into 1" lengths
1/2 c. cheddar cheese,	4 eggs, hard-cooked and sliced
grated	1/2 c. blanched almonds, roasted

Make a white cream sauce with butter, flour and milk. Add cheese, salt and pepper. Cook and drain asparagus. Put all ingredients in a greased casserole dish and bake at 350 degrees F. for 20 to 30 minutes.

Favorite Recipes, Tabitha Kunkle, p. 31

Asparagus Casserole

1 10 oz. pkg. frozen asparagus	3 T. flour
or a 1 lb. can drained asparagus	1 t. salt
or 1 lb. cooked fresh asparagus,	1/8 t. pepper
cut in 1" bias strips	2 c. milk
2 T. butter or margarine	4 to 6 eggs, hard-cooked
	and chopped

Cook asparagus as directed on pkg. until barely tender. Drain. Melt butter or margarine in small saucepan. Stir in flour, salt and pepper, blending until smooth. Add milk and cook over medium heat, stirring constantly, until thickened and bubbly. Turn half of the drained asparagus into a 1 qt. casserole. Top with half of the hard-cooked eggs. Pour half of the sauce over eggs. Repeat with remaining asparagus, eggs and white sauce. Bake at 325 degrees F. for 20 to 30 minutes, or until hot and bubbly. Serves 4.

Miriam B. Loo's Family Favorites Cookbook, p. 30

Marinated Asparagus

2 1/2 lbs. fresh asparagus
French dressing
3 T. dill, snipped
3 T. shallots, minced

1 T. parsley, minced
2 t. lemon rind, grated
salt and pepper to taste

Cook asparagus, about 40 stalks, and transfer to a shallow dish. While still warm, pour dressing over the asparagus and toss to coat well. Sprinkle with dill, shallots, parsley and lemon rind. Salt and pepper to taste and toss the mixture gently. Let the asparagus stand covered 1 hour. Serve at room temperature or chilled. Serves 4 to 6.

A Taste from Back Home, p. 66

Asparagus and Pea Casserole

1 16 oz. can peas
1 16 oz. can asparagus cuts
1 8 oz. can mushroom pieces

1 can mushroom soup
1/2 c. cracker crumbs
1/2 c. cheddar cheese, grated

Drain vegetables and mushroom pieces. Place half amount of ingredients above in order listed in a buttered casserole. Repeat layers. Bake at 350 degrees F. for 30 minutes.

Recipes from Miss Daisy's, p. 97

Country Asparagus Pie

1 1/2 lbs. fresh asparagus
  cut into 1" pieces
4 c. water
salt
3 T. margarine
3 T. flour
1 c. milk
1 chicken bouillon cube,
  crushed

1 t. instant minced onion
1/2 t. salt
1/4 t. curry powder
2 eggs, hard-cooked and chopped,
  optional
1 9" deep-dish pie shell, baked
1/2 c. Parmesan cheese
1/2 c. sharp cheddar cheese,
  shredded
paprika

Place asparagus, water and 1/2 t. salt in a 10" skillet. Bring to a boil over high heat. Reduce heat to medium-low. Cover and simmer until asparagus is fork-tender. Drain. Melt margarine in a 3 qt. saucepan over medium heat. Stir in flour until smooth. Gradually stir in milk until well blended. Cook, stirring constantly, until mixture boils and thickens. Remove from heat. Stir in bouillon cube, onion, salt and curry until bouillon cube is dissolved. Stir asparagus and chopped eggs into milk mixture until well blended. Pour into baked shell. Sprinkle with Parmesan cheese, cheddar cheese and paprika. Bake in a 350 degree F. oven 5 minutes or until cheese melts. Remove from oven.

Elizabeth Ross

Scalloped Asparagus

cracker crumbs	1/4 lb. butter
1 medium can asparagus	2 T. flour
4 to 5 eggs,	cheese, grated
hard-cooked and sliced	

Cover bottom of medium-size casserole with cracker crumbs. Drain asparagus, reserving juice. Add a layer of asparagus to casserole along with sliced eggs. Repeat to fill casserole. Melt butter and stir in flour. Add juice from asparagus and cook a few minutes. Add to casserole dish. Add crumbs on top with grated cheese or butter. Bake in a 350 degree F. oven for 30 minutes.

Mrs. Earle B. Combs, Sr.

Scalloped Asparagus

2 c. fresh asparagus	4 eggs, hard-cooked and sliced
cut in 1/2" pieces	salt and pepper to taste
1 c. Parmesan or	paprika
Swiss cheese, grated	1 pat butter
1 1/2 c. medium white sauce	unseasoned bread crumbs

Steam asparagus until a little more than crisp-tender. Fill a well-oiled baking dish with alternate layers of asparagus, cheese, white sauce and sliced eggs. Sprinkle with salt, pepper and paprika. Dot with pat of butter cut into pieces. Sprinkle with bread crumbs. Bake at 400 degrees F. for 30 minutes. Serves 6.

The Household Searchlight Recipe Book, p. 279; Elizabeth Ross

Scalloped Eggs with Asparagus

6 eggs, hard-cooked
and sliced
2 doz. fresh asparagus spears,
cooked and drained

salt and pepper to taste
1 1/2 c. medium white sauce
3/4 c. buttered bread crumbs

Fill a well-oiled baking dish with alternate layers of sliced eggs and asparagus. Season with salt and pepper. Add white sauce. Cover with buttered crumbs. Bake at 400 degrees F. until sauce bubbles. Serves 6.

The Household Searchlight Recipe Book, p. 139

Asparagus Souffle

3 T. butter, melted
3 T. flour
1 c. milk

4 eggs, separated
2 1/2 c. asparagus, cooked
and diced
3/4 t. salt

Preheat oven to 325 degrees F. Blend butter and flour. Add milk gradually. Cook slowly until thickened, stirring constantly. Beat egg yolks until thick and lemon-colored. Add asparagus and salt. Blend into sauce. Beat egg whites until stiff and fold into asparagus mixture. Pour into a greased casserole and set in pan of hot water. Bake 45 minutes. Serves 6.

Miss Daisy Entertains, p. 119

Canned Green Beans

1/2 lb. ham, bacon or smoked
pork shoulder cut in 1" cubes
1 medium-large onion,
peeled and quartered
1 28 oz. can water

1 28 oz. can Shellie beans
1 28 oz. can cut green beans
1/8 red pepper pod
salt to taste

Use a heavy 2 qt. pot with lid. Place ham in pot and add liquid drained from beans. Add onion quarters and water. Cook over medium heat for 30 minutes or until onion is soft. Now you can add corn or red potatoes, if desired. Add beans, cayenne and salt and simmer, covered, for 30 minutes. Test for seasoning and serve hot. A good winter dish.

Elizabeth Ross

Green Beans

half runner or Kentucky wonder   salt to taste
  beans, as many as you want   pepper
onion to taste   tiny piece of chili pepper pod
sugar to taste   seasoning bacon or salt pork

Snip the ends off the beans. Cut them in half. Remove the strings. Slice up the onion. Add all the ingredients in a big kettle and season the beans to your taste. Cover the beans with water. Put a top on the kettle and simmer slowly for 3 to 5 hours. For the last 1/2 hour turn up the heat and let the water cook out of the beans. Adjust the seasoning if need be.

Thelma's Treasures, p. 62

Green Beans with Meat

Allow 1 lb. of side-meat, hog jowl or cooking bacon for 2 lbs. of beans. Put the meat in a large kettle with considerable water. Add a red pepper pod. Let the meat simmer until it has given up just about all its fat and flavor. This takes at least 1 1/2 hours. Keep pot covered during this cooking time. Next, add the green beans and 1 t. salt for 2 lbs. of beans. Cook uncovered until beans are tender and the juice has cooked down. Never stir the beans with a spoon. Just shake the pot occasionally to keep them from sticking and to keep the cooking going evenly throughout. To serve, pile high on a platter and top off with slices of the bacon.

Cissy Gregg's Cook Book, vol. 1, p. 10,
The Courier Journal & Louisville Times Co., reprinted with permission

Pennyrile Green Beans

1/2 lb. ham hock	1/2 t. sugar
1 small onion peeled	dash of salt
1/2 red pepper pod	1 lb. green beans
1 1/2 pts. water	

Simmer ham, onion, pepper and water for 1 hour in heavy iron covered pot. Add sugar, salt and green beans. Simmer for 2 hours.

Recipes from Kentucky State Resort Parks, p. 27

Kentucky Wonder Beans

1/2 lb. smoked bacon	1/4 dried red pepper pod
(dry cured)	1 t. sugar
2 lbs. fresh green beans	salt and pepper

Boil bacon until it is half done, about 30 to 40 minutes. Add beans that are snapped in 1" pieces, red pepper and sugar. Barely cover with water. Simmer for at least 3 to 4 hours, adding water just to keep the beans from sticking. About 1 hour before the beans are done taste for salt and pepper. Cook very low or until almost all the broth is gone.

Recipes from Kentucky State Resort Parks, p. 22

Lima Bean Casserole

2 pkgs. frozen lima beans	8 oz. sour cream
butter	2 T. milk or cream
salt and pepper to taste	Parmesan cheese
1 medium-size can pimiento, chopped	

Cook lima beans in small amount of water. Drain and season with butter, salt and pepper. Add remaining ingredients and pour into buttered casserole. Sprinkle generously with Parmesan cheese. Bake at 325 degrees F. for 30 to 40 minutes. Serves 6 to 8.

Cooking with Curtis Grace, p. 127

Creamed Lima Beans

1 large bag frozen
  Fordhook lima beans
1 1/2 T. butter or margarine
1 T. cornstarch

1/4 t. salt
1/8 t. pepper
1 c. milk

Cook limas according to pkg. directions. Drain and set aside. Melt butter in saucepan. Blend in cornstarch, salt and pepper. Gradually add milk. Heat to boiling over direct heat and then boil gently for 2 minutes, stirring constantly. Makes 1 c. Combine with cooked limas.

Florence Ross, my Mother

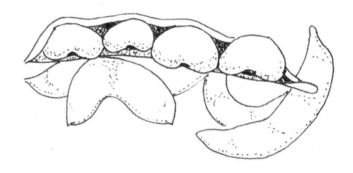

Favorite Lima Beans

1 10 oz. pkg. frozen lima beans
1 4 oz. can mushrooms
dash of paprika

1/4 t. salt
1 c. medium white sauce
1/2 c. cheddar cheese, grated

Preheat oven to 350 degrees F. Cook lima beans according to pkg. directions. Combine remaining ingredients, putting cheese on top. Bake 15 minutes or until cheese melts.

Miss Daisy Entertains, p. 121

Broccoli Casserole

2 boxes frozen chopped broccoli	4 t. onion, grated
1 c. cheddar cheese, grated	1 c. mayonnaise
1 can cream of celery soup	2 eggs, slightly beaten

Cook the broccoli as directed on the pkg. Drain and mix with the ingredients above. Pour into buttered casserole and top with buttered crumbs. Bake at 350 degrees F. for 45 minutes.

Favorite Recipes, Eva Price, p. 30

Broccoli Casserole

2 pkgs. frozen broccoli	1 jar Old English cheese spread
1/2 onion, chopped	1 can mushrooms
1/4 green pepper, chopped	1 c. cooked rice
1 can mushroom	soupcracker crumbs for top

Cook broccoli just until tender. Saute onion and green pepper in margarine until tender. Add mushroom soup, cheese spread and mushrooms (do not drain liquid from mushrooms). Stir until well blended. Add rice and cooked broccoli. Put in a 2 qt. casserole. Sprinkle cracker crumbs on top. Bake at 350 degrees F. for 30 minutes until slightly brown and bubbly.

Sharing Our Best, Dorthea Howard, p. 41

Broccoli and Mushroom Casserole

1 to 1 1/2 lbs. fresh broccoli	1 c. cheddar cheese, grated
1/2 lb. fresh mushrooms, sliced	2 c. medium white sauce
2 T. green pepper, chopped	paprika
butter	

Preheat oven to 350 degrees F. Cook broccoli 3 to 5 minutes or until tender. Drain and spread in greased baking dish. Saute mushrooms and green pepper in butter. Add with 3/4 c. cheese and paprika. Bake for 15 to 20 minutes. Makes 4 to 6 servings.

Miss Daisy Entertains, p. 123

Light and Cheesy Broccoli Casserole

1 10 oz. pkg. frozen chopped
   broccoli, thawed and drained
1 c. light sour cream
1 c. low-fat creamed cottage
   cheese
1/2 c. baking mix

1/4 c. margarine, melted
1 carton egg product
1 tomato, peeled and thinly sliced
1/4 c. Parmesan cheese, grated

Heat oven to 350 degrees F. Lightly spray a 8"x8"x2" baking dish with cooking spray. Spread broccoli in dish. Beat sour cream, cottage cheese, baking mix, margarine and egg product with hand beater for 1 minute. Pour over broccoli. Arrange tomato slices on top. Sprinkle with Parmesan cheese. Bake until golden brown and knife inserted half way between center and edge comes out clean, about 30 minutes. Cool 5 minutes. Serves 6 to 8.

Southeastern REMC Electric Consumer, February, 1989

"Mrs. Wiggs" Boiled Cabbage

1 good size head of cabbage
1 chunk of seasoning meat
   or ham hock

1 red pepper pod
salt and pepper

Put the cabbage, meat, red pepper, salt and pepper in a kettle and cover with water. Cook down real slow. Serve with cornbread.

Cabbage Patch Famous Kentucky Recipes, "Mrs. Wiggs," p. 84

Boiled Green Cabbage

Remove wilted outer leaves. Cut into 6 to 8 wedges. Cook, covered, in a small amount of boiling salted water for 10 to 12 minutes.

Elizabeth Ross

Cabbage Casserole

2 c. corn flakes, crushed
1/2 c. butter, melted
4 c. cooked cabbage, shredded
1 c. milk

1 c. cheese, grated
1/2 c. mayonnaise
1 can cream of celery soup

Mix corn flakes and butter. Put 1/2 of mixture in buttered dish. Layer cabbage on top of crumbs. Combine milk, cheese, mayonnaise and celery soup. Pour over cabbage. Top with remaining corn flakes mixture. Bake at 350 degrees for 30 minutes.

Mrs. William H. Riddell

Scalloped Cabbage

1 medium head of cabbage,
    shredded
1 c. cheese, grated
4 T. butter

4 T. flour
2 c. milk
salt, pepper and paprika
1/3 c. bread crumbs

Cook cabbage until just short of being done. Place layer of cabbage in a baking dish, sprinkled with a layer of grated cheese, then pour on a layer of sauce made of the next 3 ingredients. Add a second layer of each, seasoned with salt, pepper and paprika. Add bread crumbs as the top layer and dot with butter. Bake at 350 degrees F. until crumbs are browned.

Sauce: Melt butter in a heavy saucepan. Stir in the flour and blend well over low heat. Slowly add milk, stirring constantly. Cook 2 minutes.

Favorite Recipes, Mrs. Charles Kennedy, p. 38

Scalloped Cabbage

1 small head cabbage,
    cut into 1/2" to 3/4" wedges
1 c. cream sauce

6 slices bacon, cooked and
    crumbled
buttered bread crumbs

Cook cabbage quickly until barely tender. Drain well. Place in 1 1/2 to 2 qt. buttered casserole dish. Pour cream sauce over casserole and top with bacon, then buttered bread crumbs.

Bake at 350 degrees F. for 20 minutes or until lightly browned. This recipe can be used with left-over cooked cabbage.

Welcome Back to Pleasant Hill, p. 34

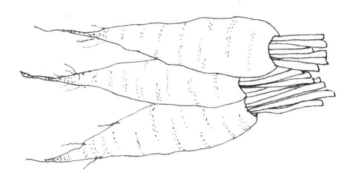

Carrots in Consomme

1 bunch carrots, peeled	1 can consomme
1/4 stick butter	

Slice carrots lengthwise in quarters or halves. Cook, with butter and consomme, covered, 12 to 15 minutes or until tender. Turn while cooking. Cook until only 1 to 2 spoonfuls of pan juices remain. Serves 4 to 6.

Elizabeth Ross

Cauliflower Au Gratin

1 head cauliflower	1 1/2 c. milk
3 T. butter	1 c. cheese, grated
3 T. flour	1 c. bread crumbs
1/2 t. salt	1/3 c. butter, melted
paprika	

Boil cauliflower in salted water until tender. In a saucepan, melt butter. Add flour, salt and a dash of paprika. Pour in milk and stir until sauce boils. Stir in grated cheese. Put layer of cauliflower in bottom of baking dish and pour sauce over it. Add another layer of cauliflower, then sauce until all is used. Sprinkle bread crumbs into melted butter and sprinkle over the top. Bake at 350 degrees F. for 30 minutes. Serves 6.

The Crowning Recipes of Kentucky, p. 124; *Miss Daisy Entertains*, p. 124

Corn on the Cob

Use freshly picked corn. It loses its sweetness and becomes starchy if it is too old. The ears should be well-filled and the kernels soft and milky. Remove husks, silks, stem ends and unfilled tips. Place in boiling salted water to cover. Cook 6 to 10 minutes or until tender. Do not overcook. A little sugar added to the cooking water will improve the flavor. Serve at once with plenty of butter, salt and pepper.

Elizabeth Ross

Roast Corn on the Cob

6 ears corn,	1 t. salt
as fresh as possible	1/8 t. pepper
1/2 c. butter, softened	heavy-duty aluminum foil

Pull husks away from cob, but do not pull off completely. Remove corn silk. Soak ears in deep pail of water for 1/2 hour. Spread corn with mixture of butter, salt and pepper. Fold husks over cob. Wrap corn in foil and seal carefully. The coals on the fire must burn down so that they look gray all over before the cooking can begin. Place corn directly on the coals. Roast 30 minutes until corn is tender, turning often. Partially unwrap and serve corn in foil. If a large crowd is to be served, line a wheelbarrow with heavy-duty foil and lay a fairly shallow charcoal fire in it. Cook as above.

Note: The soaking step may be eliminated, just clean corn completely and proceed with wrapping with foil, only double wrap.

Elizabeth Ross

Roasting Ears of Corn

12 ears sweet corn	butter, salt, pepper

Carefully pull down husks from 12 ears of freshly picked corn. Remove the silk and replace the husk. Tie, if necessary, to hold together. Place in a preheated, slow (300 degree F.) oven for 30 minutes. Serve as they are, or remove husks to serve. Be sure plenty of butter, salt and pepper is available. This rule may be varied by removing all the husks when boiling, then placing a handful of sweet inner husks in the bottom of the kettle. This greatly enhances the flavor of the corn and is far simpler than removing the husks from the very hot ear.

The Shaker Cookbook, p. 76

Fresh Corn Souffle

2 T. sweet butter	3 egg yolks
2 T. all-purpose flour	2 c. fresh corn, grated from cob
1 c. milk	3 egg whites
1/2 t. salt	1 T. sugar
1/8 t. black pepper	

Make a white sauce by melting butter and stirring in flour with a wooden spoon, over low heat. Blend well. Stir in the milk until smooth. Stir in salt and pepper. Beat the egg yolks slightly and add to the white sauce. Mix thoroughly. Stir in corn and let cool slightly. Beat egg whites until soft peaks are formed. Add sugar and continue beating until stiff peaks are formed. Fold white sauce mixture into beaten egg whites. Pour mixture into a buttered 3 qt. straight-sided casserole or souffle dish and bake in a preheated moderate, 325 degree F. oven for 45 minutes. Serve at once. Serves 6.

The Shaker Cookbook, p. 41

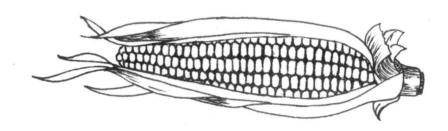

Fresh Sweet Corn

When buying fresh corn look for green husks and plump juicy kernels that will "spurt" milk when broken with the thumbnail. Refrigerate and use unhusked corn within 1 to 2 days of picking. It should not be husked until time to cook it. Adding salt or milk or overcooking toughens the kernels and takes away their sweetness. A little sugar may be added to the boiling water. White Silver Queen corn is my favorite for its sweetness and tenderness. It does not turn yellow when boiled.

The Gold Cookbook, p. 644; Elizabeth Ross

Fresh Sweet Corn in Cream

1 doz. ears of fresh corn   1/2 c. cream
1/4 c. butter   salt and pepper

Cut kernels from corn raw or after boiling. Scrape cobs with back of knife to get the milk out of cob. Add other ingredients. Heat to simmer. Cook no more than 5 minutes if using cooked corn, 10 minutes if uncooked. This dish is better if you use fresh corn, but is a good way to use left-over corn. If desired, add a pinch of salt. Also, you might want to saute a bit of onion and green pepper in the butter and add to mixture.

Source unknown

Fried Corn

6 tender ears of corn   3 T. bacon fat
1/2 c. hot water   3 T. butter
salt and pepper to taste   1/4 c. whole milk

Cut off corn and scrape cob with the back of a knife to get all the pulp and milk. Stir in hot water, salt and lots of pepper. In a heavy skillet, heat the bacon fat until hot. Pour in corn mixture. Cook 10 to 15 minutes or until water begins to evaporate. Add a lump of butter and milk. Set over low heat to form crust on bottom, stirring occasionally to keep from burning. Serves 4.

Kentucky Derby Museum Cookbook, p. 157

Fried Corn

8 ears corn (young   2 T. bacon drippings or
    field corn preferred)   lard or butter
4 T. butter   1 green pepper,
salt and pepper to taste   diced, optional

Cut corn kernels from cobs. Melt butter in skillet. Add corn and seasonings and cook until the corn is tender - about 10 minutes. Stir occasionally. Do not have the flame too high as the corn may burn. If mixture begins to brown before corn is done, add 1/2 c. of milk or cream. Keep the lid on while cooking and stir occasionally to keep from sticking. We often add a diced green pepper when the corn is put in the skillet. Makes 6 servings.

Out of Kentucky Kitchens, p. 156

Corn Fritters

3/4 c. flour, sifted	1 egg, beaten
2 t. baking powder	1/2 c. milk
1 t. sugar	2 c. corn
1/2 t. salt	confectioners' sugar

Sift together dry ingredients except confectioners' sugar. Combine beaten egg, milk and corn. Add to dry ingredients. Mix just until flour is moistened. Drop by level tablespoonfuls into deep fat (375 degrees F.). Fry until golden brown, 3 to 4 minutes. Drain well on paper towels. Dust with confectioners' sugar. Serve warm.

Note: These fritters were served at the Executive Mansion and is the recipe of the former Governor of Kentucky, Martha Layne Collins. Makes 1 1/2 doz.

The Crowning Recipes of Kentucky, p. 275

Corn Fritters

4 eggs	6 c. milk
3 1/2 T. baking powder	3 c. canned whole kernel corn
1 t. salt	powdered sugar
8 c. flour	

In a large bowl beat eggs until well combined. In a separate bowl combine dry ingredients except powdered sugar. Add to eggs along with milk. Mix well with a spoon until you have a smooth batter. Fold in the corn. In a skillet, melt shortening to a depth of 1" and heat to 325 degrees F. Using a soup ladle drop batter into hot fat and fry until golden brown on both sides. To test for doneness pierce fritter with a toothpick, if raw dough does not rise out of fritter it is done. Roll in powdered sugar and serve warm. Batter will keep in refrigerator one week. Makes 2 doz.

Donna Gill Recommends, p. 40

Corn Fritters Old Stone Inn

6 eggs
12 oz. milk
1 1/2 lbs. flour
1/2 oz. salt
1 1/2 oz. baking powder

1/2 oz. sugar
1 oz. cooking oil
2 1/2 lbs. canned whole kernel
  corn, drained
deep fat for frying
powdered sugar

In large bowl beat eggs. Add milk and blend well. Sift flour, salt, baking powder and sugar together. Add to milk mixture and beat smooth. Beat in cooking oil and then corn. Stir until well blended. Drop tablespoonfuls of the batter into deep fat and brown for 2 to 3 minutes. Roll in powdered sugar and serve while hot. Makes 25.

Dining in Historic Kentucky, vol. 1, p. 92

Kentucky Dam's Corn Fritters

2 1/2 c. fresh corn,
  grated finely
2 t. flour

1/4 t. salt
1 egg yolk, well-beaten
1 egg white

Mix corn, flour, salt and egg yolk. Beat egg white until stiff, but not dry. Fold gently into corn mixture. Drop on a hot buttered skillet by spoonfuls and cook on both sides until light golden brown. Serves 4.

Recipes from Kentucky State Resort Parks, p. 5

Old Talbott Tavern Corn Fritters

2 c. self-rising flour
1/2 t. sugar
1 egg
1/4 c. canned whole kernel
  corn, drained

milk
deep oil for frying
powdered sugar

In bowl mix all ingredients, using just enough milk to moisten. Batter should be stiff. Drop by tablespoonfuls into deep oil at 325 degrees F. Fry to a golden brown. Roll in powdered sugar and serve warm.

Dining in Historic Kentucky, vol. 2, p. 119

Corn Pudding

2 c. corn	2 eggs, well-beaten
4 T. flour	1 T. butter or margarine, melted
2 t. sugar, level	2 c. milk
1 t. salt, level	

Mix corn, flour, sugar and salt together. Combine well-beaten eggs, melted butter and milk. Mix with corn mixture. Pour into a greased baking dish. Bake at 350 degrees F. for 1 hour. Stir from the bottom 2 or 3 times during the first 30 minutes of baking time. Recipe may be doubled. Serves 4.

Cissy Gregg's Cook Book, vol. 1, p. 41,
The Courier Journal & Louisville Times Co., reprinted with permission

Corn Pudding

2 c. milk	1/2 bell pepper, diced
1/4 c. bacon drippings	1/2 c. sugar
4 slices bread	salt and pepper to taste
4 eggs, beaten until fluffy	1 c. cheddar cheese, grated
2 10 oz. pkgs. frozen whole kernel corn or creamed, if you prefer	

Combine milk and bacon drippings. Pour over bread slices and soak. Break slices into pieces, then mix in eggs. Add mixture to corn seasoned with bell pepper, sugar, salt and pepper. Bake at 325 degrees F. for 30 minutes or until slightly browned. Top with grated cheese just as you take it from the oven. Serves 8 to 10.

Cooking with Curtis Grace, p. 133

Corn Pudding

4 ears of young field corn	3 T. butter, melted
2 eggs	1/4 t. salt or more to taste
1 c. whole milk	1/8 t. black pepper or more to taste
2 t. sugar	

After the tender young ears have been shucked and the silks removed, they are washed and dried and the very tip ends of the grains cut off with a sharp knife. Then the ear of corn is held upright over a bowl and the tender inside kernels scraped out with the back edge of a dull knife. None of the husks are supposed to be scraped off the cob. Beat eggs and milk. Add corn, sugar, melted butter, salt and pepper. Pour into a greased baking dish and bake in a moderate 375 degree F. oven until pudding is just set. When it does not shake when moved, it is ready. Do not cook too long. It takes 35 to 45 minutes. Makes 4 to 5 servings.

Out of Kentucky Kitchens, p. 154

Mother's Corn Pudding

2 1/2 c. whole kernel corn, canned, fresh or frozen, drained (preferably canned white Shoepeg)
2 large eggs or 3 small ones
1 t. salt
1/8 t. pepper
2 T. margarine or butter, melted
3/4 c. cream, half & half or Pet milk
2 T. sugar (preferably 1/4 c.)
1 to 2 shakes nutmeg

If fresh corn is used, stew for 20 minutes. Beat eggs. Mix all ingredients together. Bake in greased baking dish at 350 degrees F. for 35 to 45 minutes. When pudding has cooked about 15 minutes, stir it gently to prevent corn from settling to bottom. Cook until nicely browned on top and center is set. Serve.

Note: No flour is used in this recipe, it will be lighter in texture.

Florence Ross, my Mother

Corn Souffle

2 c. fresh corn or
1 10 oz. pkg. frozen corn, thawed
2 T. flour
2 T. sugar
1/2 t. salt
1/8 t pepper
1 c. milk
2 eggs, separated
butter

Mix together corn, flour, sugar, salt, pepper and milk. Add egg yolks to mixture. Beat egg whites until stiff and fold into corn mixture. Pour into a 1 qt. casserole and dot with butter. Bake at 350 degrees F. for 45 to 50 minutes. Makes 6 servings.

Best of the Best from Kentucky, To Market, To Market, (p. 107), p. 137

Eggplant Casserole

6 c. eggplant, peeled and diced	chicken base, optional
1 c. cracker crumbs	salt
1/2 c. cheese, grated	pepper
2 c. milk	butter

Put eggplant in salted water and bring to boil. Change water twice. Drain and put eggplant in baking dish. Put in a layer of cracker crumbs then a layer of cheese. Build it up to the top of the dish. Pour milk to the top of the dish. Chicken cubes or stock may be added to the milk. Season with salt and pepper. Dot with butter. Bake at 350 degrees F. for 20 minutes.

Nancy Lee Ross

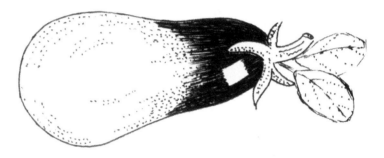

Kentucky Eggplant Casserole

2 medium eggplants	1/4 to 1/2 c. olive oil
1/2 c. flour	2 8 oz. cans tomato sauce
1/2 t. salt	1/2 c. Parmesan cheese, grated
1/8 t. pepper	1 8 oz. pkg. Mozzarella cheese, thinly sliced

Peel eggplant and cut into 1/2" slices. Sprinkle with salt. Spread out on board or paper towels. Let stand 20 minutes. Pat dry with paper towel. Dip each slice into the mixture of flour, salt and pepper. Heat olive oil and brown eggplant quickly. Cooking quickly over medium-high heat will keep eggplant from absorbing too much of the oil. Drain on paper towel. Pour 1/4 of tomato sauce in greased 2 qt. casserole. Top with 1/3 of the eggplant slices, 1/3 of the remaining tomato sauce and 1/3 of the cheese. Continue layers. Cover and bake in hot oven at 400 degrees F. for 20 minutes. Remove the cover and continue baking 20 minutes.

A Taste from Back Home, p. 96

French Fried Eggplant

eggplant	cracker meal
flour	seasoned salt
buttermilk	

Peel eggplant. Cut into thumb-size pieces. Dip into flour, then into buttermilk and finally into cracker meal. Deep fry in oil for 3 to 4 minutes at 350 degrees F. Drain on wire rack. Sprinkle with seasoned salt. Serve immediately with horseradish cocktail sauce.

F & N Steakhouse, Dayton, Kentucky

Collard Greens

Select young and tender collard greens. Wash and cut fine. Cover with salted water. Cook 1 hour. Serve at table with broth in which greens have been cooked. This is the "pot liquor." If desired, a strip of bacon may be added after 30 minutes of cooking. Serve with cornbread to dunk in the pot liquor.

Fort Lauderdale Recipes, Recipe Selection Committee, p. 217

Cooked Greens

1 lb. hog jowl or ham hock	3 lbs. collard greens,
2 c. water	washed and drained
1 t. salt	

Simmer meat in water for 45 minutes. Add salt and collard greens. Cover and cook for 25 to 30 minutes or until tender.

Historic Kentucky Recipes, p. 152

Dandelion Greens

Remove the brown leaves and roots of the dandelions and wash in at least 3 waters. Let soak overnight in cold water. Cook in a small amount of boiling salted water to which a pinch of baking soda is added when the boiling point is reached. Simmer greens 1 hour, then drain well and serve with lemon juice, vinegar or the fat from fried salt pork. Dandelions were considered to be a natural spring tonic and were dug up in the spring before the buds had opened.

Out of Old Nova Scotia Kitchens, p. 83

Kale Greens

2 lbs. kale	1 qt. water
1 ham hock or	butter
1 c. ham scraps	salt and pepper
(city or country)	

Wash kale carefully. Remove coarse stalks. Boil fat in water for 30 minutes. Strain water and return to stove. Save larger ham pieces to add to kale for flavor. Bring flavored water to a boil and add kale and ham scraps. Cook until desired tenderness. Do not over cook as leaves should be a bit crisp. Add butter, salt and pepper to taste.

Welcome Back to Pleasant Hill, p. 35

Turnip Greens

turnip greens,	salt pork with a streak of lean in it
tender and crisp	

First, pick over greens and wash them well. The little leaves go in the pot whole, the large ones strip from the stem. Into a pot, put 1 qt. of cold water for each 2 lbs. turnip greens. For this same amount use 1/4 to 1/2 lb. of salt pork. Cut the salt pork into slices 1/4" thick and drop them into the pot of cold water. Bring to a boil and simmer the meat by itself for 30 minutes, then add the greens. Cover the pot and heat to boiling again and let the turnip tops wither down. Turn the mess over in the pot at least once to complete the withering. When this has been done, press the leaves down under the surface of the water and continue cooking uncovered for another 30 to 45 minutes or until greens are tender. The actual time depends on the age and tenderness of the tops. If more water is needed to keep the leaves covered, add boiling water. The salt pork does the seasoning.

Cissy Gregg's Cook Book, vol. 1, p. 11,
The Courier Journal & Louisville Times Co., reprinted with permission

Sauteed Mushrooms and Onions

4 T. butter or margarine	1 lb. mushrooms, sliced
1 large sweet onion, sliced	salt and pepper

Melt butter in heavy skillet. Add onions and saute until translucent. Add mushrooms and saute until lightly browned. Salt and pepper to taste and serve at once. Good served with broiled or grilled steak.

Elizabeth Ross

Fried Okra

Cut okra into pieces 1/4" long and drop into milk until thoroughly covered. Lift out of milk and drop into a paper sack containing cornmeal seasoned with salt and pepper. Have oil or shortening heated in skillet. Add okra pieces and fry until golden brown.

A Taste from Back Home, p. 99

Creamed Onions

2 to 3 c. small whole onions	1/2 c. crumbs, buttered
1 1/2 c. medium white sauce	paprika

Peel onions. Place in a large amount of boiling salted water. Pierce each onion with sharp knife or ice pick in center. This keeps them from falling apart. Boil uncovered for 20 minutes or until tender. Overcooking develops strong flavor and odor. In a greased casserole arrange onions and medium white sauce in layers. Top with buttered crumbs. Sprinkle with paprika. Bake in moderate 375 degree F. oven for 25 minutes or until browned.

White Sauce:

4 T. butter	1/2 t. pepper
4 T. flour	2 c. milk
1 t. salt	

Melt butter over low heat. Add flour, salt and pepper. Stir until well blended. Remove from heat. Gradually stir in milk. Return to heat. Cook, stirring constantly, until thick and smooth. Makes 2 c.

Best of the Best from Kentucky, Stephensburg Homecoming Recipes, Jean Stewart, p. 182

Creamed Onions

Cook small onions 15 minutes. Drain. Add 1 c. thin cream and cook in a double boiler until tender. Add salt to taste when the onions are nearly done. Sprinkle with chopped, roasted peanuts or almonds.

Recipes from Kentucky State Resort Parks, p. 24

Onion Rings (Bill Boland's recipe)

Peel the onions. Use large dry onions, either silver skinned or yellow. Cut them into slices between 1/4" to 1/8" in thickness. Separate the slices into rings using only the large ones for frying. Save the smaller ones for seasoning. Keep the rings to be fried dry.

Batter:

1 egg	2 t. sugar
1 1/3 c. milk	2 t. baking powder
2 c. flour	2 t. butter, melted
2 t. salt	

Beat the egg and add the milk. Sift flour and measure. Add salt, sugar and baking powder. Sift dry ingredients together into a bowl. Gradually add the liquids and beat until smooth. Add the melted butter. Heat the fat for frying to about 360 degrees F. Don't try to fry too many rings at one time. Drop them one by one into the batter using a fork or your fingers to get the rings well covered. Gently drop them into the hot fat, turn once and lift out. Drain on absorbent paper.

Cissy Gregg's Cook Book, vol. 1, p. 10,
The Courier Journal & Louisville Times Co., reprinted with permission

Fried Onion Rings

1 c. flour
1 t. baking powder
1 1/2 t. salt
1 egg, beaten

1 c. milk
4 onions, sliced and separated
   into rings

Combine flour, baking powder, salt, egg and milk. Beat until smooth. Cover and let stand 15 minutes. Dip onion rings into batter. Fry in deep fat until light brown. Drain on paper towels.

Historic Kentucky Recipes, p. 19

French Fried Onion Rings

4 large sweet onions
milk
seasoned flour (flour with
   salt, pepper and paprika)

deep fat or use the skillet frying
   if not doing too many

Wash and peel onions and cut into 1/4" slices. Let stand in milk to cover 1 hour. Drain. Roll in flour, and that flour will be helped by a little M.S.G. added. Have the rings well coated. Heat fat to 375 degrees F. Put a few slices at a time into the hot fat. Turn once so they are well browned on both sides. Remove when golden brown and drain. Serve right away.

Cissy Gregg's Cook Book, vol. 2, p. 21,
The Courier Journal & Louisville Times Co., reprinted with permission

French Fried Onions

Peel 4 large mild sweet onions. Cut in 1/4" slices and separate into rings. Dip in milk, drain and dip in 1/2 c. flour mixed with 1/2 t. salt. Fry 4 to 6 minutes in deep fat heated to 370 degrees F. Drain on paper towels and sprinkle with salt.

Recipes from Kentucky State Resort Parks, p. 24

Peas Au Gratin

3 c. fresh peas,
  cooked and drained
2 5 oz. cans water chestnuts,
  drained and sliced

1 can cream of mushroom soup
1 1/2 c. sharp cheddar cheese,
  grated

Combine peas and water chestnuts. Mix in soup. Add cheese. Place in lightly greased casserole. Bake at 350 degrees F. for 30 minutes. Makes 6 to 8 servings.

Miss Daisy Entertains, p. 125

Peas and White Sauce

2 T. butter
1 1/2 T. all-purpose flour
1/2 t. salt

1 c. milk
1 10 oz. pkg. frozen peas, cooked
  and drained or 1 c. canned peas,
  drained

Melt butter in a saucepan. Blend in flour and salt. Add milk. Stir and cook until thick and bubbly. Add peas to hot mixture. Heat through. Makes 2 c.

Miriam B. Loo's Family Favorites Cookbook, p. 10

Quick and Easy Peas

1/4 c. onion, finely chopped
1/4 c. butter
2 c. fresh peas,
  cooked and drained

1 can cream of mushroom soup
cheddar cheese, grated

Saute onion in butter. Add remaining ingredients. Heat and serve. You may put this in a buttered casserole, top with grated cheddar cheese and bake at 350 degrees F. for 20 minutes.

Recipes from Miss Daisy's, p. 101

Peas and New Potatoes

2 lbs. new potatoes	1 c. milk
1 pkg. frozen peas,	salt and pepper to taste
fresh if available	2 green onions, chopped
1 T. margarine	parsley or paprika
1 T. flour	

Rub skin off new potatoes. Cook in salted water 20 minutes. Add peas and cook 20 minutes longer. Make white sauce of next 4 ingredients and chopped onions. Drain potatoes and peas. Mix with white sauce. Sprinkle with parsley or paprika.

Food for My Household, p. 26

Fresh Peas

Fresh peas should be available by May. When buying, 1 lb. in the shell should yield 1 c. shelled peas. Fresh peas were Thomas Jefferson's favorite vegetable and his garden book records that he grew more than 30 varieties and every spring he took great pride in being the first in his neighborhood to have them on his table. To convert a recipe: 3 c. fresh = 2 pkg. frozen peas.

Source unknown

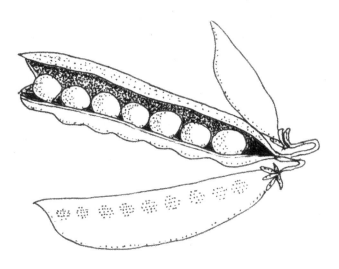

June Peas and New Potatoes

3 lbs. fresh June peas
  (3 c. shelled)
3 slices country smoked
  bacon, sliced thick
1 T. sugar

1/2 lb. small new potatoes,
  freshly cooked
salt to taste
3 T. pure butter
parsley and fresh pepper

Drop fresh peas in boiling water with bacon and sugar. Cook until peas are tender. Drain at once. Discard bacon. Add potatoes to peas. Add some salt and butter. Taste. Toss together lightly for a few minutes. Sprinkle with fresh chopped parsley and pepper. No fresh peas - use frozen.

Recipes from Kentucky State Resort Parks, Mrs. Ida Hamby, P. 22

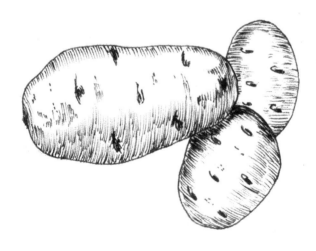

Creamed Potatoes and Peas

1 T. butter	2 1/2 c. new potatoes,
1 T. flour	cooked and cubed
1/2 t. salt	1 1/2 c. fresh peas,
1 c. milk	cooked and drained

Melt butter in medium saucepan. Blend in flour and salt. Add milk. Stir and cook until thick and bubbly. Add cooked potatoes and cooked peas to hot mixture. Garnish with a little chopped pimiento, if desired. Pour some melted butter over the top just before serving for a richer flavor. Serves 4 to 6.

Joyce Le Compte

Mashed Potato Cakes

These are made with leftover mashed potatoes. You may also beat an egg into the potatoes. Also, add 1/4 c. chopped onion if you like. Shape potatoes into flat cakes 3" to 4" wide and 1 to 1 1/2" thick. Wrap in waxed paper and chill - they must be cold. Dip each cake in flour seasoned with salt and pepper. Fry over moderate heat in butter or bacon drippings until the cakes are nicely browned on both sides. For 4 cakes you will need about 2 c. mashed potatoes and 6 T. butter. Serve hot.

Elizabeth Ross

Little New Potatoes in Jackets

Wash potatoes. Boil in salted water, cooking until a fork pierces them easily. Drain well. Add butter and chopped parsley on top of potatoes. Return to heat long enough to melt butter. Serve hot.

We Make You Kindly Welcome, p. 32

Small New Potatoes in Jackets

Select small redskinned new potatoes of even size, 1 to 1 1/2" in diameter. There is no need to pierce or cut a band of peel around middle when cooking with water. Put in a microwave cooking dish and add water to about half their depth. Cover and cook on high until a potato can barely be pierced with a sharp fork, 7 to 8 minutes for 1 lb. Drain. Let stand, covered, 5 minutes. Season with butter, salt and pepper, finely minced fresh parsley or snipped fresh dill.

Recipes Remembered, p. 169

Sweet Potato Casserole

3 c. cooked sweet potatoes, fresh or canned	1/2 t. salt
1/2 c. brown sugar	1/2 stick margarine, melted
2 eggs, beaten	1/2 c. evaporated milk
	1 1/2 t. vanilla

Topping:

1/2 c. brown sugar	1 c. pecans, chopped
1/3 c. plain flour	1/3 stick margarine, melted

Mash sweet potatoes. Add sugar, eggs, salt, margarine, milk and vanilla. Put mixture into casserole dish. Mix topping ingredients and spread over sweet potato mixture. Bake at 325 degrees F. for 30 minutes. Serves 6.

Sample West Kentucky, p. 94

deSha's Sweet Potato Casserole

3/4 c. butter, softened	dash allspice
1 c. sugar	2/3 c. heavy cream
4 eggs	1/2 t. salt
2 1/4 t. vanilla	6 c. sweet potatoes, cooked, peeled
dash cinnamon	and mashed (5 large potatoes)

Cream butter and sugar. Add remaining ingredients in order, blending well. Pour into greased 9"x13" pan and cover with topping. Bake at 350 degrees F. for 20 minutes. Serves 12.

Topping:

1 stick plus 2 T. butter	1/2 c. plus 2 T. flour
1 c. brown sugar	1 c. pecans, chopped

For topping: melt butter. Stir in brown sugar, flour and pecans. Mix well.

Dining in Historic Kentucky, vol. 2, p. 46

Iron Kettle Sweet Potato Casserole

1/2 c. butter, melted
1 c. brown sugar
1/2 c. flour
1/2 c. pecans
3 c. sweet potatoes,
   cooked and mashed

1 c. sugar
2 eggs, beaten
1/2 c. butter, melted
1/2 c. milk
1 T. vanilla

Mix first 5 ingredients together; set aside. Mix remaining ingredients together. Combine both groups of ingredients, pour into greased pan. Bake at 350 degrees F. for 30 minutes. Serves 4 to 6.

Dining in Historic Kentucky, vol. 2, p. 190

Academy Inn Sweet Potato Souffle

3 c. sweet potatoes, cooked
4 T. margarine, melted
2 eggs
1/3 c. flour

1/2 c. milk
1/2 t. salt
1/2 t. nutmeg
1 t. vanilla

Topping:

1/2 c. brown sugar
4 T. margarine

1/2 c. walnuts, chopped
1/3 c. flour

In large bowl of mixer, whip all souffle ingredients together. Pour into baking dish sprayed with vegetable oil spray. Bake at 325 degrees F. for 35 to 40 minutes. Remove from oven, sprinkle with topping and bake another 5 minutes.

For topping: Mix brown sugar, margarine, walnuts and flour until crumbly.

Dining in Historic Kentucky, vol. 2, p. 71

Kentucky Bourbon Sweet Potatoes

2 no. 2 1/2 cans sweet potatoes	1/2 t. vanilla
1 c. sugar	bourbon to taste (3 oz.)
1 stick butter or margarine	marshmallow topping

Heat potatoes until hot, drain water and mash well. Add sugar, butter, vanilla and bourbon. Beat well and pour into baking pan, top with marshmallows. Cook for about 30 minutes in 350 degree F. oven. Serves 8.

Recipes from Kentucky State Resort Parks, Mrs. Erma Bullock, p. 22

Bourbon Yams (Heaven Hill Distilleries)

4 medium yams, unpeeled	1/3 c. brown sugar
1 stick butter	1/4 c. bourbon

In a large pot boil yams gently in water to cover until tender. Cool. Peel and slice lengthwise. Layer in greased 2 qt. casserole. Melt butter in a saucepan. Add brown sugar and bourbon. Heat until sugar dissolves and pour over yams. Bake at 350 degrees F. for 20 minutes or until bubbly. May be made a day ahead. Serves 6.

Kentucky Derby Museum Cookbook, p. 168

Praline Yams

40 oz. can cut yams, drained	1/2 c. brown sugar, firmly packed
1/2 c. pecans, chopped	1/4 c. flour
1/2 c. coconut	1/4 c. margarine or butter, melted

Heat oven to 350 degrees F. Place drained yams in 2 qt. ungreased casserole or baking dish. In small bowl, combine remaining ingredients, blending well. Sprinkle over yams. Bake at 350 degrees F. for 35 to 40 minutes or until bubbly. Serves 10.

Princella can

Spinach Casserole

2 pkgs. frozen spinach,
  chopped, cooked and drained
1/2 stick butter or margarine
1 8 oz. carton French onion dip

1/2 pt. sour cream
1/2 t. salt
1/2 t. pepper
1/2 c. prepared stuffing mix,
  crushed

Cook spinach according to directions and drain well. Melt butter and add to spinach along with dip, sour cream, salt and pepper. Pour into a buttered 1 qt. baking dish. Top with crushed stuffing mix. Bake at 350 degrees F. for 20 minutes. Serves 6.

The Crowning Recipes of Kentucky, p. 142

Easy Spinach Casserole

3 10 oz. pkgs. frozen
  chopped spinach,
  thawed and drained

1 pkg. onion soup mix
1/2 c. butter, melted
1/2 t. nutmeg

Mix ingredients. Bake in buttered casserole at 350 degrees F. for 30 minutes.

Recipes from Miss Daisy's, p. 99

Spinach Souffle

2 10 oz. pkgs. chopped
  spinach, thawed and drained
2 cans mushroom soup
3 c. sharp cheddar cheese, grated

2 egg yolks
bread crumbs

Preheat oven to 350 degrees F. Mix all ingredients except bread crumbs and place in a greased casserole. Sprinkle with bread crumbs and cook for 30 minutes. Makes 6 servings.

Miss Daisy Entertains, p. 45

Baked Acorn Squash

1 medium acorn squash
butter, melted

1/4 t. salt
1/4 t. corn syrup or mixture of
  brown and white sugar

Scrub squash. Cut in half lengthwise. Scrape out seeds and stringy portion with spoon. Brush cut surface of each half with a little melted butter. Sprinkle each half with salt, 1/8 t. each half. Arrange, cut side down, in a baking pan. Bake in moderate oven at 400 degrees F. for 30 minutes then turn, cut side up, and brush well with butter mixed with corn syrup. Bake until tender, about 30 minutes. Brush often with syrup butter mixture.

We Make You Kindly Welcome, p. 33

Summer Squash

2 lbs. summer yellow neck
  squash
1 large onion

2 T. butter
sugar, salt and pepper to taste

Slice unpeeled squash, chop onion. Parboil squash and onions, in water to cover, until tender. Drain well. Cook in skillet, iron if you have one. Add butter, sugar, salt and pepper. Stir and cook until dry. Serves 6.

Recipes from Kentucky State Resort Parks, Mona Sisk, p. 22

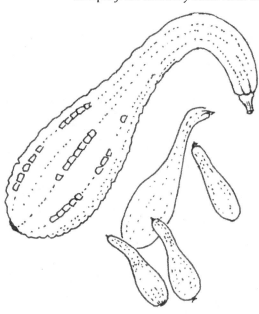

Sauteed Summer Squash

3 T. butter or margarine
1 bunch green onions

6 to 8 small-medium yellow neck
    summer squash
salt and pepper

Heat butter in large skillet with a lid. Clean and slice onions, and saute in butter until translucent. Wash and slice squash into rounds. Add to onions in skillet. Salt and pepper to taste. Cover and cook over low-medium heat until squash is as tender as desired. Add a little water if necessary. Makes 4 servings.

Elizabeth Ross

Succotash

4 T. butter or margarine
1 t. cornstarch
1/4 t. salt
1/8 t. pepper

1 c. milk
2 c. corn, cooked
2 c. lima beans, cooked

Heat butter in saucepan. Add cornstarch, salt and pepper. Gradually add milk and heat to boiling. Boil gently for 2 minutes, stirring constantly until thickened. Meanwhile, heat corn and limas together. Add milk mixture to corn and lima beans. Serve hot.

Elizabeth Ross

Escalloped Tomatoes

1 no. 2 can tomatoes or
    4 large fresh tomatoes
2 c. soft bread crumbs, toasted
2 T. butter

1 medium onion, chopped
3/4 t. salt
1 T. sugar

Combine tomatoes with the toasted bread crumbs and stir in butter, onion, salt and sugar. Turn into casserole. Bake in a moderate oven at 375 degrees F. for 15 to 20 minutes. Makes 5 servings.

Cherished Recipes, Cleo Durham, p. 53

Grilled Tomato Halves

3 medium tomatoes	1/2 t. salt
2 T. butter, melted	1/4 t. seasoned pepper
1/2 t. oregano	

Cut tomatoes in half. Brush top of each half with melted butter. Sprinkle with oregano, salt and seasoned pepper. Wrap the bottom and sides with foil wrap. Leave top exposed. Place on grill. Baste with remaining butter. Cook until tender, about 8 minutes. To broil in oven, place seasoned tomatoes in foil on broiler rack 5" from heat. Broil 4 to 5 minutes.

Source unknown

Scalloped Tomatoes

1 can tomatoes	2 T. sugar
(1 lb. regular size)	salt and pepper to taste
1 onion cut into small pieces	butter
2 slices bread, cubed	

Mix all ingredients in proper-sized buttered baking dish. Dot generously with butter. Bake, uncovered, long and slowly until bread browns a bit - at least 1 1/2 hours at 325 degrees F. Serves 4.

Bentley Farm Cookbook, p. 193

Scalloped Tomatoes

2 c. tomatoes, cooked	salt and pepper
2 T. butter	buttered bread crumbs
1 c. soft bread cubes	

Alternate layers of well-seasoned cooked tomatoes, butter and soft bread cubes in a well-oiled baking dish. Cover with bread crumbs. Bake at 350 degrees F. for 35 minutes. Serves 6.

The Household Searchlight Recipe Book, p. 274

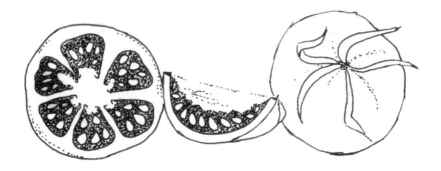

Scalloped Tomatoes

3 T. butter
1 1 lb. 3 oz. can tomatoes
1 c. coarse bread crumbs

1/2 c. sugar
salt and pepper

Melt butter in skillet. Add all remaining ingredients. Heat to a boil. Reduce heat to simmer and cook, stirring occasionally, for 1 hour. Serves 4 to 6.

A Taste from Back Home, p. 105

Southern Scalloped Tomatoes

3 c. home-canned or
   bought canned tomatoes
1/4 c. butter
3 c. medium coarse stale bread,
   crumbled

3 T. sugar
1 t. salt
1/8 t. pepper
ground allspice

Heat tomatoes and butter in saucepan over moderate heat just until butter melts. Mix in crumbs, sugar, salt and pepper. Bake at 400 degrees F. until puffy. Sprinkle allspice over top of casserole.

St. Mark's Catholic Church Cookbook, Mrs. Charles Fowler, p. 89

Stewed Tomatoes

1/2 c. green peppers, diced
1/2 c. onions, diced
10 pieces toast
1 qt. whole tomatoes, crushed

1/4 c. sugar
1/2 lb. Parmesan cheese, grated
salt and pepper

Cook green peppers and onions in plain water and drain well. Cut toast into cubes.
Combine all ingredients. Season to taste with salt and pepper. Simmer for 30 minutes.

Recipes from Kentucky State Resort Parks, Ned Weber, p. 24

Baked Stuffed Tomatoes

6 tomatoes
2 T. green pepper, chopped
1/2 c. celery, finely chopped

1 T. onion, finely chopped
bread crumbs for topping

Remove tops and scoop out tomatoes. Combine remaining ingredients and cook until
thick. Stuff tomatoes, sprinkle with bread crumbs. Bake in muffin tins so tomatoes will
stay erect. Bake at 375 to 400 degrees F. for 25 to 30 minutes.

Florence Ross, my Mother

Fried Green Tomatoes

6 medium tomatoes
  (green but turning pink)
1 c. cornmeal
1/2 t. salt

1/4 t. pepper
1/2 t. oregano
bacon drippings

Cut tomatoes into 1/4" thick slices, discarding the top and bottom slices. Mix cornmeal
with seasonings. Coat the tomatoes well. In hot skillet containing bacon drippings, add
tomato slices in 1 layer. Lower heat to medium and fry for 6 more minutes or until golden
brown on both sides. Drain on paper towels. Repeat with remaining tomato slices.
Serves 8.

The Kentucky Derby Museum Cookbook, p. 165

Fried Green Tomatoes

green tomatoes
salt and pepper to taste
brown sugar

cornmeal
bacon grease

Slice tomatoes. Sprinkle with salt, pepper and a little brown sugar. Roll in cornmeal. Fry slowly in hot bacon grease until golden brown on both sides.

Sharing Our Best, Mary Searly, p. 35

Country Fried Green Tomatoes

Slice large, firm, green unpeeled tomatoes 1/4" thick. Sprinkle with salt, pepper and sugar. Dip in cornmeal or flour and fry in a skillet containing enough bacon drippings or melted butter to be 1/4" deep in the skillet. Have the fat hot when the tomatoes are added, then reduce heat and brown on both sides.

A Taste of Back Home, p. 105

Southern-Fried Green Tomatoes

2 large green tomatoes
1 1/2 c. finely ground
white cornmeal

oil or solid vegetable shortening
for frying
salt and pepper to taste

Slice the tomatoes 1/4" thick. Dredge both sides of the tomatoes in cornmeal, pressing the slices firmly into the meal to make a good coating. Shake off excess meal. Put enough oil or shortening in a skillet to come to a depth of 1/4" and place the skillet over medium heat. Add the tomatoes to the hot oil a few at a time without crowding. Fry until golden brown or about 2 minutes. Turn. When both sides are golden brown, drain on paper towels and sprinkle with salt and pepper. Serve hot. Serves 4.

Sharing Our Best, Lucille Lowe, p. 35

Fruits & Preserves

Baked Apples

6 baking apples, cored
but not peeled
6 T. butter or margarine

3/4 c. brown sugar, packed
1 t. ground cinnamon
1/4 t. ground nutmeg

Preheat oven to 350 degrees F. Place apples in a 12"x8" baking dish. Put 1 T. butter in cavity of each apple. Fill with brown sugar. Mix cinnamon and nutmeg and spoon over each apple. Bake for 30 to 40 minutes or until apples are tender. Makes 6 servings.

Elizabeth Ross

Cinnamon Apples

6 small apples
2 c. sugar

2 c. water
1/4 c. red cinnamon candies

Wash, core and pare apples. Combine sugar, water and cinnamon candies. Boil 5 minutes. Add apples. Cook slowly until apples are tender. Stick cinnamon or cinnamon extract and red food coloring may be substituted for the red cinnamon candies. If desired, apples may be cut in half or quartered. Makes 6 servings.

The Household Searchlight Recipe Book, p. 171

Fried Apples

6 apples
1 T. sugar

1/4 t. salt
1/4 c. water

Wash apples. Remove stems, blossom ends and seeds. Slice apples. Sear in hot fat. Add sugar, salt and water. Cover and cook slowly until apples are tender. Serves 6.

The Household Searchlight Recipe Book, p. 171

Fried Apples

2 qts. small tart apples
1/3 box light brown sugar

1 good pinch cinnamon
1/3 stick butter or margarine

Cut unpeeled apples into 6 wedges from core to stem. Remove seeds. Place apples in a skillet. Sprinkle them with sugar and cinnamon. Dot with butter. Cover skillet with a lid or foil. Place it on a cold stove. Set at low heat and cook until tender, stirring only occasionally. Remove lid and cook 3 to 5 minutes longer.

We Make You Kindly Welcome, p. 4

Hardscuffle Fried Apples

Quarter 5 good, red cooking apples that will hold their shape. (Jonathans or Rome Beauties are good choices.) Do not peel. Place apples in a pot with a tight-fitting lid. Add 3 T. lemon juice, 2 T. butter and 1 3/4 c. sugar. Cook, covered, over medium heat, stirring occasionally, for 15 to 20 minutes, just until all the juices are absorbed and a nice, brown glaze has formed on the apples. Serve with country ham, sausage or any pork dish. Serves 6.

Dinwiddie Lampton, Jr., Hardscuffle Farm

Kentucky Fried Apples

2 medium tart cooking
  apples, you need 2 c.
1/2 to 3/4 c. sugar

1/4 c. margarine

With paring knife, peel a 1 1/2" strip around the center of the apple. This band will then remove about 1/3 of the apple peel. Cut the apples into quarters. Next, slice each quarter into 3 or 4 sections as you would section an orange. Place the apples, sugar and margarine in a very heavy or cooking pan. Cover and place on medium heat. When mixture begins to cook, allow 10 minutes of cooking time. Remove cover and cook 5 to 10 minutes longer until apples are tender and rather transparent. You may need to reduce the heat to low during this final cooking stage. Should your apples be juiceless, you may wish to add a small amount of water to give moisture. Makes 3 servings.

More Hougen Favorites, p. 16

Spiced Apples

1 c. water	1/4 c. cinnamon drops
1 c. sugar	6 apples

Boil water, sugar and cinnamon drops until cinnamon drops are dissolved. Peel and core apples. Slice into rings. Add to syrup and cook until tender. Remove apples and set aside. Boil syrup until thick. Pour over apples. Serve warm.

We Make You Kindly Welcome, p. 48

Stewed Apples

2 lbs. apples	1/2 c. white wine
2 T. butter	1 small piece lemon peel
1/2 c. sugar	1 T. lemon juice
1/2 c. water	

Peel and core apples. Cut in thick slices. Saute in butter 2 to 3 minutes. Sprinkle with sugar. Add water, wine, lemon peel and lemon juice. Cover and cook slowly until tender. Serves 6.

My Old Kentucky Homes Cookbook, p. 13

Fresh Cranberry Orange Relish

1 lb. raw cranberries	2 c. sugar
2 oranges	

Wash and pick over cranberries. Wash and quarter oranges, leaving the peel on. Remove seeds. Put cranberries and orange quarters through food chopper. Put in a bowl and stir in sugar to desired sweetness. Add a little lemon juice if you like. Chill and serve. Store in refrigerator.

Mrs. Earle B. Combs, Sr.

Broiled Grapefruit

Cut grapefruits in half. Remove seeds, loosen sections with a paring knife and core. Sprinkle each half with 2 t. brown sugar. Dot with butter. Place 3" to 4" from broiler unit and broil 15 to 20 minutes. Cinnamon sugar can be used instead of brown sugar, if desired. Mix 1 T. ground cinnamon with 1/2 c. sugar.

University of Kentucky Agriculture and Home Economics Extension Pamphlet, 1965

Fried Peaches

An old Kentucky recipe.

2 large freestone peaches, not too ripe	2 T. butter
	4 T. sugar

Peel and halve peaches, remove stones and place the peaches cut side down in a skillet of hot butter. When edges are nicely browned turn halves up. Sprinkle half the sugar over top side and allow the other side to brown, then turn. Sprinkle the other side with remaining sugar. Cook until sugar caramelizes slightly, turning the peaches to coat them. Serve with fowl, game or roast, or for dessert with rich cream.

Out of Kentucky Kitchens, p. 178

Spiced Peaches

5 peaches	1 stick cinnamon
2 c. brown sugar	1 t. cloves
3/4 c. vinegar	

Combine in saucepan all ingredients but peaches. Simmer for 20 minutes. Add cut and peeled peaches. Cook until tender. Store in closed container until ready to use. Makes 1 qt.

Kentucky Cooking New and Old, p. 25

Apple Butter

10 c. apple pulp	1 1/2 t. ground cloves
5 1/2 c. sugar	1 t. allspice
1 T. ground cinnamon	

Wash, quarter and cook 8 lbs. of apples. It is not necessary to peel them. Add 2 qts. water. Cover and let simmer until tender and soft. Rub through a sieve to get the pulp. Add sugar and spices to the pulp and mix thoroughly. Let simmer gently, partly covered, for 2 to 3 hours, or until desired thickness. Stir frequently. When thick, pour into hot, sterilized jars and seal at once. Makes 5 pts.

The Cincinnati Cookbook, Mrs. Wilmer Highlands, p. 271

Baked Apple Butter

12 lbs. apples,	2 lemons
Winesaps or Jonathans	1 T. cinnamon
apple cider or water	1 1/2 t. ground cloves
sugar	1 1/2 t. allspice

Wash, core and quarter apples, no need to peel. Combine them in a large kettle with cider or water to nearly cover. Bring to a boil, then lower heat and simmer gently for 1 1/2 hours or until soft. Put the pulp through a food mill or fine strainer. Measure the pulp and allow 1/2 c. sugar for each cup of apple pulp. Combine these in the large kettle and mix well. Add the grated rind and juice of the lemons, cinnamon, ground cloves and allspice. Bring to a boil on surface unit, then pour into a large roasting pan or pair of pans and bake, uncovered, in a slow, moderate oven, 300 degrees F., stirring occasionally with a wooden paddle until thickened, about 4 hours. Seal in sterilized jars for shelf storage, or simply clean jars for freezer storage.

Recipes Remembered, p. 314

Kentucky Blackberry Jam

To 1 qt. fresh blackberries, add 4 c. sugar. Cook over medium heat in a heavy 4 qt. saucepan. When berries have bubbled in a full boil for 3 minutes, add an additional 1 1/2 c. sugar. Bring to a boil rapidly until mixture thickens and forms a glaze on the spoon. Stir gently taking care not to bruise berries. Store in airtight containers, sealing while hot. Makes 3 pts.

Dinwiddie Lampton, Jr., Hardscuffle Farm

Blackberry Preserves

fresh blackberries, well washed   sugar

Mash the blackberries with a potato masher. Measure the pulp and add 1 pt. sugar to each pt. of pulp. Bring the mixture to a full bubble and cook 30 minutes. Be sure to skim the mixture with a wooden spoon while cooking so paraffin will seal properly. Ladle the preserves into sterilized jars. Melt paraffin carefully, removing all bubbles with a sterilized spoon. Pour it until it is 1/4" thick on top of each jar of preserves. Let it stand and harden.

We Make You Kindly Welcome, p. 3

Corn Relish

2 qts. corn, cut (about 18 ears)	2 c. sugar
1 c. cabbage, chopped	2 T. dry mustard
1 garlic, minced	1 T. celery seed
1 c. onions, chopped	1 T. mustard seed
1 c. sweet green peppers, chopped (about 2 medium)	1 T. salt
	1 T. turmeric
1 c. sweet red peppers, chopped (about 2 medium)	1 qt. vinegar
	1 c. water

To prepare corn: Boil 5 minutes, cut from cob. Combine with remaining ingredients and simmer 20 minutes. Bring to boiling. Pack hot into hot pint jars, leaving 1/4" head space. Adjust caps. Process 15 minutes in boiling water bath. Makes 6 pts.

Ball Blue Book, Alltrista Consumer Products, p. 34

Candied Grapefruit Peel

3 grapefruit	granulated sugar
1 qt. cold water	2 T. corn syrup
1 T. salt	

Wipe grapefruit and remove peel in 4 sections lengthwise from fruit. Soak overnight in cold water in which salt has been dissolved. Drain. Cover with cold water. Bring to a boil and boil for 20 minutes. Repeat this process 3 times and cook in the last water until soft, about 4 hours. Drain and cut into strips 1/8" wide. Weigh peel. Put an equal weight of sugar in saucepan and half as much water. Add corn syrup. Bring to a boil. Add peel. Cover and cook until peel is clear and almost dry (to 230 degrees F.). Remove to plate, taking up as little syrup as possible. Cool. Roll each piece in granulated sugar. Spread on waxed paper to dry. Store in glass jars.

We Make You Kindly Welcome, p. 52

Peach Preserves

4 lbs. peaches	1 pkg. powdered pectin
2 T. lemon juice	7 c. sugar

Peel and pit peaches, then thinly slice (about 4 c. sliced). Combine peaches, lemon juice and pectin in a large saucepot. Stir in sugar and bring to a full rolling boil. Boil hard 1 minute, stirring constantly. Remove from heat and skim foam. Pour, hot, into hot jars, leaving 1/4" head space. Adjust caps. Process 10 minutes in boiling water bath. Makes 6, 12 oz. jars.

Ball Blue Book, Alltrista Consumer Products Co., p. 56

Quick Pickled Peaches

1 can peach halves	1/2 c. vinegar
whole cloves	1/3 stick cinnamon
1 c. peach syrup	1/2 c. granulated sugar

Stud each peach half with 3 to 4 cloves. Simmer with remaining ingredients 3 to 4 minutes. Cool and refrigerate. Makes 8 servings.

Food for My Household, Catherine Cosby, p. 9

Pear Honey

Pare, core, chop and measure hard-ripe pears. Add a little water if needed to start cooking. Boil 10 minutes to each qt. chopped pears. Add 3 c. sugar, 1 T. lemon juice, 1/2 t. grated lemon rind and 1/2 t. ground ginger. Boil until thick. Pour into hot sterilized jars. Seal at once.

Note: Orange and nutmeg may be used instead of lemon and ginger.

My Old Kentucky Homes Cookbook, p. 5

Bread and Butter Pickles

16 to 20 medium cucumbers, thinly sliced	2 T. mustard seed
10 small onions, thinly sliced	2 t. turmeric
1/3 c. salt	2 t. celery seed
3 c. distilled vinegar	1 t. ground ginger
2 c. sugar	1 t. peppercorns

Combine cucumbers and onion slices in large bowl. Layer with salt and cover with ice cubes. Let stand 1 1/2 hours. Drain and rinse. Place remaining ingredients in large saucepot and bring to boiling. Add drained cucumbers and onions and return to boiling. Pack hot into hot 1 1/2 pt. jars, leaving 1/4" head space. Remove air bubbles. Adjust caps. Process 10 minutes in boiling water bath. Makes 5, 1 1/2 pt. jars.

Ball Blue Book, Alltrista Consumer Products Co., p. 32

Strawberry Preserves Deluxe

1 1/2 qts. firm,
   red ripe strawberries,
   stemmed

5 c. sugar
1/3 c. lemon juice

Berries with hollow cores should not be used. Combine strawberries and sugar. Let stand 3 to 4 hours. Bring slowly to boiling, stirring occasionally until sugar dissolves. Add lemon juice. Cook rapidly until berries are clear and syrup thickens, 10 to 12 minutes. Pour into shallow pan. Let stand, uncovered, 12 to 24 hours in a cool place. Shake pan occasionally to distribute berries through syrup. Pour into hot jars leaving 1/4" head space. Adjust caps. Process 20 minutes in boiling water bath. Makes 4, 1/2 pints.

Ball Blue Book, Alltrista Consumer Products Co., p. 57

Watermelon Rind Preserves

1 1/2 qts. prepared
   watermelon rind
4 T. salt
2 qts. cold water
1 T. ground ginger

4 c. sugar
1/2 c. lemon juice
7 c. water
1 lemon, thinly sliced

To prepare watermelon rind: Trim green skin and pink flesh from thick watermelon rind. Cut into 1" pieces. Dissolve salt in 2 qts. water and pour over rind. Let stand 5 to 6 hours if salt is used. Drain, rinse and drain again. Cover with cold water and let stand 30 minutes. Drain. Sprinkle ginger over rind. Cover with water and cook until fork-tender. Drain. Combine sugar, lemon juice and 7 cups water. Boil 5 minutes. Add rind and boil gently for 30 minutes. Add sliced lemon and cook until the melon rind is clear. Pack hot, into hot jars, leaving 1/4" head space. Remove air bubbles. Adjust caps. Process 20 minutes in boiling water bath. Makes 6, 1/2 pints.

Ball Blue Book, Alltrista Consumer Products Co., p. 57

Pies

Blackberry Cobbler

1 1/2 c. all-purpose flour	6 c. blackberries
scant 1/4 t. salt	3/4 c. sugar
5 T. unsalted butter	4 T. butter
4 T. vegetable shortening	heavy cream, whipped cream
4 to 5 T. ice water	or ice cream

Note: Chill the butter and shortening thoroughly in the freezer. Preheat oven to 425 degrees F. Have ready a 9" round oven-proof dish 2 or more inches deep. Prepare the pastry dough first, then refrigerate it while you get everything else ready. To make the dough, place the flour and salt in a food processor. Add the butter and shortening and process until completely incorporated. Add the ice water and process until the dough just begins to cling together, about 10 seconds. Gather the dough in a ball, wrap and refrigerate until ready to use. Roll out the dough in a large ragged circle, big enough to line the pan and flop a bit over the top. Add the berries, sprinkle them with sugar and dot with butter. Bring edges of the pastry over the berries. There will be a little space in the center. Bake for 45 minutes. Put a sheet of foil in the bottom of the oven because cobblers bubble over. Let cool and serve with heavy cream, whipped cream or ice cream. Serves 6.

Lee Bailey, *USA Weekend*, August 16-18, 1991

Blackberry Cobbler

3/4 c. sugar	3 c. blackberries with any
1 T. cornstarch	juice on them
1 c. boiling water	1/2 T. butter
	1/2 t. cinnamon

Mix together sugar and cornstarch in a saucepan. Gradually stir in boiling water. Bring to a boil and boil 1 minute, stirring constantly. Add blackberries. Pour into a 10"x6"x2" baking dish. Dot with butter and sprinkle with cinnamon.

Top crust:

1 c. flour	1/2 t. salt
1 T. sugar	3 T. shortening
1 1/2 t. baking powder	1/2 c. milk

Knead dough lightly. Drop by spoonfuls onto fruit. Bake cobbler 30 minutes at 400 degrees F. Serve warm with the juice and cream. Serves 6.

Betty Crocker's Picture Cook Book, p. 224, reprinted by permission of General Mills, Inc.

Blackberry Cobbler

1 9" pie crust	4 T. flour
1/2 stick (4 T.)	butterdash of nutmeg
2 c. sugar	1 qt. blackberries

Roll out the pie crust and put in a deep baking dish; reserve the extra dough for a criss-cross pattern on top of the cobbler. Dot the crust with butter. Mix up the sugar, flour and nutmeg. Place the berries alternately with the sugar and flour mixture and then dots of butter on top. Cover top with strips of dough in a criss-cross pattern. Brush top with melted butter if desired. Place cobbler in a preheated 450 degrees F. oven for 15 minutes, then turn down the heat to 350 degrees F. for another half hour or until the cobbler is bubbling.

Thelma's Treasures, p. 99

Super Blackberry Cobbler

4 c. blackberries	2 t. sugar
1 c. sugar	5 t. baking powder
1/4 c. quick tapioca	1/4 t. salt
1 1/3 c. water	6 T. shortening
2 T. butter	2/3 c. milk
2 c. flour	1/4 t. lemon extract

Combine berries, sugar, tapioca, water and butter and let stand while making crust. Sift flour, sugar, baking powder and salt together. Cut in shortening. Add milk all at once. Stir to dampen. Roll out. Cut into 8, 2 1/2" rounds. Sprinkle with sugar. Add lemon extract to berries and pour into buttered baking dish. Place rounds over berries and bake at 425 degrees F. for 30 minutes.

A Taste from Back Home, p. 280

Blackberry Stack Cobbler

Wash and pick over 8 to 10 c. fresh blackberries. Sweeten to taste and let simmer 10 minutes. Drain the juice off and into a pitcher. Have baked 5 to 6 pie shells made to fit the bottom of a 9" pie pan but not the sides. It works best if you roll the pastry a little thicker than usual, 1/4" thick. To make the 6-layer stack, use 6 c. of flour and the other ingredients to go with it for pastry, or 3 times a 2 c. pastry recipe. Brush the pastry rounds lightly with melted butter. Start with a shell on a plate. Place over it a layer of the berries. Sprinkle lightly with sugar. Repeat this procedure until all the berries and pastry rounds have been used. Set aside "to set" for 1 to 2 hours. Cut into wedges and pour the juice over it and serve at once because the serving will absorb all the juice if allowed to set any length of time. If desired, the juice may be thickened slightly with cornstarch.

Cissy Gregg's Cook Book, vol. 1, p. 36,
The Courier Journal & Louisville Times Co., reprinted with permission

Louisville Black Bottom Pie

1 1/4 c. milk	1 t. vanilla
2 eggs, well beaten	1 1/2 T. light rum
1/2 c. sugar	1 c. whipping cream
3 2/3 T. cornstarch	bitter chocolate, shaved
1 oz. bitter chocolate, melted	1 9" gingersnap crust, baked

Scald milk in double boiler, then slowly add beaten eggs and blend well. Mix sugar and cornstarch and stir into egg mixture. Cook 15 to 20 minutes in the double boiler, stirring occasionally. When the custard generously coats a wooden spoon, it is done. Take 1/3 of the hot custard and mix slowly with melted chocolate until cool. Add vanilla to chocolate custard. Stir the rest of the custard slowly until cool to avoid lumping. When cool, add rum and blend. Whip cream until it is stiff. Add chocolate custard to the cooled gingersnap crust and completely cover crust. Add the rum custard on top of the chocolate and spread evenly across pie. Top with whipped cream and sprinkle with shaved chocolate.

Gingersnap crust:
16 gingersnaps, chopped fine   5 T. butter, melted

Mix ingredients and pat evenly into 9" pie pan. Bake at 300 degrees F. for 10 minutes. Cool completely.

A Taste from Back Home, p. 250

Caramel Pie

2 c. sugar	2 c. cream or rich milk
1 c. boiling water	4 T. sugar
1/2 c. flour	1/3 t. salt
4 eggs, separated	1 t. vanilla

Put 1 c. of sugar in an iron skillet and let it come to a golden brown syrup, stirring constantly. Add the boiling water and cook slowly until it is free of lumps. Mix the remaining c. of sugar with the flour. Beat egg yolks and add the cream. Stir the sugar and flour mixture in the syrup and add the cream and egg yolks. Beat the egg whites; add sugar, salt and vanilla. Use for meringue. Pour the pie filling into baked crusts. Cover with meringue. Put in slow oven, 300 degrees F., and let meringue bake 15 minutes. Makes 2 pies.

Sharing Our Best, Ruby Mae Litsey, p. 91

Caramel-Nut Pie

4 T. flour	2 c. milk
1 c. brown sugar	1/2 c. nuts, chopped
1/4 t. salt	1 t. vanilla
1 T. butter	1 9" pie shell, baked
2 eggs, separated	

Mix flour, sugar, salt, butter and egg yolks and beat well. Add to hot milk and cool until thick, stirring constantly. Add nuts and vanilla. Pour into baked shell. Make meringue.

Meringue:

2 egg whites	3 T. powdered sugar

Beat the egg whites until soft peaks are formed. Gradually beat in powdered sugar. Beat until stiff peaks are formed, all sugar is dissolved and mixture has a glossy appearance. Pile on top of pie, making sure edges are sealed. Bake at 350 degrees F. for 13 to 15 minutes.

Prairie Recipes and Kitchen Antiques, p. 123

Chess Pie

1 T. flour, level	1/4 c. water
1 c. white sugar	1 t. white vinegar
1/4 t. salt	1/2 c. butter, melted
2 egg yolks	unbaked pie shell
1 whole egg	

Mix flour, sugar and salt together. Beat the 2 egg yolks and the one whole egg together adding water, vinegar and melted butter. After beating the above mixture well, add the flour, sugar and salt mixture. Pour into pie shell and bake at 350 degrees F. until set, about 35 minutes. Use the 2 egg whites left from yolks for meringue. Use 1 T. white sugar to each egg white. Beat with electric mixer until stiff. Spread on top of pie and brown for 12 minutes in a 250 degree F. oven.

Beaumont Inn Special Recipes, p. 110

Chess Pie

5 eggs	1/2 c. heavy cream
1 1/2 c. sugar	1 T. vanilla
2 T. cornmeal	9" pie shell, unbaked
1/4 c. melted butter	

Beat eggs, sugar and cornmeal. Gradually add remaining ingredients and blend well. Pour into pie shell. Bake at 350 degrees F. for 30 minutes or until set.

Donna Gill Recommends, p. 31

Chess Pie

1 9" pie crust

Filling:

1 stick (8 T.) butter, softened	2 c. sugar
3 eggs, separated	1 t. white vinegar
3 whole eggs	1/2 c. half & half cream

Meringue topping:
3 egg whites   6 T. sugar

Preheat oven to 350 degrees F. Let butter come to room temperature. Add the egg yolks to the 3 whole eggs and mix with the sugar and the softened butter. Beat with a mixer until fluffy. Add white vinegar and half & half. Beat. Beat very well. The beating is the secret. Pour the mixture into the prepared pie crust. Bake at 350 degrees F. for 45 minutes or until firm in the center. Just before the pie is ready to come out of the oven, beat the 3 egg whites with the sugar, adding the sugar gradually. Pour the meringue mixture on top of the pie when it comes out of the oven. Put the pie back in and bake 15 minutes at 350 degrees F. or until golden brown on top.

Thelma's Treasures, p. 96

Chess Pie

1 1/2 c. sugar   1 1/2 t. cornmeal
1/2 c. butter, melted   1 1/2 t. vinegar
3 eggs   9" unbaked pie shell

Use mixer at low speed for combining ingredients and do not mix too much. Combine sugar and melted butter. Add eggs and remaining ingredients. Pour into pie shell. Preheat oven to 450 degrees F. Put pie in oven and turn immediately to 400 degrees F. Cook at 400 degrees F. for about 15 minutes, then at 300 degrees F. for about 20 minutes. Filling for pie will puff up full. Give a little jiggle to be sure center is firm before removing it from oven. Place it on a rack to cool. Pie may be browned before serving.

Note: Cooking time varies as to oven and eggs — if eggs are fresh, it takes longer.

We Make You Kindly Welcome, p. 36

Chess Pie for Posterity (Beaumont Inn)

1 level T. flour   3 T. water
1 c. white sugar   1 t. white vinegar
1/4 t. salt   1/4 lb. (1/2 c.) butter, melted
2 egg yolks   2 egg whites
1 whole egg   2 T. white sugar

Mix flour, sugar and salt together. Beat the 2 egg yolks and the 1 whole egg together, adding water, vinegar and melted butter. Beat together well, then add the sugar-flour mixture. Pour into an unbaked pie shell and bake at 350 degrees F. for 35 minutes. The companionate 2 egg whites to the 2 egg yolks used in the filling go to make the meringue. Use 1 T. of white sugar for each egg white and beat in electric mixer to form a meringue. Spread on top of the pie and brown-off for 12 minutes in a 350 degree F. oven.

Cissy Gregg's Cook Book, vol. 1, p. 33,
The Courier Journal & Louisville Times Co., reprinted with permission

Lemon Chess Pie (Kitty Cornett)

3 c. sugar	1/4 c. lemon juice
1 T. flour	1/4 c. butter, melted
1 T. white cornmeal	1/4 c. milk
4 eggs	9" pastry shell, unbaked
1 T. lemon rind, grated	

In large bowl of electric mixer, stir together sugar, flour and cornmeal. Add eggs. Beat until thick. Add lemon rind, juice and butter. Beat just enough to mix. Add milk and beat to mix. Pour into pastry shell. Bake in preheated oven at 350 degrees F. for 50 to 60 minutes or until knife inserted comes out clean.

Cookbook of Treasures, Ruth Luxon, p. 81

Lemon Chess Pie

1/2 c. butter or margarine	4 eggs
2 c. sugar	1 T. lemon rind, grated
2 T. cornmeal	1/4 c. lemon juice
1/4 t. salt	9" pie shell, unbaked

Cream together butter and sugar until fluffy. Beat in cornmeal and salt. Add eggs, one at a time. Beat well. Beat in lemon rind and lemon juice. Turn in pie shell. Bake on lowest shelf of oven at 375 degrees F. for 35 minutes until filling is golden brown. Cool to room temperature. Serve in small wedges as this pie is very rich.

Cookbook of Treasures, Mary Keene, p. 81

Lemon Chess Pie

2 c. sugar
2 T. flour
2 T. white cornmeal
4 large eggs
1/4 c. butter, melted

1/4 c. heavy cream
1 T. lemon rind, grated
1/4 c. fresh lemon juice
9" pastry shell, unbaked

Combine sugar, flour and cornmeal in mixing bowl. Add eggs, butter, cream, lemon rind and lemon juice. Beat until well blended. Pour into pie shell. Bake in 350 degree F. oven 40 to 50 minutes or until just set. Serve topped with blueberry sauce.

Donna Gill Recommends, p. 34

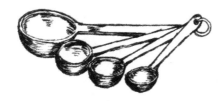

Kentucky Chocolate-Nut Pie

2 eggs, lightly beaten
1 c. sugar
1/2 c. flour
1 stick butter, melted and cooled

1 c. English walnuts or pecans
1 t. vanilla
1 c. semi-sweet chocolate chips
unbaked pie shell

Mix eggs, sugar, flour, butter, nuts, vanilla and chocolate chips in order. Mix well and spread in pie shell. Bake at 325 degrees F. for 30 to 35 minutes.

Sharing Our Best, Kathleen Forrister, p. 98

Coconut Cream Pie

4 T. sugar
2 1/2 T. flour
1/4 t. salt
2 c. milk
2 egg yolks, slightly beaten
1 c. shredded coconut

2 t. vanilla
9" pie shell, baked
2 egg whites
4 T. sugar
1/2 c. shredded coconut

Combine sugar, flour and salt in top of double boiler, add milk and egg yolks, mixing thoroughly. Cook over boiling water for 10 minutes, stirring constantly. Remove from heat, add coconut and vanilla. Cool slightly, then turn into pie shell. Beat egg whites until foamy throughout. Add sugar, 2 T. at a time, beating after each addition until sugar is blended, then continue beating until stiff. Pile lightly on filling, sprinkle with coconut. Bake at 350 degrees F. for 15 minutes or until light brown.

A Taste from Back Home, p. 257

Boone Tavern Jefferson Davis Pie

2 c. brown sugar
1 T. flour, sifted
1/2 t. nutmeg
1 c. cream
4 eggs, slightly beaten

1 t. lemon juice
1/2 t. lemon rind, grated
1/4 c. margarine, melted
whipped cream for garnish
9" pie shell, unbaked

Sift sugar with flour and nutmeg. Add cream and mix well. Add eggs and mix well. Add lemon juice, rind and margarine. Beat well. Pour into pie shell and bake at 375 degrees F. for 45 minutes. Serves 8.

Dining in Historic Kentucky, vol. 1, p. 33

Kentucky Pie

1/2 c. butter
3 c. light brown sugar
3 eggs
1/2 c. cream

1 t. vanilla
pinch of salt
9" pie shell, unbaked

Cream butter, sugar and eggs. Add other ingredients and mix well. Pour into pie shell and bake in 350 degree F. oven for 30 to 45 minutes. Very rich.

Cooking with Curtis Grace, Ema Noble, p. 167

Kentucky Lemon Pie

6 eggs
1 1/2 c. corn syrup
1 t. cornstarch
3/4 c. sugar

juice of 2 lemons
rind of 1 lemon
1/8 c. butter, melted
1 pie shell, unbaked

Beat eggs well. Add syrup and mix well. Mix cornstarch with the sugar. Add to the syrup mixture. Add lemon juice and grated rind. Add melted butter. Beat together until well mixed. Pour into unbaked pie shell. Bake on lower shelf of oven at 375 degrees F. for 15 minutes then reduce the temperature to 300 degrees F. for 40 minutes or until pie is set.

Look No Further, p. 178

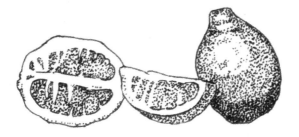

deSha's Lemon Ice Box Pie

3 eggs
pinch of salt
1 1/3 cans sweetened
  condensed milk

3/4 c. lemon juice
9" graham cracker crust

Beat eggs with salt, add condensed milk, then lemon juice, mixing well. Pour into crust and bake at 350 degrees for 15 minutes. Chill.

Dining in Historic Kentucky, vol. 2, p. 47

Lemon Meringue Pie

7 T. cornstarch	1 t. lemon peel, grated
1 1/2 c. sugar	2 T. butter or margarine
1/4 t. salt	9" pie shell, baked
1 1/2 c. hot water	1 T. lemon juice
3 egg yolks	3 egg whites
1/2 c. fresh lemon juice	6 T. sugar

Mix cornstarch, sugar and salt in a saucepan. Stir in hot water gradually and bring to boil over direct heat. Cook for 8 to 10 minutes over medium heat, stirring constantly until thick and clear. Remove from heat. Stir several spoonfuls of this hot mixture into beaten egg yolks. Mix well. Pour egg yolks back into saucepan. Bring to boil, then cook over low heat 4 to 5 minutes, stirring constantly. Remove from heat. Gradually add lemon juice, lemon peel and butter. Cool filling and pour into cooled baked pie shell. Top with meringue.

For the meringue add lemon juice to egg whites along with sugar. Spread the cooled meringue over the cooled filling. Start with the edges and work toward center of pie. Be sure to attach meringue securely to edges of crust. Bake at 350 degrees F. for 15 to 20 minutes. Cool before serving.

Cissy Gregg's Cook Book, vol. 2, p. 24,
The Courier Journal & Louisville Times Co., reprinted with permission

Old-Fashioned Lemon Pie (Doe Run Pie)

1/2 c. butter or margarine	2 lemons
2 c. sugar	9" pie shell, unbaked
4 eggs	

Cream well butter and sugar, adding the eggs, one at a time. Grate peel from the lemons, then cut and juice. Add juice and all of rind. The grated rind is what makes the crust on top. Pour into pie shell and bake in a preheated 350 degree F. oven at least 30 minutes. From that point, test with a knife or by shaking. Remove from oven just before it gets firm. It will firm up some as it cools.

Sharing Our Best, Hazel Woosley, p. 105

Shaker Lemon Pie

2 large lemons	9" pie shell, unbaked
2 c. sugar	1 top crust, unbaked
4 eggs, well beaten	

Slice lemons as thin as paper, rind and all. Combine with sugar and mix well. Let stand 2 hours or longer, blending occasionally. Add beaten eggs to lemon mixture. Mix well. Turn into pie shell, arranging lemon slices evenly. Cover with top crust. Cut several slits near center. Bake at 450 degrees F. for 15 minutes. Reduce heat to 375 degrees F. and bake for 20 minutes or until silver knife inserted near edge of pie comes out clean. Cool before serving.

Historic Kentucky Recipes, Ruth Payne, p. 39

Fresh Sliced Peach Pie

3 to 4 large ripe peaches	confectioners' sugar
9" deep dish pie shell,	whipped cream or topping
pre-cut into slices	

Bake pie shell until nicely browned. Peel peaches and slice 1/2" thick. Sprinkle with confectioners' sugar to taste. Refrigerate until well chilled. When ready to serve, drain peach slices and arrange in baked pie shell. Cover with whipped cream. Serve at once so pie crust does not get soggy.

Elizabeth Ross

Pecan Pie

3 eggs, slightly beaten	1 t. vanilla
1 c. white corn syrup	1 1/2 c. pecans
1 c. sugar	9" pie crust, unbaked
1 T. margarine, melted	

In large bowl, combine eggs, syrup, sugar, margarine and vanilla until blended. Stir in pecans. Pour into pie crust. Bake at 350 degrees F. for 50 to 55 minutes. May be served topped with whipped cream or vanilla ice cream. This pecan pie is very close to the one served at the Canary Cottage, a famous Lexington, Kentucky restaurant.

Sharing Our Best, Debbie Decker, p. 107

Bourbon Pecan Pie

1/4 c. butter	1/2 c. chocolate chips
1 c. sugar	1/2 c. black walnuts or pecans,
3 eggs	chopped
3/4 c. white corn syrup	2 T. bourbon
1/4 t. vanilla	9" pie shell, unbaked

Cream butter and sugar. Add eggs, syrup and vanilla. Add chocolate chips, nuts and bourbon. Pour into pie shell and bake at 375 degrees F. for 40 to 50 minutes. Serve warm with whipped cream.

A Taste from Back Home, p. 262

Chocolate Pecan Pie

1 c. sugar	2 T. bourbon
1/4 c. margarine, melted	1 t. vanilla
3 eggs, slightly beaten	1/2 c. pecans, chopped
3/4 c. light corn syrup	1/2 c. chocolate chips
1/4 t. salt	9" pie shell, unbaked

Cream sugar and margarine. Add eggs, syrup, salt, bourbon and vanilla. Mix until blended. Spread pecans and chocolate chips in bottom of pie shell. Pour filling into shell. Bake at 375 degrees F. for 40 to 50 minutes.

Fountain Favorites, p. 79

Pumpkin Pie

2 eggs	1 t. ground cinnamon
1 16 oz. can pumpkin	1/2 t. ground ginger
(about 2 c.)	1/2 t. ground cloves
1 14 oz. can sweetened	1/2 t. salt
condensed milk	9" pastry shell, unbaked

Preheat oven to 425 degrees F. Beat eggs lightly in a large bowl. Stir in pumpkin, milk and seasonings. Mix well and pour into pie shell. Bake 15 minutes. Reduce temperature to 350 degrees F. and bake for 35 to 40 minutes longer or until knife inserted in center comes out clean. Cool on a wire rack. Garnish as desired. Refrigerate leftovers. Makes 1 pie.

Elizabeth Ross

Kentucky Shoo Fly Pie

3/4 c. dark molasses	1/2 t. baking soda
3/4 c. boiling water	1/4 c. butter
1 1/2 c. flour	pastry for 1 crust
1/2 c. brown sugar, packed	

Mix molasses with hot water and blend well. Prepare crumb mixture by sifting together flour, sugar and soda. Cut in butter until the mixture resembles coarse meal. Line 9" pie dish with pastry. Pour in 1/3 of molasses mixture and top with 1/3 of the crumb mixture. Repeat layering process twice more, alternating layers of syrup and crumbs, ending with crumbs on top. Bake in a preheated oven (375 degrees F.) for 35 minutes.

The Shaker Cookbook, p. 124

Old Talbott Tavern Pie

3/4 c. sugar	1/2 c. orange juice
1/2 c. flour	2 T. lemon juice
1/4 t. salt	1 T. orange rind, grated
1 1/4 c. water	9" pie shell, baked
2 egg yolks, beaten	whipped cream

Combine sugar, flour and salt in top of double boiler. Add water and stir until smooth. Cook and stir over direct heat for 5 minutes. Remove from heat, add yolks and cook 5 minutes longer over boiling water, stirring constantly. Remove from heat and add fruit juices and rind. Chill and turn into pie shell. Top with whipped cream. May also be topped with meringue instead of whipped cream. Top meringue with orange slices, peeled, and 3/4 c. coconut. Serves 8.

Cissy Gregg's Cook Book, vol., 1, p. 41,
The Courier Journal & Louisville Times Co., reprinted with permission;
Dining in Historic Kentucky, vol. 2, p. 119

Shaker Sugar Pie

1 1/4 c. flour	just a little vanilla
1 c. brown sugar	1/4 c. butter, softened
9" pie shell, unbaked	pinch of nutmeg
2 c. light cream	

Mix flour and sugar and place in bottom of pie shell. Add cream, vanilla and soft butter in small pieces. Sprinkle nutmeg over top. Bake at 350 degrees F. for 40 to 45 minutes or until firm.

The Golden Lamb Hotel, Lebanon, Ohio

Transparent Pie

pastry for pie crust	5 T. cream
2 T. butter or margarine	1 t. vanilla
1 c. white sugar	3 egg whites
3 egg yolks, beaten	

Make a 1-crust pie pastry, fit it into pie pan and crimp the edges. Have the butter or margarine at room temperature and work it into the sugar. Add egg yolks and cream. Add flavoring. Pour into the unbaked pie crust and bake in a 375 degree F. oven for 30 minutes or until the filling is firm and light brown. Take the 3 egg whites which accompanied the egg yolks used in the filling and beat into a meringue using an extra 6 T. of sugar which are added gradually. Spread over the filling and brown lightly in a 350 degree F. oven for 15 minutes. It is a rich pie and should be dealt out in small portions.

Cissy Gregg's Cook Book, vol. 2, p. 24,
The Courier Journal & Louisville Times Co., reprinted with permission

Transparent Pie

2 c. granulated sugar
3/4 c. butter
4 eggs

2 t. all-purpose flour
1/2 c. cream
unbaked pie shell

Cream sugar and butter. Beat in eggs, flour and cream. Pour into pie shell. Bake at 350 degrees F. for 45 minutes or until set.

Welcome Back to Pleasant Hill, p. 81

Apple Deep Dish Pie

1 c. brown sugar
2 T. flour
1/8 t. salt
1/4 t. nutmeg
1/4 t. cinnamon

1 t. lemon juice
2 t. butter
6 c. Granny Smith apples, pared,
   cored and sliced 1/4" thick
pastry for single crust

Preheat oven to 425 degrees F. Combine sugar, flour, salt, nutmeg, cinnamon, lemon juice and butter. Arrange apples in a 10"x6"x2" (1 1/2 qt.) baking dish. Sprinkle with sugar mixture. Roll pastry to fit top of dish with 1/2" overhang. Lay pastry loosely over apples. Fold overhang under. Press onto rim firmly with upturned tines of floured fork. Cut several small slits for steam vents. Bake 40 minutes or until apples are done. Makes 6 servings.

Elizabeth Ross

Fried Apple Pies

Fried pie dough:
    4 c. self-rising flour
    1 1/2 c. solid shortening

2 1/2 to 3 c. ice water

Mix well. Turn onto waxed paper. Wrap and refrigerate for 8 hours or more.

Apple pie filling:
    1 T. cornstarch
    1/2 c. sugar
    pinch of salt

1/4 t. vanilla
2 c. apples, fresh, frozen or canned

Mix starch, sugar, salt and vanilla together and add to cooked apples. Bring to a boil. Cool before putting into pies. Roll dough out thin and cut into 6" round circles (a saucer works well as a pattern). Place apple filling in the center of each circle. Fold over and press ends together with fingertips or with the edge of a fork. Fry in a skillet of shortening deep enough for pies to float, but shortening does not have to cover the pies. The grease should be hot enough to sizzle. Test the grease by dropping in a small piece of dough. If the grease is too hot the pies will brown too fast and will not cook all the way through. Brown each pie on both sides, remove from grease and drain on paper towels. Sprinkle each with sugar and serve warm. Makes 14 pies.

Moonlite Bar-B-Q Cookbook, p. 75

Fried Apple Pies

2/3 c. shortening	3/4 t. salt
2 c. flour, sifted	4 to 6 T. cold water

Filling:

2 c. apples or 1 can	1 T. cinnamon
of pie apples or applesauce	butter
1/2 c. brown sugar	

Combine shortening, flour, salt and water to make pastry. Roll very thin and cut into circles the size of a saucer. Combine apples, brown sugar, cinnamon and butter to make filling. Cut apples with a pastry blender until smooth. Add 2 T. filling to center of circles. Fold until edges are even and press together firmly with fork. Fry quickly in hot fat, covered until golden brown. Drain.

Source unknown

Cakes
&
Frostings

Kentucky Black Cake

2 c. flour	1/2 t. soda
1/2 c. seeded raisins	1/4 t. cloves
1/2 c. dates, chopped	1 t. cinnamon
1/2 c. figs, chopped	1/4 t. allspice
2 T. whiskey	1/2 t. nutmeg
1 c. butter	1/2 c. raspberry or blackberry jam
1 c. brown sugar, packed firm	1/2 c. nuts, pecans, almonds or
2 eggs, well-beaten	English walnuts, chopped
1/3 c. sour cream	

Brown flour in oven until golden brown. Stir occasionally to prevent sticking. Set aside and cool. Sift. Mix the raisins, dates and figs. Pour whiskey over the fruit and mix well. Let stand 2 hours or until all liquor has been absorbed. Cream butter with sugar. Add the beaten eggs and sour cream. Sift the flour once more with the soda and spices. Pour the liquid ingredients into the dry, stirring constantly to prevent lumping. Add the jam, chopped nuts and the whiskey-soaked fruit. Pour into a greased and floured tube pan or a loaf pan and bake in a moderate 375 degree F. oven for 1 1/2 to 2 hours or until cake tests done. Remove from oven and let cake cool in pan before turning out. Makes a 3 lb. cake.

Out of Kentucky Kitchens, p. 257

Kentucky Butter Cake

3 c. all-purpose flour, sifted	1 1/2 c. granulated sugar
3 t. baking powder	1 c. milk
1/4 t. salt	1 t. vanilla
3/4 c. butter	3 egg whites, beaten until stiff

Sift flour, baking powder and salt together. Cream butter and sugar until very light. Add alternately flour and milk. Stir in vanilla. Fold in egg whites. Pour into 2 greased and lightly floured 9" cake pans. Bake at 350 degrees F. for 30 minutes. If desired, ice before serving.

Welcome Back to Pleasant Hill, p. 81

Chocolate Cake, Old Kentucky Style

Mix in large bowl:

    2 c. sugar   1 t. soda

    2 c. self-rising flour   1 t. cinnamon

In saucepan:

    melt 2 sticks margarine   add 4 T. cocoa and
                                        1 c. water

Boil these ingredients 1 minute. Pour over flour mixture.

Then add:

    2 whole eggs   1 t. vanilla

    1/2 c. buttermilk

Mix well, do not use mixer. Batter will be thin. Bake at 350 degrees F. for 30 to 40 minutes or until done.

Frosting:

    1 stick butter   6 T. milk

    4 T. cocoa

Melt in saucepan and add:

    1 box confectioners' sugar   1 t. vanilla

    1 c. chopped nuts

Stir until smooth and frost cake.

Nancy Ballard McQuerry

Pleasant Hill Christmas Cake

3 c. all-purpose flour, sifted	1 c. milk
3 t. baking powder	1 t. vanilla
1/4 t. salt	3 egg whites, beaten until stiff
3/4 c. butter	1/2 c. black walnuts, hickory nuts
1 1/2 c. granulated sugar	or pecans, chopped

Sift flour, baking powder and salt together. Cream butter and sugar until very light. Add alternately flour and milk. Stir in vanilla. Fold in egg whites then nuts. Pour into 2 greased and lightly floured 8" cake pans. Bake at 350 degrees F. for 30 minutes. Frost with Maple Syrup Frosting (see Frostings).

Welcome Back to Pleasant Hill, p. 60

Fresh Coconut Cake

1 c. shortening, half butter	1/2 t. salt
2 c. sugar	1 c. milk
4 eggs	1 1/2 t. vanilla flavoring
2 2/3 c. cake flour, sifted	milk from 1 coconut
2 t. baking powder	

Cream shortening, adding sugar gradually. Cream until mixture is very fluffy. Add eggs, beat mixture until light and fluffy. Sift flour, baking powder and salt together. Add to mixture alternately with milk until milk and dry ingredients have all been added. Mix in vanilla. Pour into 3 greased cake pans. Bake at 350 degrees F. for 30 to 35 minutes. Pour coconut milk into layers by sticking a knife into them several times and pour milk in, using it all. Let cool and frost.

Icing:

2 c. white sugar	1/2 t. vanilla
1/2 c. water	1 coconut, grated
1/4 t. salt	1/2 t. lemon flavor
2 T. white corn syrup	2 egg whites

Combine sugar, water, salt and corn syrup. Boil slowly without stirring until mixture spins a thread when dropped from spoon. Add vanilla, part of grated coconut and lemon flavor. Beat egg whites until stiff. Pour cooked icing over egg whites, a small amount at a time. Beat well after each addition. Spread icing between each layer and over cake, sprinkle coconut over top of icing and sides of cake.

My Old Kentucky Homes Cookbook, p. 29

Granny's Black Fruit Cake

1 pkg. dates	1 t. cinnamon
1/4 lb. cherries or figs	1/2 t. nutmeg
1/4 lb. raisins	1/2 t. allspice
1/4 lb. citron	1/4 t. ground cloves
1/4 lb. lemon peel	1/2 t. salt
1/4 lb. orange peel	1 t. soda
1 c. nuts	3 eggs
2 1/2 c. flour	1/2 c. molasses
1/2 c. butter or solid shortening	1 c. blackberry jam
1 c. brown sugar	1/2 c. whiskey or fruit juice

Cut up fruit and break nuts. Put flour on fruit and nuts. Cream butter, adding sugar gradually. Add spices, salt, soda, beaten eggs, molasses and jam. Add floured fruit and nuts alternately with liquid. Pour into paper lined pan. If baking, put a pan of water under pan. Bake or steam at 275 degrees for 3 hours.

Bess Hamilton, my Grandmother

Jennie Benedict's Fruitcake

A prized Kentucky cake.

1 lb. butter	1 T. allspice
1 lb. sugar	1/2 c. wine
1 c. New Orleans style molasses	1/2 c. brandy
12 eggs	1/2 lb. citron
1 lb. flour	2 lbs. raisins
2 t. baking powder	1 lb. currants
1 c. light cream or top milk	1/2 lb. figs
2 nutmegs, grated or 2 full t.	1/2 lb. candied pineapple
ground nutmeg	1/2 lb. candied cherries
1 T. cinnamon	2 lbs. blanched almonds

Cream butter and sugar together. Add molasses, then eggs which have been beaten separately. Add flour which has been browned - spread flour in shallow pan, place in slow oven and brown, stirring frequently. Dissolve 2 t. baking powder in 1 c. light cream or top milk. Add to mixture. Add the spices which have been dissolved in the c. of liquors. Chop fruits and nuts and dredge with flour. Add these to batter last. Bake at 250 to 300 degrees F. for 4 hours. This makes 2 large fruitcakes or about 12 lbs. of fruitcake altogether.

Cissy Gregg's Cook Book, vol. 1, p. 36,
The Courier Journal & Louisville Times Co., reprinted with permission

White Fruitcake

1 lb. white raisins	1 t. baking powder
1/2 lb. citron, cut fine	1/2 t. salt
1/2 lb. candied orange peel	1 c. butter
1/2 lb. candied pineapple	1 1/2 c. sugar
1/2 lb. candied red cherries	1 T. lemon juice
1/2 lb. candied green cherries	1 c. grated coconut
4 c. flour, sifted	1 lb. blanched almonds, slivered fine
1/2 t. soda	10 egg whites, beaten stiff

Assemble all the fruit and have them cut up before starting in on mixing the cake. Sift flour and measure. To the measured flour add soda, baking powder and salt, then sift all together 3 times. Sift 1 c. of this flour mixture over the fruit. Cream butter, gradually add the sugar and cream together thoroughly. Add remaining flour to this mixture. Beat until smooth. Add lemon juice, fruits and nuts. Fold in stiffly beaten egg whites. Pour into greased paper lined tube pan and bake in a slow oven. Keep the temperature to 250 degrees F. for 2 1/2 hours and then increase it to 300 degrees F. and bake 15 minutes longer. This makes 1, 6 lb. cake.

Cissy Gregg's Cook Book, vol. 1, p. 35,
The Courier Journal & Louisville Times Co., reprinted with permission

Kentucky White Fruitcake

1/2 lb. butter	1/4 lb. candied cherries
1 lb. white sugar	1 t. soda
1 lb. flour	2 t. cream of tartar
1 lb. citron, cut in strips	12 egg whites, well-beaten
1/4 lb. candied pineapple	1 coconut, fresh grated
2 lbs. almonds, blanched and cut fine	

Cream butter and gradually add sugar, then gradually work in about 3/4 of the flour (3 c.). Add 1/2 of the fruits. Sift soda and cream of tartar with remaining flour (1 c.) and use this mixture for dredging the remaining fruits. Fold in egg whites, then the floured fruits. Bake in a greased, unglazed, paper-lined and greased-again pan. Bake at 275 degrees F. for 2 1/2 hours or until done according to the toothpick test.

Cissy Gregg's Cook Book, vol. 1, p. 34,
The Courier Journal & Louisville Times Co., reprinted with permission

Jam Cake

6 eggs
1 c. butter, melted
4 T. buttermilk
2 c. brown sugar
1 c. blackberry jam
3 c. all-purpose flour,
    sifted before measuring
2 t. cinnamon

2 t. allspice
2 t. nutmeg
1 t. soda
1 c. English walnuts or
    pecans, chopped
1 c. raisins
bourbon

Mix whole eggs, which have been beaten, with the melted butter, buttermilk, brown sugar and blackberry jam. Add flour, which has been sifted with the cinnamon, allspice, nutmeg and soda. Add nuts and raisins and fold in. Bake in a 9" tube pan greased with a mixture of 1 part flour and 2 parts shortening rubbed together. Bake at 325 degrees F. for 1 1/2 to 2 hours or until done. Let cool 5 minutes and turn it out on a cake rack. While still warm, add bourbon to the bottom of the cake.

Cissy Gregg's Cook Book, vol. 2, p. 26,
The Courier Journal & Louisville Times Co., reprinted with permission

Jam Cake

1 c. shortening
2 c. sugar
3 egg yolks, well-beaten
1 c. blackberry jam
3 c. flour

1/2 t. salt
1 t. soda
1 t. cinnamon
1 c. buttermilk
3 egg whites, stiffly beaten

Cream shortening and sugar. Add egg yolks and jam and beat well. Sift dry ingredients and add alternately with buttermilk. Beat vigorously after each addition. Fold in egg whites and pour into a 9" greased cake pan or mold. Bake in moderate 350 degrees F. oven for 30 minutes. Cool and ice.

Florence Ross, my Mother

Jam Cake

2 c. blackberry jam	1 1/2 t. cloves
1 c. vegetable oil	1/2 t. allspice
2 c. white sugar	1/2 t. nutmeg
1 c. buttermilk	1 c. nuts
1 t. baking powder	1 c. raisins
3 eggs	3 c. plain flour

Mix all ingredients well. Bake at 350 degrees F. for 1 hour.

Speedwell Christian Church Cookbook, Dixie Wilhoit, Mary Butler, p. 73

Christmas Jam Cake

1 c. butter or shortening	1 c. buttermilk
3 c. sugar	3 c. flour
6 eggs	1 t. allspice
1 c. blackberry jam	1 t. nutmeg
2 c. strawberry jam	1 t. cinnamon
1 1/2 t. soda	1 c. pecans, chopped

Cream butter and sugar. Add eggs, one at a time. Blend well. Do not use mixer for balance of the cake or it will be crumbly. Stir in jam. Stir soda into buttermilk. Sift dry ingredients together 2 times. Add dry ingredients alternately with buttermilk mixture. Begin and end with flour mixture. Fold in pecans. Pour into 3 layer cake pans lined with foil and then greased and floured. (The foil prevents a heavy crust from forming.) Bake in a 300 degree F. oven for 1 hour and 15 minutes. Test for doneness with toothpick. Frost between layers and on sides with caramel or other favorite icing.

Best of the Best from Kentucky, What's Cooking for the Holidays, p. 204

Mrs. Creason's Jam Cake

1 c. butter or shortening	1/4 t. salt
2 c. sugar	1 t. soda
5 eggs, beaten	1 c. buttermilk
3 c. flour	1 c. raisins or dates, chopped
1/2 t. cinnamon	1 c. nuts, chopped
1 1/2 t. cloves	1 c. jam
1 1/2 t. allspice	

Cream butter and gradually add the sugar. Cream together until light and fluffy. Add well-beaten eggs. Sift flour before measuring and add to it the spices and the salt. Dissolve soda in buttermilk and add it and the flour mixture alternately to the egg-sugar-butter mixture and beat after each addition. Lightly dredge the fruit and nuts with extra flour and add. Next, add the jam. Stir to get good distribution. Grease and paper-line 2 9" cake pans. Batter fills pans 2" deep. Bake at 325 degrees F. for 40 minutes. Ice with caramel icing or whatever you like.

Cissy Gregg's Cook Book, vol. 1, p. 43,
The Courier Journal & Louisville Times Co., reprinted with permission

Jiffy Jam Cake

1 1 lb. 2 oz. pkg.	eggs, oil and liquid
spice cake mix	as directed on pkg.
	1 c. blackberry jam

Preheat oven to 350 degrees F. Combine cake mix, eggs, oil and liquid in large mixer bowl and beat as directed on pkg. Add blackberry jam and beat only to mix until smooth. Pour into ungreased 9"x13"x2" oblong cake pan. Bake on middle oven rack for time given on cake mix pkg. or until cake begins to break from pan sides and toothpick stuck in center will come out clean. Cool in pan on a cake rack. Cut in squares to serve, either plain or with a lemon or caramel sauce or spread the cooled cake with caramel icing. Makes 12 to 15 pieces.

Recipes Remembered, p. 224

Kentucky Blackberry Jam Cake

1/2 c. butter	1 t. cinnamon
1 c. brown sugar	1/2 t. allspice
2 eggs, well beaten	1/2 t. nutmeg
1 c. blackberry jam with seeds	1/4 t. ground cloves
2 c. all-purpose flour	1/2 c. buttermilk
1 t. baking powder	1/2 c. pecans or English walnuts,
1 t. baking soda	chopped
	1/2 c. seedless raisins, optional

Cream butter and sugar. Add eggs and mix well. Stir in jam. Sift flour and other dry ingredients. If using nuts and raisins, toss them with a few T. of the flour mixture. Add flour mixture alternately with the liquid to the sugar mixture. Mix until just combined. Fold in nuts and raisins. Turn into 2 greased and floured 9" layer cake pans, a 11"x14"x2 1/2" sheet cake pan or a 9" tube pan. Bake in a preheated moderate 350 degrees F. oven for 30 minutes for layers or 40 minutes for sheet cake until cake leaves sides of pan. Let cool slightly, 5 minutes, and turn out on a cake rack. Frost with caramel icing.

Elizabeth Ross

Kentucky Pecan Cake (100 year old recipe)

6 eggs, beaten	1 lb. pecans
1 lb. sugar	1 lb. dates, pitted
2 sticks butter	1 c. Maker's Mark bourbon
4 c. flour	1 t. baking powder
2 T. nutmeg	1/2 t. baking soda
2 lbs. raisins	1/4 c. warm water

Preheat oven to 350 degrees F. Dissolve baking soda in warm water. Grease and flour large cake pan or several smaller loaf pans. Mix all ingredients together well. Pour batter into the greased and floured pan and place in the oven on the middle rack. On the bottom rack beneath it set a pan of water for steam. Cook for 3 1/2 hours. Let cake get cold before unmolding it. Pour on enough bourbon until cake is good and moist. Wrap up tightly in cheesecloth and then in foil wrap. It will keep a long time like this.

Thelma's Treasures, p. 89

Kentucky Pecan Bourbon Cake

1 1/2 c. flour
1 lb. shelled pecans,
  chopped coarsely
1/2 lb. seeded raisins,
  cut in half
1 t. baking powder
1/2 c. butter

1 c. plus 2 T. sugar
3 eggs, separated
2 t. nutmeg, freshly grated
1/2 c. bottled-in-bond
  Kentucky bourbon whiskey
jumbo pecan halves and candied
  cherries for decorating

Measure the flour after sifting once, then sift twice more. Take 1/2 c. of this flour and mix with the nuts and raisins. Add the baking powder to the rest of the flour and sift again. Cream butter and sugar. Add yolks of eggs, one at a time, beating until mixture is smooth and lemon-colored. An electric beater is excellent for this. Soak the nutmeg in the whiskey for at least 10 minutes, then add to the butter mixture, alternating with the flour and beating as the batter is being blended. When it is finished it looks and tastes a lot like eggnog. Slowly fold the raisins and nuts into the batter with a large spoon. Last of all, fold in the egg whites, stiffly beaten with a few grains of salt. Grease a metal tube pan and line it with brown paper, greased on both sides. Pour batter into pan and let it stand for 10 minutes allowing mixture to settle into the pan. In the meantime, decorate the top of the cake with the candied cherries and jumbo pecan halves. Cook in a warm 325 degree F. oven for 1 1/4 hours. If top seems to brown too quickly, put a piece of brown paper over the surface. Test the cake by pressing with the fingers. If it is firm and the indentation does not show, the cake is ready to remove from the stove. It should be slightly moist and a few crumbs may adhere to a straw even though the cake is ready. Let the cake stand in the pan for 30 minutes before trying to remove it. Place a plate a little larger than the pan over the surface and quickly turn the pan upside down. Gingerly turn the cake right side up on another plate, being careful not to disturb the decorations on top of the cake. Cut the slices with a saw-edged knife as it crumbles easily. Makes 1, 3 lb. cake.

Out of Kentucky Kitchens, p. 257

Kentucky Pecan Bourbon Cake

1 lb. pecans, coarsely chopped	3 egg yolks
1/2 lb. raisins, chopped	2 t. nutmeg
1 1/2 c. flour, sifted	1/2 c. bourbon
1 t. baking powder	candied cherries
1/2 c. butter	nuts
1 1/8 c. sugar	3 egg whites

Combine pecans and raisins and dredge in 1/2 c. of the flour. Add the baking powder to the other 1 c. of flour and sift again. Cream butter and gradually add sugar and cream until fluffy. To this add egg yolks, one at a time, beating after each until the mixture is smooth and yellow. Combine nutmeg and bourbon and let stand 10 minutes. Add this mixture to the butter-egg mixture alternately with the sifted flour beating thoroughly to blend. Fold in raisins and pecans with a wooden spoon. Beat egg whites and fold in when stiff. Grease a large tube pan and line it with lightly greased paper. Pour batter into pan and allow to settle for 10 minutes. Top with candied cherries and nuts. Bake in preheated oven at 325 degrees F. for 1 1/4 hours. Cover the top with brown paper if it browns too quickly. Let cake stand 1/2 hour before removing from pan. Cool on cake rack. Wrap with bourbon-soaked cloth and then metal foil to store.

A Taste from Back Home, p. 236

Pineapple Upside-Down Cake (easy way)

1 15 1/2 oz. can crushed pineapple	1 c. brown sugar
1 stick butter or margarine	1 box yellow cake mix

Drain pineapple, reserving syrup. Melt butter in baking pan. Add brown sugar and 1 T. pineapple syrup. Add water to remaining syrup to make amount called for in cake mix directions. Arrange pineapple in bottom of pan. Prepare yellow cake mix according to pkg. directions. Pour cake mix over pineapple in pan. Bake in oven according to pkg. directions. Cool 5 to 10 minutes. Cover with foil wrap and invert onto a plate. Serve warm.

Teresa Conklin

Miss Jennie's Rum Cake

1 c. butter	8 egg whites, beaten stiff
2 c. granulated sugar	but not dry
1 c. milk, not too cold	3 1/2 t. baking powder
3 1/2 c. cake flour,	1 t. vanilla
sifted once before measuring	1 pinch salt

Cream the butter and add the sugar, a little at a time. Cream until fluffy. Add 1/3 each of the milk, flour and egg whites, in the order named, beating after each addition and beating well and long after the last addition. But mark this - keep out 2 T. flour, into which mix the baking powder and add this when all the beating is over, the pans greased and lined with paper and the batter is ready to go in the stove. At the very last, add the vanilla and salt. The beating should have special attention. Bake in 2 9" greased and paper-lined cake pans for 20 to 25 minutes at 350 degrees F. Turn out on racks and allow to cool before adding the filling.

Take 2 1/2 c. powdered sugar, 1/3 c. soft, creamed butter. Blend and beat until soft and smooth. Sifting the powdered sugar makes the blending lighter to work, too. Add 4 oz. rum. Mix well again. Put into refrigerator until firm enough to spread. The filling should be 1/2 to 3/4" thick. After the filling is spread on the cake and top layer placed in position, put the filled cake into the refrigerator until the filling is set and the top frosting is ready to cover all.

Cissy Gregg's Cook Book, vol. 1, p. 36,
The Courier Journal & Louisville Times Co., reprinted with permission

Spice Cake

1 c. seedless raisins	1 t. baking soda
1 c. water	1 t. cinnamon
1/2 c. salad oil	1 t. nutmeg
1 egg, beaten	1 t. allspice
1 c. sugar	1/2 t. ground cloves
1 3/4 c. flour	1/2 c. pecans, chopped
1/4 t. salt	

Bring to boil raisins and water in a pan large enough to hold whole recipe. Stir in oil. Cool. Combine egg and sugar. Add to raisin mixture. Combine remaining ingredients and mix well. Add to raisin-sugar mixture. Pour into well-buttered 9"x12" pans. Bake in preheated 375 degree F. oven for 25 minutes. Cool completely in the pan on a rack. Frost if you like. Leave in pan until ready to serve. Cut into 24 squares.

Bentley Farm Cookbook, p. 237

Stack Cake

4 c. flour	1 c. sorghum molasses
1 t. salt	3 eggs
1/2 t. soda	1 c. milk
2 t. baking powder	3 c. applesauce seasoned with
3/4 c. shortening	spices, cooked down to thicken
1 c. sugar	

Thoroughly mix flour, salt, soda and baking powder by sifting at least 3 times. Cream shortening, then add sugar a little at a time, blending well. Add sorghum and mix thoroughly. Add eggs, one at a time, beating after each addition. To this add flour and milk alternately and beat until smooth. Place mixture 3/8" deep in 9" greased and floured pans. Bake in a 375 degree F. oven for 18 minutes. This should make 6 layers. When cool, stack up layers using applesauce generously between each layer.

Cissy Gregg's Cook Book, vol. 1, p. 44,
The Courier Journal & Louisville Times Co., reprinted with permission

Old-Fashioned Stack Cake

1/2 c. sugar	2 t. baking powder
1/2 c. shortening	1/2 t. salt
1/2 c. buttermilk	1/2 t. soda
1 egg, well beaten	1 t. ginger
1/3 c. molasses	1 t. vanilla
3 1/2 c. flour	sweetened applesauce or
	dried apples, cooked

Cream sugar and shortening together. Add the egg, molasses and buttermilk. Mix well. Sift flour, baking powder, salt, soda and ginger together and add to the other mixture. Mix well. Add vanilla. It makes a dough. Roll out as for pastry. Cut to fit a 9" cake pan or heavy skillet. Bake at 350 degrees F. for 10 to 12 minutes. When cool, stack the layers with highly spiced and sweetened applesauce or, better still, old-fashioned dried apples, cooked, sweetened and spiced.

Cissy Gregg's Cook Book, vol. 1, p. 44,
The Courier Journal & Louisville Times Co., reprinted with permission

The Original Kentucky Whiskey Cake

1 lb. red candied cherries, cut in pieces or halves	1 lb. white sugar
	1 c. brown sugar
1/2 lb. golden raisins, cut in half or use 1/2 lb. dates, chopped	6 eggs, beaten separately
	5 c. flour, sifted before measuring
	2 t. nutmeg
1 pt. Kentucky bourbon whiskey	1 t. baking powder
3/4 lb. butter	1 lb. shelled pecans

Soak cherries and raisins in bourbon overnight. Cream butter and sugar until fluffy. Add egg yolks and beat well. Add soaked fruit, remaining liquid and the flour, reserving a small amount of flour for the nuts. Add to butter-sugar-egg yolk mixture. Add nutmeg and baking powder. Fold in beaten egg whites. Add the lightly floured pecans last. Bake in a large greased tube pan lined with greased paper for 3 to 4 hours in a slow 250 degrees F. oven. Watch baking time. To store when thoroughly cool, place in tightly covered container. Stuff center hole with cheesecloth soaked in bourbon whiskey. Wrap in heavy waxed paper. Keep very cool, in refrigerator if necessary.

Cissy Gregg's Cook Book, vol. 2, p. 26,
The Courier Journal & Louisville Times Co., reprinted with permission

Caramel Frosting

Cook together 2 c. brown sugar and 1 c. cream until the mixture reaches the soft ball stage. Beat until creamy. If the frosting gets too hard before you get it all on, beat in a little cream.

Cissy Gregg's Cook Book, vol. 1, p. 40,
The Courier Journal & Louisville Times Co., reprinted with permission

Caramel Frosting

1 small can evaporated milk	3 T. butter
1 lb. brown sugar	1 t. vanilla

Mix milk and sugar well. Bring to a boil and boil 3 minutes. Remove from heat. Add butter and vanilla. Beat until cool and of spreading consistency.

Speedwell Christian Church Cookbook, Bobbie Jones, p. 73

Mrs. Howard's Caramel Icing

10 T. brown sugar
8 T. cream
4 T. water

2 T. butter
confectioners' sugar

Combine ingredients in pan over high heat. Stir when it comes to a boil and boil hard 5 minutes. Let cool and add enough powdered sugar to thicken to right consistency to spread easily.

Bess Hamilton, my Grandmother

Mother's Caramel Icing

1 c. light or dark brown
   sugar, packed
2 T. butter, 3 T. Spry
   shortening, mixed well
   or all margarine

1/3 c. milk
2 c. confectioners' sugar, sifted

In a saucepan, mix brown sugar and butter/Spry mixture. Stir until it boils. Add milk. Boil 1 minute. Cool to lukewarm. Add confectioners' sugar. Cream and spread.

Aunt Nora gave Mother this recipe. It was on a Spry advertisement.

Simple Caramel Frosting

3/4 c. butter
1 1/2 c. brown sugar
1/4 c. plus 2 T. milk

3 c. powdered sugar
1 t. vanilla

Melt butter and add brown sugar. Add milk and bring to a boil. Turn off heat and let cool. Add powdered sugar and vanilla. Beat until creamy and smooth.

We Make You Kindly Welcome, p. 22

Maple Syrup Frosting

1 c. maple syrup
2 egg whites, unbeaten

1/4 t. salt
1/2 c. black walnuts, hickory nuts
or pecans, chopped

Cook maple syrup to 242 to 248 degrees F. on candy thermometer or until a firm ball forms when dropped into cold water. Pour syrup slowly into egg whites beating all the time. Add salt and beat until thick. Frost cake and sprinkle nuts on top of frosting. This icing does not set hard.

Welcome Back to Pleasant Hill, p. 60

Cookies & Candies

Applesauce Cookies

1 c. brown sugar, firmly packed	1 t. cinnamon
2/3 c. butter or margarine	1/2 t. nutmeg
2 eggs	1 c. applesauce
1 3/4 c. flour	1 c. rolled oats, quick cooking
1 1/2 t. baking powder	1 c. chocolate covered raisins, chocolate chips or nuts

Beat together brown sugar, butter and eggs until light and fluffy. Combine flour, baking powder, cinnamon and nutmeg. Stir into beaten mixture. Add applesauce, oats and nuts. Stir to combine. Drop by 1/4 cupfuls onto greased cookie sheets, flattening slightly with spatula and allowing for cookies to spread. Bake at 375 degrees F. for 12 to 15 minutes. Cool on wire racks. Makes 20 cookies.

Seneca Foods Corp.

Confection Bites

3/4 c. butter	1 T. milk
4 T. sugar	2 t. vanilla
2 c. flour	powdered sugar
1 c. nuts, chopped	

Cream butter and sugar. Work in flour and nut meats. Add milk, practically drop by drop. Add vanilla. Chill. Break and form into small rolls. Bake in 400 degree F. oven. When crisp, roll in powdered sugar.

Cissy Gregg's Cook Book, vol. 1, p. 21,
The Courier Journal & Louisville Times Co., reprinted with permission

Stuffed Date Drops

2 1 lb. boxes dates	1 egg
pecan halves for stuffing dates	1/4 c. flour
3/4 c. light brown sugar	1/2 t. soda
1/4 c. butter	1/2 c. sour cream

Stuff dates with nuts before starting. Cream sugar and butter. Beat in egg. Sift dry ingredients, then add sour cream. Fold in dates. Drop on greased cookie sheet one date at a time. Bake at 350 degrees F. for 8 to 10 minutes. Cool. Top with icing.

Frosting:

1/2 c. butter	3/4 t. vanilla
3 c. confectioners' sugar	3 T. water

Slightly brown butter and remove from heat. Slowly beat in sugar, vanilla and water to make spreading consistency.

Nancy Lee Ross

Gingerbread Cookies

1/2 c. butter or margarine, softened	4 1/2 c. all-purpose flour
3/4 c. brown sugar, firmly packed	2 t. baking soda
	2 t. ground cinnamon
1 egg	2 t. ground ginger
3/4 c. molasses	1/2 t. ground cloves
	1/2 t. ground nutmeg

Cream butter and sugar. Beat in egg and molasses. Mix flour, baking soda and spices. Stir in butter and sugar mixture. Dough should be stiff and smooth. Divide dough and chill at least 2 hours in refrigerator. Roll out 1/2 of dough onto well floured board to 1/8" thickness. Cut into desired shapes. Place on greased and lightly floured cookie sheets. Bake in preheated 350 degree F. oven for 8 to 10 minutes. Do not overbake. Cool on wire racks. Decorate as desired. Makes 4 doz.

Mary Ann Lane

Old-Fashioned Gingersnaps

1 c. sugar	1 c. sorghum
1 c. lard	1 egg
1 T. baking soda	1 T. ginger
4 c. flour	

Mix ingredients in order given. Roll into small balls. Roll balls in sugar. Place on baking sheets and bake at 350 degrees F. for 8 minutes. These cookies need to be stored for a week to develop their delicious flavor.

Hart-County Sorghum, Munfordville, Kentucky

Hermits

1/2 c. vegetable oil	1/2 t. nutmeg
3/4 c. brown sugar, firmly packed	1/2 t. baking soda
2 eggs	1/4 t. salt
2 T. milk	1/4 t. allspice
1 1/2 c. all-purpose flour	1/4 t. ground cloves
3/4 t. cinnamon	1 1/3 c. Muscat raisins, cut to pea size
	1/2 c. pecans, chopped

Preheat oven to 350 degrees F. Combine oil and brown sugar in large bowl at medium speed of electric mixer. Add eggs one at a time. Beat well after each addition. Mix in milk. Combine flour, cinnamon, nutmeg, baking soda, salt, allspice and cloves. Add slowly to creamed mixture. Stir in raisins and nuts. Grease a teaspoon, dip up a level spoon of batter and push with back of another greased teaspoon 2" apart onto well-oiled baking sheets. Bake 8 to 9 minutes or until a delicate brown. Transfer to cooling rack. Cool and store in airtight containers. These cookies freeze well and are better if they are aged several days before eating.

Florence Ross, my Mother

Hermits

1 c. butter, softened	1 lb. raisins, Muscats if possible.
1 1/2 c. dark brown sugar	If not, yellow raisins. They
1/2 c. sour milk or sour cream	remain softer and chewier
1/2 t. baking soda	after baking.
1 t. cinnamon	1 lb. or 1 c. nut pieces,
1 t. allspice	pecans are best
1 t. nutmeg	2 eggs
	3 c. flour, enough to make a
	stiff batter

Mix ingredients to make a stiff batter. Drop onto cookie sheet with spoon. Make the size of a medium egg. Bake in 375 degree oven for 15 to 20 minutes or until a delicate brown - do not overdo it - cookies should be fairly moist, soft and chewy.

Bess Hamilton, my Grandmother

Coconut Macaroons

1 1/3 c. (3 1/2 oz.)	2 T. flour or use 3 T. and
Baker's angel flake coconut	omit almonds
1/2 c. almonds, chopped	1/8 t. salt
1/3 c. sugar	2 egg whites
	1/2 t. almond extract

Heat oven to 325 degrees F. Mix coconut, almonds, sugar, flour and salt in large bowl. Stir in egg whites and almond extract until well blended. Drop by teaspoonfuls onto lightly greased cookie sheets. Bake 20 minutes or until edges of cookies are golden brown. Immediately remove from cookie sheets. Cool on wire racks. Note: Recipe can be doubled. Makes 1 1/2 doz.

Reprinted with permission of Kraft General Foods, Inc.

Melting Moments

1 c. flour	1 c. margarine or butter, softened
2 T. cornstarch	1 1/3 c. (3 1/2 oz.) Baker's
1/2 c. confectioners' sugar	angel flake coconut

Heat oven to 300 degrees F. Mix flour, cornstarch and sugar in small bowl. Cut in butter to form a soft dough. Cover and refrigerate, if necessary, until dough is firm enough to handle. Shape into 3/4" balls. Roll in coconut. Place 1 1/2" apart on ungreased cookie sheets. Flatten with lightly floured fork, if desired. Bake 20 to 25 minutes or until lightly browned. Makes 3 doz.

Reprinted with permission of Kraft General Foods, Inc.

Oatmeal Cookies

2 c. sugar	1/2 t. allspice
2/3 c. brown sugar	1/4 t. ground cloves
1 c. butter or margarine,	1/2 t. salt
softened	2 c. one minute oats
4 large eggs	1 c. pecans, chopped
4 c. flour	1 1/2 c. raisins
1 t. cinnamon	2 t. vanilla

Gradually mix sugar with shortening. Beat eggs one at a time and gradually mix into sugar mixture. Add flour mixed with spices, oats, pecans and raisins. Add vanilla. Mix well and drop by spoonfuls onto greased cookie sheet. Bake at 350 degrees for 10 to 12 minutes until brown.

Verna Ross Bellamy

Peanut Butter Cookies

1/4 c. shortening	1 egg
1/4 c. butter, softened	1 1/4 c. all-purpose flour, sifted
1/2 c. peanut butter	1/2 t. baking powder
1/2 c. sugar	3/4 t. soda
1/2 c. brown sugar	1/4 t. salt

Combine shortening and butter. Add peanut butter, sugar, brown sugar and egg. Mix together thoroughly. Sift together flour, baking powder, soda and salt. Stir into peanut butter/sugar mixture. Chill dough. Roll into balls the size of a large walnut. Place 3" apart on lightly greased baking sheet. Flatten with fork dipped in flour. Crisscross. Bake at 375 degrees F. for 10 to 12 minutes until set, but not hard.

Betty Crocker's Picture Cook Book, p. 204

Pecan Cookies from the Green Tree

1 1/2 c. butter	1 1/2 c. flour
1 1/2 c. brown sugar	pinch of nutmeg
3 eggs	1 1/2 c. pecans

Cream butter and sugar. Add eggs, flour, nutmeg and pecans. Drop on greased pans. Bake at 350 degrees F. The Green Tree Shop was a Lexington, Kentucky tearoom.

Out of the Kitchen into the House, p. 32

Sand Tarts

2 c. butter	1 egg white, slightly beaten
2 1/2 c. sugar	1/2 c. confectioners' sugar
2 eggs, well beaten	2 t. ground cinnamon
4 c. flour, sifted	pecan halves

Cream butter until soft. Slowly add sugar. Cream until fluffy. Add eggs in thirds. Beat well after each addition. Add flour in fourths, beating after each addition. Fold in egg white. Chill dough overnight. Combine confectioners' sugar and cinnamon. Use a small amount of dough at a time. Roll out 1/16" thick on a lightly floured surface. Cut out cookies or roll into balls and place on cookie sheet. Dust with sugar/cinnamon mixture and press a pecan half on each cookie. Bake at 350 degrees F. for 9 minutes. Makes 17 1/2 doz.

Elizabeth Ross

Sand Tarts

2 c. butter or margarine
1/4 c. confectioners' sugar
4 t. vanilla extract
2 T. water

4 c. flour, sifted
2 c. pecans, chopped
confectioners' sugar

Cream butter and sugar. Add vanilla and stir in water and flour. Blend well. Fold in pecans. Form into 1 1/2" balls. Place on ungreased baking sheet and bake at 300 degrees F. for 20 minutes. Remove from oven and dust with confectioners' sugar while hot.

Recipes from Miss Daisy's, p. 122

Mexican Wedding Cookies

1/2 c. margarine
1/2 c. solid shortening
1 t. vanilla

2 c. flour
6 T. powdered sugar
1 c. pecans, chopped

Cream margarine and shortening. Add vanilla. Stir in flour and sugar. Add pecans. Refrigerate. Roll into small balls. Bake on ungreased cookie sheet at 400 degrees F. for 10 to 12 minutes. While warm, roll in powdered sugar.

Cookbook of Treasures, Mary Unterecker, p. 107

Jennie Benedict's Lemon Wafers

1 stick butter
1/2 c. sugar
2 eggs

1 c. plus 2 T. flour
1 T. lemon flavoring

Cream butter and sugar together until light and fluffy. Add well-beaten eggs and beat until the creamed butter, sugar and eggs are well mixed and the mass is fluffy. Add sifted flour and beat until smooth. Add flavoring. Drop batter from a t. on greased cookie sheet, keeping the cookies at least 2" apart for spreading. Bake in a moderate 350 degree F. oven for 7 minutes or until lightly browned around the edges and done in the middle. Serve with eggnog. Makes 5 doz.

Cissy Gregg's Cook Book, vol. 1, p. 21,
The Courier Journal & Louisville Times Co., reprinted with permission

Bourbon Balls

To 1 c. of vanilla wafer crumbs (vanilla wafers rolled fine), add 1 c. chopped pecans, 1 c. powdered sugar, 2 T. cocoa. To 2 jiggers (1/4 c.) of bourbon whiskey add 1 1/2 c. white corn syrup. Mix whiskey and corn syrup with crumbs, nuts and cocoa. Form into small balls and roll in powdered sugar. Keep cool until ready to serve.

Cissy Gregg's Cook Book, vol. 1, p. 36,
The Courier Journal & Louisville Times Co., reprinted with permission

Bourbon Balls

1 lb. confectioners' sugar	pecan halves
1 T. butter, softened	1 12 oz. pkg. semi-sweet
1/4 t. salt	chocolate bits
1 t. vanilla	1/2 block paraffin
bourbon whiskey	

Mix the first 4 ingredients, adding enough bourbon to make a base as thick as dough. Roll into balls and place 1/2 pecan on the top of each ball. Place on waxed paper to harden. Melt together over a double boiler the chocolate bits and 1/2 block paraffin. Using a toothpick, dip balls in chocolate and place on waxed paper.

Cookbook of Treasures, p. 121

Bourbon Balls

3 c. vanilla wafers	3 T. light corn syrup
1 c. pecans	1 1/2 T. cocoa, optional
1 c. confectioners' sugar	1/2 c. bourbon

Grind wafers and nuts fine in food chopper. Mix with other ingredients thoroughly. Roll into balls the size of large cherries. Dust with confectioners' sugar. Makes 30 to 35 balls.

Florence Ross, my Mother

Kentucky Bourbon Balls

2 T. cocoa	2 T. corn syrup
1 c. powdered sugar	1 c. vanilla wafer crumbs
1/3 c. bourbon	1 c. pecans, crushed

Mix together all ingredients. Make into small balls and roll in additional powdered sugar. Let sit in a cool place in a tin before serving. Makes 80 balls.

The Crowning Recipes of Kentucky, p. 230

Kentucky Bourbon Balls

1 c. vanilla wafers, ground	2 T. white corn syrup
1 c. powdered sugar	1/4 c. whiskey, more if desired
1 c. nuts, chopped	

Mix ingredients and roll into small balls. Cover with powdered sugar. Store in covered container.

A Taste from Back Home, p. 198

Kentucky Bourbon Balls

1/2 c. butter	pecan halves
3 1/2 to 4 c. powdered sugar	4 squares semi-sweet chocolate
4 T. bourbon, or less	1/4 bar paraffin

Cream butter. Add sugar gradually. Beat well. Slowly add bourbon, blending well. Chill 1 hour or more. Roll in 1" balls and place on waxed paper. Lightly press a pecan half on top of each ball. Chill for 1 hour or more. In top of double boiler melt chocolate and paraffin. Stir to blend. With a fork, dip each ball into chocolate mixture and place on waxed paper. Chill. Store in tins in refrigerator. Note: Strength of bourbon flavoring depends on proof and taste. If creamed mixture seems too sticky to handle, beat in a little more powdered sugar.

Welcome Back to Pleasant Hill, p. 63

Kentucky Colonel Bourbon Balls

1 c. pecans, finely chopped
2/3 c. bourbon
1 stick butter or margarine

2 lbs. confectioners' sugar
6 squares bitter chocolate
1 square paraffin, about 1"

Let nuts stand in bourbon overnight. Work butter and sugar together until mixture is in fine crumbs like meal. Add bourbon, a little at a time. Work in pecans. Form into balls about the size of large marbles and chill in refrigerator on a cookie sheet until crusty, 1 hour. Put bitter chocolate and paraffin in top of double boiler and melt over hot water. Do not let water boil. Dip balls in chocolate. Put on waxed paper to cool. Store in refrigerator. Note: This mixture will be very sticky and hard to form into balls. It is easier if you keep your hands cold by running water over them. Use only bonded bourbon, any proof. Do not use a blended whiskey. Makes 90 balls.

The Cincinnati Cookbook, Mrs. George H. Hills, p. 267

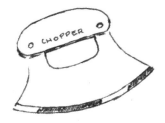

Kentucky Colonels Bourbon Balls

1 lb. confectioners' sugar
1 T. butter, softened
1/4 t. salt
1 t. vanilla

bourbon whiskey
pecan halves
1 pkg. semi-sweet chocolate

Mix first four ingredients. Add enough bourbon to make a batter resembling biscuit dough. Roll in palms of hands to balls the size you want. Place a pecan half on top of each ball. Place candies on waxed paper. Refrigerate 30 minutes. Meanwhile, melt chocolate in double boiler over hot water. Dip each chilled ball in melted chocolate. Place on waxed paper to dry. 3 lbs. confectioners sugar and 1 pt. of bourbon makes 150 pieces.

Favorite Recipes, Mrs. Robert D. Lackey, p. 118

Bourbon Candy

1 box confectioners' sugar, sifted	pecan halves
5 T. margarine	3 cakes bitter chocolate
1/4 to 1/3 c. bourbon	3 cakes semi-sweet chocolate
	5 T. paraffin

Knead sugar, margarine and bourbon and roll into balls. Add a nut to each ball. Cool. Melt chocolates and paraffin over hot water, not boiling. Use a fork or toothpick to dip the balls into the chocolate mixture and place on waxed paper to cool.

Best of the Best from Kentucky, Best Made Better Recipes, vol. II, p. 229

Kentucky Bourbon Candy

2 c. nuts	1 c. butter
1/2 to 3/4 c. bourbon	3 large boxes semi-sweet chocolate
4 lbs. powdered sugar	1 T. paraffin to a box of chocolate
1/2 c. Eagle Brand milk	

Chop nuts and add to bourbon and let soak for several hours. Mix sugar, milk, butter, bourbon and nuts and form into balls. Melt chocolate and paraffin and dip balls in the mixture. Put on waxed paper until set. Makes 5 lbs.

A Taste from Back Home, p. 198

Caramels

2 c. sugar	1/2 t. salt
1 c. light corn syrup	1/2 t. vanilla
2 c. heavy cream, warmed and divided	1/2 to 1 c. pecans, chopped

In large heavy saucepan, mix sugar, syrup and 1 c. of cream. Cook 10 minutes, stirring thoroughly to dissolve sugar before it comes to a strong boil. Insert candy thermometer. Thereafter, stir only when necessary to prevent scorching. Add the other c. of cream slowly so as not to stop cooking. When candy reaches 230 degrees F., cook more slowly to 244 degrees F. Remove from heat, add salt and vanilla, stirring only enough to blend flavors. Add chopped pecans and pour in oiled 8"x8" pan. Cool. Refrigerate until hard. Cut into small squares and wrap in waxed paper. Store in tins in refrigerator. This will be difficult to remove from pan so lift each corner and remove entire square, then cut into smaller squares on a cutting board. Makes 2 1/2 doz.

Kentucky Derby Museum Cookbook, p. 247

Coconut Balls

2 egg whites	1 c. shredded coconut
1/2 c. granulated sugar	1 t. vanilla extract
1 c. dates, snipped	1/2 t. almond extract
1 c. walnuts, chopped	1/3 c. maraschino cherries, finely chopped

Preheat oven to 300 degrees F. Beat egg whites until stiff. Gradually beat in sugar. Fold in dates, nuts, coconut and extracts. Mix well. Spread in ungreased 8"x8"x2" pan. Bake 20 minutes. Remove mixture from oven and turn into a bowl. Add cherries. Let mixture cool until it can be handled. Form into balls. Roll each one in granulated sugar. I prefer powdered sugar.

Florence Ross, my Mother

Cream Candy

3 pts. sugar	1 t. salt
3 T. thick cream	butter, size of a walnut
3 T. vinegar	1 pt. boiling water

Add first 5 ingredients to the boiling water. Stir well. Pour into a heavy aluminum saucepan. Boil until a ball tested in cold water cracks against the cup. Candy should not be stirred so reduce heat as soon as it begins to boil to prevent burning. As soon as mixture reaches hard ball stage, pour it onto a buttered marble slab or enamel table top. Do not scrape the pan. Allow it to cool until it can be handled. Butter the hands and pull candy until it is too stiff to pull any more. Twist candy into a slender rope 1" thick. Cut into 1 1/2" long pieces with a scissors. It will be chewy at first but will cream in a few hours. Wrap each piece in waxed paper and store in tightly closed container.

Favorite Recipes, Mrs. Richard Cobb, Jr. p, 118

Cream Candy

3 c. white sugar	1 T. butter
1 c. boiling water	1/8 t. soda
1 c. whipping cream	1/2 t. salt

Cook ingredients, without stirring, slowly until a spoonful will crack real hard when put in cold water or cook by candy thermometer to 250 degrees F. Pour out on marble slab or greased cabinet top. When cool enough, pull out into a rope and cut into pieces. Individual pieces must be wrapped in plastic wrap and stored in metal containers.

Valeria Ross

Cream Pull Candy

3 c. white sugar	1 c. thick cream
1/2 T. salt	2/3 c. boiling water
1/4 t. soda	1 t. vanilla

Mix sugar, salt and soda with cream, then add boiling water and stir until it begins to boil. Don't stir any more. Boil to 255 degrees F. Add vanilla and pour on large slab or large meat dishes. When cool, pull until it is a dull color. Cut with scissors. Let cool in box, not crowded. It takes about 24 hours before it creams.

Cookbook of Treasures, Mrs. Richard Cobb, Jr., p. 122

Cream Pull Candy

3 pts. granulated sugar	1/4 t. baking soda
boiling water,	1 pt. cream
enough to dissolve sugar	1/4 lb. butter
1 t. salt	1 t. vanilla

Put sugar in a kettle. Add water to dissolve sugar, then while boiling good, add salt, soda and cream 1 T. at a time. Add butter a little at a time. Do not allow candy to stop boiling while doing this. When done, candy will crack against glass when cooled in water. Remove from fire and pour on greased marble slab. When cold, pull 30 minutes. When pulling, add vanilla.

Courtesy of the Ruth Hunt Candy Co., Mt. Sterling, Kentucky

Cream Pull Candy

1 c. water	1 c. cream
3 c. white sugar	1/4 t. soda
1/2 t. salt	butter, size of an egg

Place 1 c. water in deep kettle. Bring to a boil and add sugar and salt. Cook until mixture will spin a thread. Add cream with soda dissolved in it, slowly. Add butter. Bring to a hard boil, cooking until it forms a hard ball in cold water. Pour on marble slab and cool. Pull until it holds its shape. Cut with scissors and place in tin.

Sharing Our Best, Mary Searly, p. 152

Kentucky Pull Candy

3 c. sugar	1 t. salt
4 T. thick cream	1 T. butter
1 t. vinegar	1 c. boiling water

Stir all ingredients together until dissolved. Put on the fire and cover. Cook until it reaches a boil. Remove the cover and cook, without stirring, until hard and glassy. Flavor to taste with lemon or vanilla. Pour on a cold platter and when cool enough to handle, pull until white and firm. Cut with greased scissors in sticks of the desired length. May be colored a delicate pink with a drop of food coloring if desired.

Kirksville Historical Cookbook, Mrs. Earle B. Combs, Sr., p. 36

Fondant

2 c. sugar	1/2 c. water
1/8 t. cream of tartar	

Combine sugar and cream of tartar. Add water. Stir until sugar dissolves. Cover and boil 5 minutes. Uncover. Boil without stirring to 234 to 238 degrees F. or soft ball stage. Wipe all crystals from sides of pan with a damp cloth. Pour into a shallow pan. Cool to room temperature. Beat only until stiff enough to knead. Knead until smooth. Place in a bowl. Cover with waxed paper. Allow to ripen for 24 hours before using. Tint, flavor or shape into pieces. This candy may be used to stuff dates or figs. Roll in confectioners' sugar.

The Household Searchlight Recipe Book, p. 71

Smith College Fudge

1 c. sugar	1/2 c. light cream
1 c. brown sugar, firmly packed	2 squares (2 oz.) unsweetened chocolate
1/4 c. molasses	1/4 c. butter
	1 1/2 t. vanilla

Combine the sugars, molasses, cream and coarsely chopped chocolate in a saucepan. Stir until sugar and chocolate have melted over moderate heat. Cook until mixture reaches 238 degrees F. Do not stir. Remove from heat. Stir in butter and vanilla. Cool slightly. Beat until candy begins to harden. Pour onto well-buttered platter. Cut into squares. Makes 1 1/4 lbs.

Phoebe Ann Hammond, Class of 1947

Tom's Fabulous Fudge

3 c. sugar	3 T. Karo syrup, light
4 T. cocoa	1 1/2 t. vanilla extract
5 to 6 T. butter	1 12 oz. can evaporated milk

Sift together dry ingredients into cooking pan. Melt butter and add Karo syrup and vanilla extract, mix well. Pour evaporated milk into mixing bowl and add the butter mixture, mixing well. Pour into the dry ingredients. Stir until well blended. Cook at medium to medium-high heat, stirring constantly, for 15 to 20 minutes after it starts to boil or until the mixture forms a firm ball in a c. of cool water. Do not overcook. Fill a sink with 3 to 4" of cool water. Place pan in the water and beat the mixture until it loses its glossiness, about 10 to 15 minutes. Quickly pour the mixture into a buttered dish, 8"x10", and allow to cool before cutting. After cooling, cut into pieces and place in an airtight container. Some prefer to store in refrigerator.

Tom Raybourn, his Grandmother's recipe.

Hard Candy

2 c. sugar	1/2 c. corn syrup
1 c. water	1/2 t. each of flavoring and coloring

Mix the sugar, water and corn syrup. Boil on high heat to 300 or 310 degrees F. or until mixture is ready to burn. Add flavoring and coloring. Stir. Pour onto buttered platter. Cut into pieces with scissors. Toss lightly with powdered sugar.

Source unknown

Peanut Brittle

2 c. sugar	1 T. butter
1 c. light corn syrup	1 t. vanilla
1/2 c. water	2 t. baking soda
2 c. peanuts	

Use a heavy skillet. Combine sugar, syrup and water. Cook over low heat until mixture reaches 230 degrees F. on candy thermometer. Stir in peanuts. Continue cooking to 300 degrees F. Remove from heat. Stir in remaining ingredients. Pour onto a greased platter. Spread as thin as possible. Cool until hard. Break into pieces. Old time candy makers, using doeskin gloves to protect their hands, were able to flip sheet of candy over during cooling so peanuts stood out on both sides.

Mary Ann Lane

Peanut Butter Fudge

1 c. brown sugar	1 T. vinegar
1 c. white sugar	1/2 c. peanut butter
1/2 c. milk	7 marshmallows, finely cut
2 T. corn syrup	1 t. vanilla

Boil brown sugar, white sugar, milk, corn syrup and vinegar until soft ball forms in cold water. Remove from heat and cool. Add peanut butter and marshmallows. Add vanilla. Beat until creamy. Turn into a greased pan and cut into squares.

Food for My Household, Mrs. Billy Cosby, p. 102

Peanut Butter Fudge

2 c. granulated sugar	1 c. chunk-style peanut butter
2/3 c. milk	1 6 oz. (1 c.) pkg. semi-sweet
1/2 pt. marshmallow creme	chocolate
	1 t. vanilla

Butter sides of heavy 2 qt. pan. Combine sugar and milk in it. Stir over medium heat until sugar dissolves and mixture boils. Cook to soft ball stage, 234 degrees F. Remove from heat and quickly add marshmallow creme, peanut butter, chocolate and vanilla. Stir until blended. Pour into buttered 9"x9"x2" pan.

Nancy Lee Ross

Modjeskas

1 batch of basic caramel without nuts	36 to 40 marshmallows

Pour the caramel, as soon as it has been flavored and stirred, onto an oiled marble slab. Cut the marshmallows in half with wet scissors. When the caramel has cooled slightly, use a spatula to pick up a small sheet of caramel and wrap around each marshmallow half, molding with oiled fingers to cover each. Wrap each candy separately in waxed paper. Store tightly in tin boxes. This method gets lots of caramel on each candy.

Kentucky Derby Museum Cookbook, p. 244

Modjeskas

2 c. sugar	1 t. vanilla
1 c. white corn syrup	1/2 t. salt
2 c. heavy cream	36 to 40 large marshmallows

In heavy saucepan, mix sugar, syrup and 1 c. of the cream. Cook about 10 minutes, stirring until sugar is dissolved. Add the other c. of cream slowly and stir just enough to prevent scorching. Cook over high heat until thermometer reaches 230 degrees F. Reduce heat and cook to 244 degrees F. on thermometer. Remove from heat and add vanilla and salt. Beat until smooth and cool. Cut marshmallows in half and dip in caramel until well coated. When completely cooled, wrap each piece in waxed paper.

A Taste from Back Home, p. 203

Creamy Pralines

2 c. sugar
1 small can milk
1/2 c. white corn syrup
1/4 t. baking soda

1/2 stick butter
1 t. vanilla
2 c. pecans

Mix sugar, milk, syrup and baking soda and cook in double boiler. Stir frequently and cook to soft ball stage. Remove from heat at this point and add butter and vanilla and beat with spoon until shine has gone and it is cool. Add the pecans and drop on waxed paper.

A Taste from Back Home, p. 207

Desserts

Banana Nut Bread

1 c. sugar
1/2 c. shortening
2 eggs, beaten
2 c. all-purpose flour
1 t. baking soda

1/4 t. salt
1 t. vanilla
3 ripe bananas, mashed
1 c. pecans, chopped

Cream sugar and shortening. Add eggs and combine well. Add 1 c. flour and beat well. Add 1 c. flour mixed with soda and salt. Add vanilla and bananas and combine well. Add nuts last and mix well. Pour into a greased and floured loaf pan. Bake at 350 degrees F. for 60 minutes or until straw comes out clean when used as a tester. Let cool slightly and turn out onto wire rack to cool completely.

The Hillforest Sampler, Margaret Pitts, p. 36

Old-Fashioned Date and Nut Bread

2 1/2 c. all-purpose flour
1 t. salt
1 t. soda
1 c. nutmeat halves
1/4 c. shortening

2 T. vinegar
1 1/2 c. boiling water
1 c. pitted dates, cut in half
1 egg, beaten
1 1/2 c. brown sugar

Sift together flour, salt and soda. Mix in nutmeat halves. Add shortening and combined vinegar and boiling water to make 1 1/2 c. Pour over dates and let stand 10 minutes. Combine eggs and brown sugar. Add dry ingredients to egg mixture with dates and liquid mixture. Turn into greased 9 1/2"x5"x3" pan. Bake at 350 degrees F. for 1 hour and 15 minutes. Makes one 9 1/2"x5"x3" loaf.

Food for My Household, Lillian Earnest, p. 61

Date Nut Bread

1 c. brown sugar
1 lb. dates, chopped
1 T. butter
1 c. nuts
1 c. boiling water

2 c. flour
1/2 t. baking powder
1/2 t. salt
1 t. soda
1 egg

Mix sugar, dates, butter and nuts. Pour boiling water over mixture. Sift flour, baking powder, salt and soda together. Add well-beaten egg last. Bake in greased loaf pan 1 hour at 350 degrees F. Makes 1 loaf.

Cookbook of Treasures, Jane Cobb, p. 68

deSha's Date Nut Bread

2 t. baking soda	2 t. vanilla
2 c. boiling water	2 eggs
2 c. dates, chopped	2 2/3 c. flour
6 T. butter	1 c. pecans, chopped
2 c. sugar	

Mix soda and boiling water. Pour over dates and set aside. Cream butter and sugar, beat in vanilla and eggs, then flour. Fold in date mixture and pecans. Pour into greased and floured loaf pan and bake at 350 degrees F. for 45 to 50 minutes. Cool in pan.

Dining in Historic Kentucky, vol. 2, p. 47

Lemon Bread

1 c. butter or margarine	1 1/4 c. milk
2 c. sugar	1 c. nuts, finely chopped
4 eggs, separated	lemon peel from 2 lemons, grated
3 1/4 c. flour	fresh lemon juice from 2 lemons
2 t. baking powder	1/2 c. sugar
1 t. salt	

Cream butter. Gradually add sugar, creaming well. Add egg yolks and beat well. Blend together the dry ingredients and add to egg yolk mixture alternately with milk. Blend just to mix. Fold in stiffly beaten egg whites, chopped nuts and lemon peel. Turn into 3 greased and lightly floured 8 1/2"x4 1/2"x2 1/2" loaf pans. Bake at 350 degrees F. for 55 to 60 minutes or until wooden pick inserted in center comes out clean. Combine lemon juice and remaining 1/2 c. sugar. Prick all over top of loaves with wooden pick. Immediately spoon lemon juice mixture over hot loaves. Cool 1 hour before removing from pans. Do not cut for 24 hours so it will slice easily. Makes 3 loaves.

Miriam B. Loo's Family Favorites Cookbook, p. 77

Gingerbread

1 c. sorghum molasses	1/4 t. allspice
1/2 c. sugar	1/2 t. salt
1/2 c. fat, melted	2 1/2 c. plain flour
1 egg	1 1/2 t. soda
1 t. ginger	1 c. boiling water
1/2 t. cloves	

Mix together molasses, sugar, melted fat and well-beaten egg. Add spices and salt to sifted flour. Sift again into molasses mixture. Stir until flour is just dampened. Quickly mix the soda and hot water. Pour into mixture. Beat until smooth. Pour into a shallow pan or 2, 9" cake pans. Bake in moderate 350 degree F. oven for 35 minutes.

Speedwell Christian Church Cookbook, Myrtle Lakes, p. 46

Little Colonel's Christmas Crullers

1 c. butter, softened but not melted	rind of 2 lemons, grated or 1 t. vanilla
2 c. granulated sugar	6 c. flour, measured after sifting
6 egg yolks	6 egg whites
2 whole nutmegs, grated	powdered sugar for dusting

Cream butter and sugar. Slowly add the egg yolks, grated nutmegs, grated lemon rind or vanilla. Stir the butter-egg mixture into flour. Fold in the well-beaten whites. The dough is soft but can be handled. If too soft, put in a covered bowl in the refrigerator for several hours before using. Roll small amounts at a time, although more flour may have to be added. The cruller dough should be rolled thin, 1/4" thick. Cut into strips 1" wide by 6" long. Use a knife or a pastry wheel. Fold these strips in half and twist together. Fry until golden brown in deep hot melted lard or vegetable shortening, heated to 375 degrees F. As soon as the crullers are golden brown, lift out of the fat with a skimmer and drain on absorbent paper. Dust heavily with powdered sugar. These crullers, also called "raggedy britches," keep fresh for a long time and are good served with eggnog, hot chocolate or coffee. Makes 6 1/2 doz.

Out of Kentucky Kitchens, p. 206

Boiled Custard

3 c. milk, scalded	4 eggs, well beaten
1 c. sugar	1 c. whipping cream, unwhipped

Use a heavy saucepan. When the milk has reached the scalding point, remove from heat. Stir in sugar and eggs, then the whipping cream. Return to heat and cook, stirring constantly, until the mixture coats a wooden spoon. This is often served with fresh coconut cake.

My Old Kentucky Homes Cookbook, p. 29

Kentucky Kisses

4 egg whites	1 2/3 c. granulated sugar
few grains of salt	1 t. vanilla
1/4 t. cream of tartar	3 squares semi-sweet chocolate, grated

Combine egg whites, salt and cream of tartar in a mixing bowl of electric beater. With electric mixer on high speed, beat for 5 minutes, then add 1 c. of the sugar gradually. This will take another 5 minutes. Fold in the remaining 2/3 c. sugar, vanilla and the grated chocolate. Drop by teaspoonfuls onto brown paper. Bake in very slow 200 degree F. oven for 15 minutes. If they turn from white to tan, they are cooking too fast.

Cissy Gregg's Cook Book, vol. 2, p. 23,
The Courier Journal & Louisville Times Co., reprinted with permission

Mint Julep Kisses

2 egg whites	2 drops green vegetable coloring
3/4 c. sugar	6 oz. chocolate bits
1/2 t. peppermint extract	

Preheat oven to 325 degrees F. Beat egg whites until stiff, gradually adding sugar. Add peppermint and green coloring. Stir in chocolate bits. Drop by spoonfuls on cookie sheet. Put in preheated oven and turn off immediately. Leave in oven overnight or for several hours. Store in tin box. Makes 2 doz.

The Kentucky Derby Museum Cookbook, p. 237

Meringues (Egg Kisses)

6 egg whites
1/8 t. salt
2 c. granulated sugar

1 t. vinegar
1 t. vanilla extract

Let egg whites stand at room temperature for 1 hour. Add salt to egg whites. With electric mixer on high speed, beat egg whites until they hold their shape. At low speed, add sugar 2 T. at a time, beating 2 minutes each time. This should take 30 minutes altogether. Preheat oven to 275 degrees F. Add vinegar and vanilla. At high speed, beat 10 minutes longer. Drop by heaping T. onto buttered cookie sheet. Bake 45 minutes. Reduce heat to 250 degrees F. and bake another 15 minutes. Cool on rack. Store in layers with waxed paper in between.

Note: Mother made a "well" in the meringues before baking for fruit, ice cream, etc.

Florence Ross, my Mother; Millie Beacham

Meringues

1 t. vinegar
1/2 t. cream of tartar
4 egg whites

1 1/2 c. white sugar
powdered sugar

Preheat oven to 275 degrees F. Mix vinegar and cream of tartar into the egg whites and beat the whites until stiff. Gradually add the sugar, beating. Put a brown paper sack on a baking sheet (make sure there is no writing on the sack) and sprinkle with powdered sugar. Drop the meringue batter by spoonfuls onto the paper. Bake for 45 minutes. Makes 1 doz. depending on the size of the spoonfuls.

Thelma's Treasures, p. 106

Pots De Creme

1 6 oz. pkg. chocolate chips
2 T. sugar
pinch of salt
1 egg

1 t. vanilla
2 t. dark rum or 1 t. instant coffee
3/4 c. milk
whipped cream

Place first 6 ingredients in blender. Blend briefly. Heat milk to boiling. Add to blender, cover and blend 1 minute. Pour in Pots De Creme cups, demitasse, or sherbet glasses. Chill several hours. Top with whipped cream. Serves 4.

Source unknown

Banana Pudding

3/4 c. sugar
1/3 c. all-purpose flour
dash of salt
4 eggs, separated at
   room temperature
2 c. milk

1/2 t. vanilla
35 to 45 vanilla wafers
5 to 6 medium fully ripe bananas,
   sliced
reserve 1 banana and 10 to 12
   wafers for topping

Mix sugar and flour in a bowl. Add salt. Beat egg yolks, add milk and mix with flour mixture. Cook in microwave oven on high 3 minutes. Stop and stir. When it starts to thicken, stop and stir every 30 seconds. Total cooking time is 10 minutes or until desired thickness. Add vanilla and a few drops of yellow food coloring if desired. Pour mixture into 1 1/2 qt. glass baking dish. Cover with layers of vanilla wafers and sliced bananas. Top with meringue.

Fountain Favorites, p. 83

Science Hill Inn Bread Pudding

3 T. (3/8 stick) butter, melted
8 slices homemade bread
4 c. milk
1 1/2 c. sugar

4 large eggs
1/3 c. golden raisins
bourbon sauce, see below, optional

Preheat oven to 350 degrees F. Pour melted butter into 12"x8"x2" baking pan. Tear bread into small pieces and place in large mixing bowl. Add milk and soak 5 minutes. Combine sugar, eggs and raisins and mix well with bread and milk. Pour into prepared pan and bake 1 hour. If desired, serve with bourbon sauce.

   Bourbon sauce:

1/2 c. (1 stick) butter
1 c. sugar
1/4 c. water

1 egg, beaten
1/3 c. bourbon whiskey

Melt butter in small saucepan over medium heat. Add sugar and water and cook, stirring constantly, 2 minutes. Gradually add butter and sugar to egg, beating constantly. Slowly stir in bourbon. Makes 6 to 8 servings.

Science Hill Inn, Shelbyville, Kentucky

Woodford Pudding

This pudding has been made by cooks in Woodford County in the Bluegrass region of central Kentucky since the Civil War or before. It is closely related to an old English jam pudding.

1/2 c. butter or margarine	1/2 c. sour milk
1 c. sugar	1 c. flour
3 eggs, slightly beaten	1 t. cinnamon
1 t. soda	1 c. blackberry jam

Cream the butter or margarine with the sugar until light. Add the slightly beaten eggs and mix well. Dissolve the soda in the sour milk. Add the flour which as been sifted, measured and sifted with the cinnamon to the sugar-egg mixture along with the soda and sour milk mixture. Blend in the jam. Bake in a greased, shallow baking dish, 7 1/2"x12", for 40 minutes in a 325 degree F. oven. Cut in squares and serve with a brown sugar butterscotch sauce.

Cissy Gregg's Cook Book, vol. 1, p. 33,
The Courier Journal & Louisville Times Co., reprinted with permission

Woodford Pudding

1/2 c. butter or margarine, softened	2 t. baking powder
	1 t. cinnamon
1 c. sugar	1/2 t. nutmeg
3 egg yolks	1/4 t. cloves
1 1/2 c. blackberry jam	1 c. milk
1 c. flour	3 egg whites, well beaten

Cream the butter or margarine with the sugar. Add egg yolks and blackberry jam. Sift flour with baking powder and spices. Add the milk and the butter mixture alternately to the flour mixture. Fold in the well-beaten egg whites. Pour into a greased mold or Pyrex dish and bake in a moderate 375 degree F. oven until pudding sets, 30 to 45 minutes. Serve hot with pudding sauce. Makes 6 servings.

Out of Kentucky Kitchens, p. 194

Woodford Pudding

1 c. all-purpose flour, sifted	1 egg
1/2 t. soda	1/2 c. sugar
1/4 t. salt	1/2 c. thick blackberry jam
1/2 t. cinnamon	1/4 c. (1/2 stick) butter or
1/2 t. nutmeg	margarine, melted
1/8 t. ground cloves	1/2 c. buttermilk

Grease a 5 1/2"x9"x1 1/2" baking dish. Preheat oven to 350 degrees F. Sift flour once. Measure and sift with soda, salt, cinnamon, nutmeg and cloves onto waxed paper. In medium sized mixing bowl, beat egg until light and fluffy. Beat in sugar. Add blackberry jam and beat vigorously to blend. With a spoon, stir in melted butter or margarine, then the sifted dry ingredients alternately with the buttermilk. (Stick to buttermilk in the recipe - it gives better flavor and has a thicker consistency than when you stir vinegar or lemon juice into milk.) Beat to mix well. Pour into prepared baking dish - batter should be 1/2" deep. Bake until wooden pick inserted into center comes out clean - about 30 minutes.

Lemon custard filling:

1 c. milk	juice of 1 lemon and rind, grated
1/2 c. sugar	2 egg yolks
2 T. flour	1 T. butter
1/4 t. salt	

Heat milk in double boiler over boiling water. Mix sugar, flour and salt and stir into milk. Cook, stirring frequently, over boiling water until mixture is thickened and smooth. Grate lemon rind into egg yolks. Add lemon juice and beat well. Add 1/4 c. of hot mixture to yolks. Beat smooth, then stir egg yolk mixture into rest of hot mixture and cook and stir over boiling water until thickened a bit more - just a couple of minutes. Remove from hot water. Add butter and cool. One hour before serving, spread cooled lemon filling over baked pudding. Top with meringue.

Meringue:

Add 1/4 t. each of salt and cream of tartar to 2 egg whites. Beat until whites begin to form soft mounds. Gradually beat in 1/3 c. sugar and continue beating for 2 to 3 minutes after sugar has been added. Meringue should be stiff and glossy. Spread over lemon filling making attractive peaks with the tip of a spoon. Bake in a preheated hot oven, 425 degrees F., until lightly browned, 3 to 5 minutes.

Fern Storer

Woodford Pudding

1/2 c. butter	1 c. sugar
1 c. flour	1 c. blackberry jam
1 t. soda	1/2 c. sour milk
1 full t. cinnamon	3 eggs

Mix all ingredients together well. Bake in pudding dish at 375 degrees F. for 40 minutes or until lightly firm.

Note: To make sour milk add 1/2 t. baking soda to sweet milk.

We Make You Kindly Welcome, p. 70

Date Nut Roll

18 graham crackers	12 marshmallows, chopped
1 c. dates, chopped	1 c. heavy cream
1 c. pecans, chopped	whipped cream

Crumble or grind crackers. Add dates, nuts, marshmallows and cream. Mix well. Mold with hands into a long roll and wrap in lightly oiled waxed paper. Refrigerate for 24 hours before serving. After roll is set and cold it may be rolled in graham cracker crumbs. Slice and serve with whipped cream. Serves 12.

Beaumont Inn Special Recipes, p. 114

Kentucky Sally Lunn

1/2 c. butter	2 c. flour
1/4 c. sugar	1/2 c. milk
2 eggs, separated	1/2 yeast cake
1/2 t. salt	

Cream butter and sugar. Add well-beaten yolks, salt and flour, alternating with milk that has been heated until lukewarm and mixed with yeast. Fold in well-beaten whites. Put in a greased pie pan, either glass or pottery, and let stand until it doubles its bulk, 2 1/2 to 3 hours. Bake 25 to 30 minutes in a 375 degree F. oven. When bread is golden brown and tests done, remove from oven, cut into pie-shaped wedges and butter while hot. Leftover Sally Lunn can be buttered and toasted under the broiler. Brown on buttered side only. Makes 6 servings.

Out of Kentucky Kitchens, p. 59

Brown Sugar Shortbread

1 c. (2 sticks) unsalted butter	1 t. vanilla extract
1 c. light brown sugar, firmly packed	2 1/4 c. all-purpose flour, sifted

Preheat oven to 325 degrees F. Butter a 9" round cake pan. Beat the butter, brown sugar and vanilla together until fluffy. Add the flour in 4 batches, combining well after each addition. (You may do this with your hands.) Scrape the dough into the prepared pan with a spatula and pat into an even layer. Prick the surface of the dough all over with a fork. Score in wedges with a knife before baking (don't cut all the way through the dough) so it will be easier to break apart for serving. Bake in the upper third of the oven for 30 minutes or until the top is puffy and lightly browned. Makes 8 servings.

Lee Bailey, *USA Weekend*, August 16-18, 1991

Carrie Todd's Derby Cake or Scotch Shortbread

1/2 lb. flour (about 2 c.)	1/4 lb. butter (about 1/2 c.)
1/4 lb. sugar (about 1/2 c.)	

Rub ingredients together and blend with the fingers. The dough is too short to roll. Press it into 2, 9" pie or square pans and flatten with the palms of the hands so that the dough is 1/3 to 1/2" thick. Prick the surface with a fork and bake in a hot 450 degree F. oven like pie crust for 10 to 15 minutes or until golden brown. Mark into wedges or squares at once and leave in pan until cold. Dust with powdered sugar and remove sections to a platter using a pancake turner. These cakes can be topped with fresh strawberries and cream for dessert or served plain with tea or wine.

Out of Kentucky Kitchens, p. 207

Old-Fashioned Strawberry Shortcake

Pastry:

2 c. all-purpose flour	3/4 c. solid shortening
1 t. salt	5 T. cold water

Combine flour and salt in bowl. Cut shortening into flour with a pastry blender to form pea-size chunks. Sprinkle with water 1 T. at a time. Toss lightly with a fork until dough forms a ball. Press down to form a "pancake." Flour each side. Place between 2 sheets of waxed paper. Roll dough out 1/8" thick. Sprinkle flour on dough if it sticks. Turn for even rolling. Remove top piece of waxed paper. Using a saucer as a guide, cut out rounds 4 to 5" across with a paring knife. Prick each round with a fork. Bake at 450 degrees F. for 8 to 10 minutes. Watch closely so they don't get too brown.

Topping:

fresh strawberries	whipped cream or whipped topping
confectioners' sugar	

Wash and trim berries. Drain and sprinkle liberally with sugar. Chill until ready to serve. To serve, place a layer of berries on bottom pastry round. Cover with top round and cover with more berries. Top with whipped cream.

Elizabeth Ross

Shortcakes

1/2 c. shortening	1/2 t. salt
2 c. flour	1/4 c. sugar
3 t. baking powder	1 egg beaten into 1/2 c. milk

Cut shortening into flour, baking powder and salt. Add sugar and egg mixture and stir until blended. Drop onto greased baking sheets. Bake at 350 degrees F. for 15 to 20 minutes. Use for strawberry shortcake.

Judy and Chuck Hagedorn

Peach Ice Cream

1/2 pkg. unflavored gelatin
1 can peaches or 1 c. of
   pre-sweetened fresh fruit
   per qt. of ice cream
dash of salt

3 T. cornstarch
1/2 gal. milk
4 egg yolks
2 1/2 c. sugar
1 pt. cream

Dissolve gelatin in cold water according to directions. Blend fruit in blender. Add salt and cornstarch and cook together until thick. Heat milk to steaming, but do not allow to boil. Beat egg yolks until foamy and along with sugar and gelatin add to hot milk. Cook to make a custard. If lumpy, strain through sieve or any strainer. If not lumpy, add stiffly beaten egg whites. Combine fruit, custard and cream in freezer to 5" from top and freeze according to freezer directions. If you blend the fruit it makes the ice cream smoother. Preparing the ice cream mixture the day before makes the ice cream smoother and increases yield. Makes 1 gal.

Verna Ross Bellamy

Peach Ice Cream

5 eggs
3 c. sugar
dash of salt
5 c. peach pulp

3 T. lemon juice
1 T. vanilla
1/4 t. almond extract
milk

Mix first 3 ingredients well. Add peach pulp to which the lemon juice, vanilla and almond extract have been added. Add milk or cream to fill ice cream freezer and follow appliance directions. Freeze. Makes 1 gal.

A Taste from Back Home, p. 296

Peppermint Stick Candy Ice Cream

1/2 lb. red striped
   peppermint stick candy
2 c. single cream

1 pt. double cream
few grains of salt

Soak the crushed candy in the single cream overnight. If it does not dissolve, heat slightly. Cool. Combine the unbeaten double cream with the peppermint cream mixture and salt and freeze until stiff. Use an electric or old-fashioned crank freezer, but it will probably freeze in the refrigerator freezer. Makes 6 to 8 servings.

Out of Kentucky Kitchens, p. 187

Lime Sherbet

1 pkg. lime gelatin
1 c. sugar
1 c. boiling water

3 small lemons
1 qt. milk

Dissolve gelatin and sugar in boiling water. Add grated rind and juice from lemons. When cool, beat in milk. Pour into ice trays and when partially frozen, put in a bowl. Beat with egg beater until smooth. Return to trays and freeze.

Florence Ross, my Mother

Fresh Lime Sherbet

1 c. light corn syrup
1 c. sugar
3 c. water
2/3 c. lime juice (Persian)

2 T. lime peel, grated
2 egg whites, beaten stiff
1/2 pt. heavy cream, whipped thick

Combine corn syrup, sugar and water in saucepan. Bring to boil and boil 5 minutes without stirring. Cool, add lime juice and lime peel. Put in freezer. When frozen, beat until mushy. Fold in beaten egg whites and the whipped cream. Return to freezer and freeze for at least 4 hours before serving. Note: Key lime may be substituted for the Persian lime. Use 1/2 c. Key lime juice and 1 T. of rind.

Fort Lauderdale Recipes, Mrs. Mary Tsolas, p. 67

Bourbon Sauce

4 egg yolks	1/2 c. Wild Turkey 101 proof
1/2 c. sugar	bourbon
	1 c. heavy cream

Combine egg yolks and sugar in a stainless steel or copper bowl and beat well. Place bowl over a pan of simmering water. Cook, stirring constantly with a wire whisk, until mixture is thick and pale yellow. Remove from heat and stir in bourbon. Transfer mixture to another bowl and chill thoroughly. Whip cream to stiff peaks and fold into sauce. Store refrigerated. Serve on warm fruit cobbler. Makes 2 1/2 c.

Courtesy of CCM, Inc., Wild Turkey Distillery, Lawrenceburg, Kentucky

Browned-Butter and Bourbon Sauce

2 T. butter	2 T. bourbon whiskey or more
1 c. brown sugar	1 c. double cream
1/8 t. salt	

Brown butter in a heavy metal skillet. Add sugar and salt. Heat until smooth. Set aside to cool. Add whiskey and whipped cream just before serving. A pre-Civil War Kentucky recipe excellent for gingerbread, cinnamon bread or plum pudding.

Out of Kentucky Kitchens, p. 198

Butterscotch Sauce

Mix 1 1/2 c. dark brown sugar with 4 T. flour. Add 1 c. boiling water and a dash of salt. Stir and cook for 6 to 8 minutes. If too thick, add a little more boiling water. Remove from heat and add 4 T. butter or margarine and 2 T. cream. Add 1/2 t. vanilla and blend well. Keep warm until used. The double boiler is a great aid in this.

Cissy Gregg's Cook Book, vol. 1, p. 33,
The Courier Journal & Louisville Times Co., reprinted with permission

Hard Sauce

Cream 1/2 c. fresh butter, then add 1 c. granulated sugar gradually, beating with a spoon until very light. A pinch of salt may be added if you like. Flavor with vanilla or 2 T. brandy. Whipped cream may be added or stiffly beaten white of 1 egg will make the sauce very light. Very often, for color and added richness, a beaten egg yolk is added. Hard sauce is sometimes made with brown sugar and flavored with rum. Hard sauce can be flavored with grated lemon rind, or to make it orange flavored, add a little orange juice and grated orange rind.

Cissy Gregg's Cook Book, vol. 1, p. 36,
The Courier Journal & Louisville Times Co., reprinted with permission

Kentucky Sauce

1 c. brown sugar	1 c. pecans, broken
1 c. granulated sugar	1 orange
1 c. water	1 lemon
1 c. strawberry preserves	1 c. bourbon

Combine sugars with water and cook until syrup reaches 240 degrees F. on a thermometer or until it almost spins a thread. Remove from heat and stir in preserves and pecans. Remove rind from orange and lemon with potato parer and chop real fine. Cut off and discard white membrane from fruit and remove sections. Cut section into small pieces. Add cut-up rind, fruit and bourbon to first mixture. Set in refrigerator to ripen. Keeps indefinitely. Must do ahead. Serve over ice cream, gingerbread, plain cake or anything that calls for a topping. Makes 1 qt.

The Best of the Best from Kentucky, Mountain Laurel Encore, p. 209

Old-Fashioned Lemon Sauce

1 c. sugar
1/2 c. butter or margarine
1/4 c. water

1 egg, well-beaten
3/4 t. lemon peel, grated
3 T. lemon juice

In medium saucepan, combine all ingredients. Heat to boiling over medium heat, stirring constantly. Delicious over gingerbread. Makes 1 c.

The Best of the Best from Kentucky,
Campbellsville College Women's Club Cookbook, p. 210

Tangy Lemon Sauce

1 c. sugar
2 1/2 T. cornstarch
2 c. water
2 egg yolks, beaten

1/2 c. lemon juice
1 T. lemon peel, grated
2 T. butter or margarine

Combine sugar and cornstarch in saucepan. Gradually add water, blending until smooth. Cook over medium heat, stirring constantly, until mixture becomes thick and clear. Remove from heat. Stir small amount of hot mixture into egg yolks. Add to hot mixture in saucepan and cook 2 minutes. Add lemon juice, peel and butter. Blend well. Serve warm or cold. Good over warm gingerbread. Makes 2 3/4 c.

Miriam B. Loo's Family Favorites Cookbook, p. 52

Woodford Pudding Sauce

1/4 c. butter, softened
(no substitutes)
1/2 c. sugar

1 egg, well-beaten
1/4 c. brandy or whiskey or
more to taste

Cream butter with sugar. Add egg. Put into double boiler and stir until mixture thickens, but do not boil. Add brandy or whiskey. Serve at once.

Out of Kentucky Kitchens, p. 194

Bibliography

The Ball Blue Book by permission of the Alltrista Consumer Products Company, Muncie, IN, 1984.

Beaumont Inn Special Recipes by Mary Elizabeth Dedman and Thomas Curry Dedman, Jr., Beaumont Inn, Harrodsburg, KY, 1992.

Bentley Farm Cookbook by Virginia Williams Bentley, by permission of Victoria W. Bentley, Dallas, TX, 1974.

Best of the Best from Kentucky edited by Gwen McKee and Barbara Moseley, Quail Ridge Press, Brandon, MS, 1988.

        Best Made Better Recipes, Volume II by the Lincoln County 4-H Council, P.O. Box 326, Stanford, KY, 40484.

        Campbellsville College Women's Club Cookbook by the Campbellsville College Women's Club, 200 College Street, Box 561, Campbellsville, KY, 42718.

        The Corn Island Cookbook by the International Order of E.A.R.S., Inc., 11905 Lilac Way, Middletown, KY, 40243.

        Country Cookbook by the WDFB Christian Radio Station, P.O. Box 106, Danville, KY, 40422.

        Entertaining the Louisville Way, Volume II by the Queens Daughters Inc., 3022 Wellbrooke Road, Louisville, KY, 40205.

        Kentucky Kitchens by the Kentucky Chapter #32, Telephone Pioneers of America, 534 Armory Place 3W, P.O. Box 32410, Louisville, KY, 40232.

        Let Them Eat Ice Cream by Karen Rafuse and Margaret Minster, Amity Unlimited, Inc., P.O. Box 15697, Cincinnati, OH, 45215.

        Mountain Laurel Encore by the Bell County Extension Homemakers, P.O. Box 430, Pineville, KY, 40977.

        Seasons of Thyme by the Charity League of Paducah, 1921 Broadway - P.O. Box 7123, Paducah, KY, 42001.

        Stephensburg Homecoming Recipes by the Stephensburg Homemakers Club, 204 Wonderland Cavern Road, Cecelia, KY, 42724.

        To Market, To Market by the Junior League of Owensboro, Kentucky, Inc., P.O. Box 723, Owensboro, KY, 42302.

        What's Cooking for the Holidays by Irene Hayes, P.O. Box 98, Hueysville, KY, 41640.

Betty Crocker's Picture Cookbook, McGraw-Hill Book Co., New York, 1950. Reprinted with the permission of General Mills, Inc.

Cabbage Patch Famous Kentucky Recipes by the Cabbage Patch Circle, 1196 Innes Court, Louisville, KY, 40204, 1952.

Cherished Recipes by the Youth Committee of First Baptist Church, First Baptist Church, Richmond, KY, 40475.

The Cincinnati Cookbook by the Co-operative Society of the Children's Hospital, Cookbook, Children's Hospital, 240 Bethesda Avenue, Cincinnati, OH, 45229, 1972.

Cissy Gregg's Cook Book Volume 1, Oct. 4, 1953 reprinted by permission of The Courier-Journal & Louisville Times Co., 525 W. Broadway, Louisville, KY, 40201.

Cissy Gregg's Cook Book Volume 2, Nov. 1, 1959 reprinted by permission of The Courier-Journal & Louisville Times Co., 525 W. Broadway, Louisville, KY, 40201.

Civil Wah Cookbook from Boogar Hollow by Nick Powers, Country Originals, Lindale, GA, 30147, 1972.

A Cookbook of Treasures by the Christian Women's Fellowship, Group VI, First Christian Church, Richmond, KY, 40475, 1992.

Cooking with Curtis Grace by Curtis Grace, McClanahan Publishing House, Kuttawa, KY, 1985.

The Courier-Journal Kentucky Cookbook, 525 W. Broadway, Louisville, KY, 40201.

The Crowning Recipes of Kentucky by Madonna Smith Echols, Marathon International Book Co., Madison, IN, 47250-0032, 1986.

Culinary Classics by the Altar Society, St. Mark Catholic Church, Richmond, KY, 40475.

Dining in Historic Kentucky by Marty Godbey, McClanahan Publishing House, Kuttawa, KY, 1985.

Dining in Historic Kentucky by Marty Godbey, McClanahan Publishing House, Kuttawa, KY, 1992.

Dixie Dishes by Marion W. Flexner, by permission of her son, Dr. John Flexner, Nashville, TN, 1941.

Donna Gill Recommends by Donna Gill, Science Hill Inn, Shelbyville, KY.

Favorite Recipes by the Christian Women's Fellowship, First Christian Church, Richmond, KY, 40475, 1974.

Food for My Household by the CYF Cookbook Committee, First Christian Church, Richmond, KY, 40475, 1985.

Fort Lauderdale Recipes by the Fort Lauderdale Historical Society, 219 Southwest 2nd Avenue, Fort Lauderdale, FL, 33301, 1986.

Fountain Favorites, 5 Points Drugstore, Franklin, TN, 37064.

The Gold Cook Book by Louis P. DeGouy by permission of his daughter, Jacqueline S. DeGouy Dooner, Yonkers, NY, 1948.

The Hillforest Sampler by the Hillforest Historical Foundation (registered on the list of Historical Places), Aurora, IN, 47001, 1990.

Historic Kentucky Recipes by the Mercer County Humane Society, Box 423, Harrodsburg, KY, 40330, 1976.

Historical Cook Book by the Ladies Aid Society of the Kirksville Christian Church, Kirksville, KY, 40461, 1929. Reprinted 1989 by the Christian Women's Fellowship.

The Household Searchlight Recipe Book by *The Household* Magazine, Capper's, c/o Stauffer Communications, Inc., Topeka, KS, 66609, 1942.

Kentucky Cooking New and Old, The Colonettes, Louisville Junior Chamber of Commerce, 1402 Eastridge Court, Louisville, KY, 40223, 1958.

The Kentucky Derby Museum Cookbook, Kentucky Derby Museum Corporation, P.O. Box 3513, Louisville, KY, 40201, 1986.

The Kentucky Encyclopedia edited by John Kleber, The University Press of Kentucky, 663 South Limestone Street, Lexington, KY, 40508, 1992.

Look No Further by Richard T. Hougen by permission of Curtis Reppert, 186 Cumberland Street, Berea, KY, 40403, 1955.

Miriam B. Loo's Family Favorites Cookbook, Current, Inc., Box. 2559, Colorado Springs, CO, 80901, 1977.

Miss Daisy Entertains © 1980 by Daisy King, published by Rutledge Hill Press, Nashville, TN, 37219.

Moonlite Bar-B-Q Cookbook by the Moonlite Bar-B-Q Inn, 2840 W. Parrish Avenue, Owensboro, KY, 42301, 1994.

More Hougen Favorites by Richard T. Hougen by permission of Curtis Reppert, 186 Cumberland Street, Berea, KY, 40403, 1971.

My Old Kentucky Homes Cookbook by Lou Delle McIntosh, Mrs. Lou Delle McIntosh Thomas, 3295 Versailles Road, Frankfort, KY, 40601.

Old Farmer's Almanac Colonial Cookbook by Yankee Books, a Division of Yankee Publishing Inc., Dublin, NH, 1982.

Old-Fashioned Bread Recipes by J.S. Collester, Bear Wallow Books, Publishers, Inc., Nashville, IN, 1987.

Old-Fashioned Muffins & Biscuits by J.S. Collester, Bear Wallow Books, Publishers, Inc., Nashville, IN, 1993.

Out of Kentucky Kitchens by Marion Flexner, by permission of her son, Dr. John Flexner, Nashville, TN, 1949.

Out of Old Nova Scotia Kitchens by Marie Nightingale, Nimbus Publishing Limited, Halifax, Nova Scotia, Canada, B3K 5N5.

Out of the Kitchen into the House receipts of Elizabeth Kinkead Battaile compiled by Matilda B. Moore, Lexington, KY, 1971.

Philadelphia Main Line Classics by the Junior Saturday Club, P.O. Box 521, Wayne, PA, 1982.

Pleasures of Cooking, Vol. 1, Number 12, by Suzanne S. Jones, CHC of Connecticut, Inc., Greenwich, CT, 1979.

Prairie Recipes and Kitchen Antiques by Wilma Kurtis and Anita Gold, Bonus Books, Inc., Chicago, IL, 1978.

Recipes from Kentucky State Resort Parks published by Glenn Durham in cooperation with Kentucky Department of Parks, Harlan, KY, 1978.

Recipes from the Miller's Wife by Mollie Wiseman, Wiseman's Mill, Paris, KY, 40361.

Recipes from Miss Daisy's by Daisy King, published by Rutledge Hill Press, Nashville, TN, 1978.

Recipes Remembered by Fern Storer, Highland House Books, Covington, KY, 1989.

Sample West Kentucky edited by Paula Cunningham, McClanahan Publishing House, Kuttawa, KY, 42055.

The Shaker Cookbook: Recipes and Lore from the Valley of God's Pleasure by Caroline Piercy and Arthur Tolve, P.O. Box 141, Gabriel's Horn Publishing Co., Bowling Green, OH, 43402, 1984.

Sharing Our Best by the Grayson County Homemakers, 126 South Clinton, Leitchfield, KY, 42754, 1993.

Southern Style by Jane Bradley, The American Cooking Guild, Gaithersburg, MD, 1987.

Speedwell Christian Church Cookbook by the Cookbook Committee, Richmond, KY, 1990.

A Taste from Back Home by Barbara Wortham, Marathon International Book Co., Madison, IN, 47250-0032, 1983.

Thelma's Treasures by Susanna Thomas, Little Barter Press, Harrodsburg, KY, 1992.

We Make You Kindly Welcome by Elizabeth C. Kremer, Pleasant Hill Press, Harrodsburg, KY, 1970.

Weisenberger Cookbook II published by Weisenberger Mills, Inc., Midway, KY.

Welcome Back to Pleasant Hill by Elizabeth C. Kremer, Pleasant Hill Press, Harrodsburg, KY, 1977.

What's Cooking in Kentucky by Irene Hayes, P.O. Box 98, Hueysville, KY, 41640, 1982.

INDIVIDUAL CONTRIBUTORS

Mrs. Lucian C. Adams (Elizabeth McIlvaine), Orlando, FL; Mrs. Clifford Amyx (Dee Rice), Lexington, KY; Dr. Jay A. Anderson, Utah State University, Logan, UT; Mrs. Leeds Ballard (Ruth Ross), Lancaster, KY; Mrs. John Beacham (Mildred) Cincinnati, OH; Mrs. Robert L. Bellamy, Sr., (Verna Ross), Richmond, KY; Mrs. James C. Carr by permission of her daughter, Mrs. George Lee Smith, Richmond, KY; Mrs. Albert B. "Happy" Chandler, (former First Lady of Kentucky) by permission of her son, Albert B. "Ben" Chandler, Jr., Versailles, KY; Mrs. Earle B. Combs, Sr., (wife of the late N.Y. Yankee Hall-of-Fame baseball player) by permission of her daughter-in-law, Mrs. Pauline C. Combs, Richmond, KY; Mrs. Teresa Conklin, Lawrenceburg, IN; Mrs. Cecil Dunn (Louise), Richmond, KY; Ms. Katherine Giles, Versailles, KY; Ms. Margaret Fant Gwynne, Richmond, KY; Judy and Chuck Hagedorn, Aurora, IN; Mrs. James W. Hamilton (Bess Coyle, my grandmother), Richmond, KY; Ms. Phoebe Ann Hammond, New Hope, PA; Mrs. Wesley Jackson (Diane), Lawrenceburg, IN; Mr. Dinwiddie Lampton, Jr., Hardscuffle Farm, Goshen, KY; Mrs. J.H. Lanier, Jr., (Ava), Murrels Inlet, SC; Ms. Mary Ann Lane, Guilford, IN; Mrs. Robert LeCompte (Joyce), Lawrenceburg, IN; Mrs. Bruce Maggard (Faye Davis), Richmond, KY; Ms. Mary Louise Moore, Louisville, KY; Mrs. Robert McQuerry (Nancy Ballard), Harrodsburg, KY; Mr. Tom Raybourne, Versailles, KY; Mrs. William H. Riddell (Sarah), Berea, KY; Mrs. Andrew J. Ross (Florence Hamilton, my mother), Richmond, KY; Ms. Nancy Lee Ross (my sister), Fort Lauderdale, FL, and Clay's Ferry, KY; Mrs. Earnest L. Ross (Valeria), by permission of her daughter, Linda Ross Boardman, Richmond, KY; Dr. Shirley Snarr, Eastern Kentucky University, Richmond, KY; Mr. Mark Sohn, Pikeville, KY; Mrs. Fern Storer, Covington, KY; Mrs. Louis Taylor (Elaine), Guilford, IN; Mr. H Thomas Tudor, "Tudor Hall", Richmond, KY; Mrs. Charles Utter (Emily), Lexington, KY; Mrs. John Vann (Lucille), Richmond, KY.

PERIODICALS

Back Home in Kentucky
P.O. Box 681629
Franklin, TN 37068-1629
"Beaten Biscuits with Lard and Love" by Sara C. Willis

Southern Living magazine
2100 Lakeshore Drive
Birmingham, AL 35201
"A Mint of Southern Tradition"
"Roots of Southern Food" by John Egerton

OTHER PRINTINGS

Ashland - Henry Clay Estate
120 Sycamore Road
Lexington, KY 40502

Lee Bailey
New York, N.Y. 10011

Home Economics Extension Service
Scovell Hall, College of Agriculture
University of Kentucky
Lexington, KY 40546-0064

Louisville *Courier-Journal*
525 W. Broadway
Louisville, KY 40201-7431
"The Real Hot Brown"

Frances Price, R.D., *One and Only Cook*
Reisertown, MD 21136

Cammie Vitalle
Dallas, TX 75214

RESTAURANTS AND CLUBS

The Ballard Store
2449 Baseline Avenue
Solvang, CA 93463

F&N Steakhouse
Rt. 8 East
Dayton, KY 41074
(606) 261-6766

The Golden Lamb
27 S. Broadway
P.O. Box 28
Lebanon, OH 45036

The Pendennis Club, Inc., © 1994
218 W. Muhammed Ali Blvd.
Louisville, KY 40202

COMMERCIAL PRODUCTS

Allen Canning Co. (Princilla Yams)
Siloam Springs, AR 72761-0250

General Mills, Inc. (Gold Medal Flour)
P.O. Box 1113
Minneapolis, MN 55440

Hulman & Co., Manufacturers (Clabber Girl Baking Powder)
P.O. Box 150
Terre Haute, IN 47808

Kraft General Foods (Bakers and Angel Flake Coconut)
White Plains, NY 10625

Martha White Foods (Martha White Flour)
240 Preston Street
Jackson, TN 38301

Reynolds Metals Co. (Cooking Bags)
Richmond, VA 23261

Seneca Foods Corp. (Applesauce)
Marion, NY 14505-0997

White Lily Food Co. (White Lily Flour)
P.O. Box 871
Knoxville, TN 37901

Note: Unfortunately, there were some cookbooks I was not allowed to use. They are noticeable by their absence.

Food Source Guide

BEVERAGES

Ale-8-One Bottling Co.
25 Carol Road
Winchester, KY 40391
(606) 744-3454
Specialty: Carbonated ginger beverage. They have bottled their secret formula since 1926 and have a catalog of gift items and special recipes using Ale-8-One.

Austin Nichols Distilling Co.
US 60 East
1525 Tyrone Road
Lawrenceburg, KY 40342
(502) 839-4544
Specialty: Wild Turkey Bourbon 101 Proof, Rare Breed and Kentucky Spirit. Their products can be ordered anywhere by calling 1-800-BE THERE. They have recipe cards.

Coffee Times
2572-2753 Regency Road
Lexington, KY 40503
(606) 277-9140
(606) 277-6490 Fax
Specialty: Gourmet coffees and a wide range of coffee and tea giftware and accessories. They sell gift combinations and will ship anything for you.

Maker's Mark Distillery, Inc.
3350 Burks Spring Road
Loretto, KY 40037
(502) 865-2881
Specialty: Maker's Mark Bourbon, Maker's Mark VIP (personalized bottle) and Maker's Mark Mint Julep which is available in Spring. Not sold by catalog.

Oldenberg Brewery
400 Buttermilk Pike
Ft. Mitchell, KY 41017
(606) 341-7223
Specialty: Fine Beer. Unfortunately, this micro-brewery does not sell by mail order.

BREADS

Jackson Biscuit Co.
John and Judy Jackson
725 Terry Drive
Winchester, KY 40391
(606) 745-2561
Specialty: Beaten biscuits. Recognized by the state as the true "Kentucky food product" they make and sell beaten biscuits by mail order and at many central Kentucky groceries. A family business, everything is done by hand, using an old-fashioned biscuit machine and one special biscuit cutter.

Kern's Baking Co.
Knoxville, TN 37901
(800) 247-5376
Specialty: Salt-rising bread. Widely available at grocery stores in Kentucky. Call for information about availability.

CANDIES

Ann's Candy Shop
5450 Mount Sterling Road
Winchester, KY 40391
(606) 744-1540
Specialty: Fancy homemade candies. Yes, they do sell by mail order.

Bauer's Candies
3800 Murphy Lane
Mt. Eden, KY 40046
(502) 738-5237
Specialty: Modjeska candies. They sell them by mail order, so call for prices and shipping information.

Mom Blakeman's Candy, Inc.
P.O. Box 228-209 Lexington Street
Lancaster, KY 40444
(606) 792-3464
(800) 542-4607
Specialty: Cream pull candy. They sell it plain, chocolate dipped and peppermint flavored. Call them for mail order instructions.

The Bourbon Ball
2307 Newmarket Drive
Louisville, KY 40222
(502) 896-9967
(800) 280-0888
Specialty: Hand-dipped bourbon chocolates. Made with Old Forester bourbon, sweet cream and English walnuts. Call them for ordering information.

Ehrler's Candies
1370 Belmar Drive
Louisville, KY 40213
(502) 459-1070
Specialty: Maker's Mark bourbon chocolates.

Gilliam Candy Co.
P.O. Box 1060-2401 Powell
Paducah, KY 42002-1060
(502) 443-6532
(502) 442-1922 Fax
Specialty: Old-fashioned hard candies. Although they sell wholesale only, their candy is available at many Kentucky food markets.

Old Kentucky Candies
450 Southland Drive
Lexington, KY 40503
(606) 278-4444
Specialty: Jim Beam bourbon chocolates and truffles, chocolate bourbon cherries, pulled creams, fruit and pecan cakes. They will send their catalog and mail order form upon request.

Rebecca-Ruth Candies
P.O. Box 64, 112 E. Second Street
Frankfort, KY 40602-0064
(502) 223-7475
(800) 444-3766
Specialty: The World Famous Bourbon Balls. This third generation company makes bourbon candy. They ship all year-round and just about everywhere. Just call for their catalog.

Ruth Hunt Candies
426 W. Main
Mt. Sterling, KY 40353
(800) 927-0302
Specialty: The Official Bourbon Ball of Churchill Downs, pull candy and the Blue Monday candy bar. They have a catalog/price list they will send upon request.

Sharp's Candies
2021 Regency Road
Lexington, Kentucky 40503
(606) 276-4625
(606) 276-2025
Specialty: Bourbon creams, pulled cream candy, pecan rolls, caramels, divinity and seafoam candy. This company sells by mail order.

CHEESES

Best of the Bluegrass
423 Fayette Park
Lexington, KY 40508
(606) 255-5225
Specialty: Beer cheese, both hot and mild, which needs no refrigeration; mint julep syrup, which can be used in iced tea; and bourbon and berries dessert topping. Sold in many stores.

Bloemer Food Sales Co., Inc.
925 S. 7th
Louisville, KY 40203
(502) 589-2325
Specialty: Pimiento cheese spread, BBQ sauce, BBQ beef and pork and chili products. Although this company does not sell by mail order their products are widely available in Kentucky food markets.

Castano Foods Inc.
P.O. Box 206
Nicholasville, KY 40356
Specialty: Kentucky beer cheese spread. This company distributes its cheese throughout Kentucky and has a recipe card and ideas on serving beer cheese spread.

Gethsemani Farms, Inc.
Box KGC
3642 Monks Road
Trappist, KY 40051
Specialty: A wonderful Trappist cheese that is served at the White House! The monks suggest crumbling their fruitcake and adding it to butterscotch or vanilla pudding. They have world-wide mail order service.

Hallman International, Inc.
2935 St. Xavier Street
Louisville, KY 40212
(502) 778-0459
(800) 274-4255
Specialty: Two famous Kentucky products, Hall's Beer Cheese and Hall's Benedictine Cheese, are distributed by this company. They are both available at retail grocers throughout Kentucky especially in Kroger and Winn-Dixie stores.

CORNMEAL AND FLOUR

Hodgeson Mill, Inc.
P.O. Box 430
Teutopolis, IL 62467
(217) 347-0105
(800) 500-0202
Specialty: Kentucky Colonel Seasoned Flour, an excellent product! They have two recipe folders and a mail order price list for all of their products.

Weisenberger Mills, Inc.
Box 215
Midway, KY 40347
(606) 254-5282
(606) 254-0294 Fax
Specialty: Cornmeal and flour. Also biscuit, cornbread, hushpuppy and spoonbread mixes. In business since 1864, they have a mail order list they will send and a fine cookbook you can order.

White Lily Food Co.
Box 871
Knoxville, TN 37901
(615) 546-5511
(800) 264-5459
Specialty: Flour and cornmeal. Also, biscuit, cornbread, muffin and pancake mixes. White Lily flour is made from 100% pure soft wheat and their extra milling steps produce an unusually soft tender texture. They sell by mail order.

Wiseman's Mill
384 Winchester Street
Paris, KY 40361
(606) 987-4757
Specialty: Old-fashioned ground cornmeal. They often grind and sell their meal at fairs and festivals in Kentucky. They sell by mail order.

COUNTRY HAM

Broadbent's
B&B Food Products, Inc.
6321 Hopkinsville Road
Cadiz, KY 42211-9987
(502) 235-5299 KY Residents
(800) 841-2202 Out-of-State
(502) 235-5182 Fax
Specialty: Country ham cured with honey, sugar and salt for 9 to 12 months. Seven-time winner of the Kentucky State Fair Grand Champion County Ham Award. They also sell sausages, country bacon, smoked turkey and gourmet food packs. Call for their mail order catalog.

Claudia Sanders Dinner House
3202 Shelbyville Road
Shelbyville, KY 40065
(502) 633-5600
Specialty: This restaurant specializes in country ham, fried chicken and homemade yeast rolls. Country hams can be ordered by mail.

Critchfield Meats
2254 Zandale Shopping Center
Lexington, KY 40503
(606) 276-4964
Specialty: Fine meats, country hams, cakes, pies and salads. They have a mail order catalog and ship worldwide.

Finchville Farms
Margaret Davis and Bill Robertson, Jr.
P.O. Box 56
Finchville, KY 40065
Specialty: The country hams from this company are the Kentucky State Fair Grand Champion of 1994. They sell by mail order and have an excellent recipe booklet.

Froelich's Farm
6215 Hwy. 142 (at Ensor)
Philpot, Ky 42366
(502) 281-5222
(800) 851-5908
Specialty: Country hams, smoked turkey and smoked sausage. They sell by mail order and have a recipe folder.

Gatton Farms
P.O. Box 98
Bremen, Ky 42325
(502) 523-3437
Specialty: Sugar and salt cured country hams. The will send a recipe folder and mail order price list upon request.

Harper's Hams and Bacon
P.O. Box 122
Clinton, KY 42031
(800) 264-3380
Specialty: Country hams, sausage, bacon and gift baskets. Mail order catalog is available upon request.

Meacham Hams
705 O'Nan Dyer Road
Sturgis, Ky 42459-9735
(502) 333-6924
(800) 552-3190
Specialty: Their country ham is the Official Ham of the Kentucky Derby and was judged best tasting ham at the 1993 Kentucky State Fair. They have ham snacks and sell by mail order.

Newsom's Old Mill Store
208 East Main Street
Princeton, KY 42445
(502) 365-2482
Specialty: Natural cured, aged, country hams, smoked bacon and sausage, relishes, preserves, sorgum and other gourmet items. Since 1917, Newsom's has grown and food editors nationwide have "discovered" this mail order ham business.

Penn's Ham Shop
Big Hill Plaza
Richmond, KY 40475
(606) 625-0319
Specialty: Although they do not sell by mail order, you can purchase ham by the pound or even a sandwich at this shop.

PRESERVES, RELISHES AND SAUCES

Applecreek Orchards
P.O. Box 8383
Lexington, Ky 40533
(800) 747-8871
Specialty: The finest preserves, butters, unique cakes in a jar, marinades, relishes and chocolate fudge sauces, some made with bourbon.

Bourbon County Products
4012 Dupont Circle, Suite 304
Louisville, Ky 40207
(502) 893-0690
Specialty: Makers' Mark BBQ sauce. They sell by mail order and have a recipe booklet with 20 recipes.

Golden Kentucky Products
P.O. Box 246
Livingston, KY 40445
(800) 578-9829
Specialty: Sweet sorghum, wildflower honey, biscuit mixes, raspberry mustard, honey bourbon mustard, barbecue sauce and assorted candies. They have gift baskets and sell by mail order.

Haddon House Food Products, Inc.
P.O. Box 907 - Old Marlton Pike
Medford, NJ 08055
(609) 654-7901
(609) 654-0412 Fax
Specialty: Sweet pickle watermelon rind, among many other products. These pickles taste very much like homemade and can be found in many speciality and gourmet food stores.

Ky's Smokin Grill
c/o David L. Kleckner
170 Marie Street
Danville, KY 40422
(606) 236-3609
Specialty: Spicy honey mustard. They have mail order service and a brochure of recipes using their mustard and mild or hot sauce.

Miss Penny's Southern Delicacies
P.O. Box 345
Franklin, KY 42135
(502) 586-7388
Specialty: Award winning Maker's Mark flavored marinade. Also cakes, brownies, dessert toppings and speciality nuts. They have a recipe brochure, but sell wholesale only.

Moonlite Bar-B-Q Inn
2840 West Parrish Avenue
Owensboro, KY 42301
(502) 684-8143
Specialty: Smoked BBQ sauce, but their main products are barbecued meats and burgoo. They sell by mail order and have a cookbook/price list they will send.

SORGHUM MOLASSES

Brown's Produce
Box 545
Campton, KY 41301
Specialty: Sorghum and honey.

Hart-County Sorghum
999 Logsdon Valley Road
Munfordville, KY 42765
Specialty: Sorghum. They do sell by mail order.

Loyd Roe Farms, Distributor
Pomeroyton, Menifee County, KY 40364
(606) 768-3455
Specialty: Sorghum molasses.

VEGETABLES AND FRUIT

Garrett's Country Market
Shannon Run Road at Pickard Pike
Versailles, KY 40383
(606) 873-3819
Specialty: Fresh vegetables and fruit in season (picked and U-pick). Also, they sell fruit and gourmet gift baskets. Note: Their fresh asparagus in Spring is wonderful!

Windstone Farms
3948 Pleasant Springs Road
Carlisle, KY 40311
(606) 289-5349
Specialty: Blackberry jam cake, blackberry jam, seedless blackberry jam and blackberry cobbler mix. They do sell by mail order.

OTHER SOURCES

Dolfinger's
3738 Lexington Road
Louisville, KY 40207
(502) 893-3634
Specialty: Although this is a fine jewelry and accessory store, they also sell classic silver mint julep cups. Write or call them for prices.

Party Kits & Equestrian Gifts
P.O. Box 7831
8007 Vinecrest, Suite 9
Louisville, KY 40222-8965
(502) 425-2126
(800) 993-3729
(502) 425-5230 Fax
Specialty: Everything needed for a Derby party: Invitations, plates, napkins, glasses, decorations, bourbon candies, country ham, beaten biscuits and even sweatshirts and pins. Write for their handsome mail order catalog.

Renfro Valley Grist Mill County Store
Refro Village, I-75, Exit 62
Renfro Valley, KY 40473
(606) 257-2638
(800) 765-7464
Specialty: Jellies, jams, sorghum, honey, stone ground cornmeal, country ham, gifts and gadgets.

Index of Recipes

CAKES

CANDIES